# REVIEWS

"What a treasure! Mona Ketner's daily devotional intimately speaks to women facing separation and divorce about their pain while reminding them of their hope in Christ. Drawing from everyday issues that often become painful reminders of a marriage lost, Mona offers help and hope through practical strategies and Biblical guidelines that will help women heal and live life more abundantly."

> -W. Ellen Fox, LPC, LMFT
> Licensed Marriage and Family Therapist
> Director of the Marriage and Family Enrichment
> Center of Western Avenue Baptist Church
> Statesville, North Carolina

"This devotional is encouraging and inspirational! It will show you how to walk in a godly manner through an ungodly situation. It will set you on God's path for your life, both now and for the future. I wish it had been available as I went through separation and divorce."

> -Tori Hagaman
> Winston-Salem, North Carolina

"We have continued to look for resources for people enduring separation and divorce. I will use this devotional without hesitation, and it will be a primary resource. The everyday situations are helpful to women."

> -Rev. Dr. Worth Green
> Pastor, New Philadelphia Moravian Church
> Winston-Salem, North Carolina

"Alone can be a terrible place if you are not seeking solitude. Alone and facing unwanted change can be frightening. In her book of meditations, Mona Ketner, a divorced mother of two, writes about the beauty and opportunities God provides us if we only step out of the darkness and into the light with faith. When we realize we are never truly alone . . . when in our solitude of daily meditations we can 'be still and listen to God' . . . we come to realize that all things are truly possible for those who love the Lord. Few things are more devastating than realizing that your 'happily ever after' has come apart before your eyes. Separation or divorce is life-changing and with any change there is apprehension and yes . . . real fear of the unknown.

"Mona brings home the reality that we are made in the image of a Creator who loves us and who is always with us . . . a God who takes care of us even when we are not taking the time to pray. Mona offers real, concrete suggestions for getting through those hard times. Bring yourself closer to God through these daily meditations and Bible readings. You are much stronger than the limitations you put on yourself. Break those chains . . . walk in faith . . . to love and serve the Lord and watch the person you were meant to be evolve in a new light."

> -The Reverend Sealy Cross
> Vicar, The Church of the Ascension
> Advance, North Carolina

"I highly recommend Mona Brown Ketner's *A Devotional for Women in Separation and Divorce.* I recommend it because it breathes hope, it is biblically saturated, and it centers on the reality of Christ. For example, on April 11, she writes, 'Joyfully and openly tell your children of Jesus' resurrection and our incredible hope through him.' That one sentence underscores the core value of this book. It is filled with biblical hope and pulsates with redemptive energy."

> -Rev. Conrad "Buster" Brown, Jr.
> Senior Pastor, East Cooper Baptist Church
> Mount Pleasant, South Carolina

*for Shelley*

# A Devotional

# For Women

*in* Separation *and* Divorce

*God's blessings and peace ~ Mona*

Mona Brown Ketner

*February 2011*

Grateful Steps, Inc.
Asheville, North Carolina

Grateful Steps, Inc.
1091 Hendersonville Road
Asheville, North Carolina 28803

Copyright © 2009 by Mona Brown Ketner

Ketner, Mona Brown
*Devotional for Women in Separation and Divorce*

Cover design by Mona Brown Ketner and Sundara Fawn

ISBN 978-1-935130-10-9 Paperback

Printed by *BP* Solutions Group, Inc.
Asheville, North Carolina
in the process of becoming a green business

Unless otherwise noted, Scriptures are taken from the HOLY BIBLE New Revised Standard Version, used by permission granted by the gratis policy. Scriptures noted NIV are taken from the HOLY BIBLE New International Version®, Copyright© 1973, 1978, 1984 by International Bible Society. Used by permission of Zondervan www.zondervan.com. All rights reserved. Scriptures noted KJV are taken from the King James Version of the Bible.

Library of Congress Cataloging-in-Publication Data

Ketner, Mona Brown.
  A devotional for women in separation and divorce / Mona Brown Ketner. -- 1st ed.
       p. cm.
   ISBN 978-1-935130-10-9 (pbk. : alk. paper)
  1. Divorced people--Religious life. 2. Separated people--Religious life. 3. Christian women--Religious life. I. Title.
   BV4596.D58K48 2009
   242'.6433--dc22

                                                2009003755

www.gratefulsteps.com

*To Adam and Amanda*
*who make my heart sing*

# Acknowledgments

I am eternally grateful to my parents, Leonard and Hazel Brown, for their phenomenal support throughout my entire life and especially, during my separation and divorce. My siblings and their spouses—Charles, Nadja and Mark, David and Martha—have also been incredible sources of strength, humor and acceptance. Many extended family members have been wonderfully helpful since my separation—Aunt 'Ree, Uncle Conrad and Aunt Martha, Foy and Julia, Buster and Sara. Thank you *all* for your love and for helping me stay strong!

Many wonderful female friends have supported me in countless ways through the past few years—Lisa, Miriam, Sally, Linda, Mary, Tricia, Sandy, Camille, Nancy, Frieda, Pat, Debbie, Shelia, Kay, Phyllis, Sealy, Georgena, Kristen and Cindy. Thanks to all of my Perinatal Outreach colleagues. Each of you has helped to keep me focused.

Thank you to members of my faith community who provided encouragement—Lib, Tori, Pattie and Sam, Dermont, Rosemary, Beverly, Larry and Janice, Florence, Donna, Anita, Sarah and Steve, Mary and Gene, David and Rhonda, Betty and Steve, Ellen and Sara. I owe immense gratitude to the Discovery Sunday School class and the entire congregation at New Philadelphia Moravian Church. Many thanks to Ann and our church aerobics gang! I am deeply appreciative of our pastoral staff—Rev. Dr. Worth Green, Rev. Dr. David A. Marcus, Jr. and Rev. John G. Rights.

I am thankful to Micki Cabaniss Eutsler at Grateful Steps Publishing, for her belief in this devotional book and the assistance it could provide many women. Her guidance, time and editing skills helped make this book possible.

I acknowledge all women who have lived through separation and divorce.

Finally, I cherish memories of my mother, Peggy Sue Myers Brown.

# Introduction

Separation and divorce can be unbelievably devastating. Genesis 2:24 tells us that God's ideal is that "man leaves his father and his mother and clings to his wife, and they become one flesh."

However, many circumstances such as infidelity, abandonment, domestic violence or addictions may leave you with no option other than separation. With God's love, help and reassurance, you can continue with life to the best of your ability one day—or even one hour—at a time. I was married to my high school sweetheart for 22 years before separation and am aware of the pain and heartache associated with separation and divorce. My faith, family and friends were essential ingredients to my health and survival.

This devotional book is intended for use as daily encouragement for all women in marital difficulty—living alone in a marriage, separated or divorced. All quoted scripture passages are taken from the New Revised Standard Version, except where indicated.

I pray that this devotional will help bring you God's strength, peace, joy and hope.

Did you make a New Year's resolution? As a woman who is separated or divorced, it can be very helpful to establish a few concrete goals.

Set one or two goals for the New Year that has just dawned, and write them down in a place so that you can see them. Don't write too many goals, as it may be impossible to fulfill a long list at this point in your life. And remember to take it easy; you need to be gentle with yourself during this time of transition and not expect too much at one time.

Your goals might deal with any area of your life—marriage, family, children, work, neighborhood, church, community involvement or finances. Just set a goal of some kind—have a target! This should be your own personal goal, and not one for someone else. Also, make sure that your goal is realistic. Perhaps you shouldn't plan to be reconciled within one month after separation because it may be that you never live with your husband again as man and wife. Neither should you expect to lose 15 pounds of excess weight that you've carried for years during this tumultuous time of separation or divorce.

Your New Year's resolution may be as simple as potting a plant, or it might be to pamper yourself. How about finding fifteen minutes to indulge in a bubble bath? Or you can make the time to use that gift certificate for a massage that someone gave you as a Christmas gift. Your goal may be to establish a daily prayer time with God, or it may be one of service to your community as a volunteer. Or you could plan to spend ten minutes with your child every day—simply talking.

Remember that God loves you and has a plan for your life that will be revealed. Keep this in mind through this coming year.

*Jeremiah 29:11*

*For surely I know the plans I have for you,*
*says the Lord, plans for your welfare and not*
*for harm, to give you a future with hope.*

Talking with God is an absolutely vital part of a Christian woman's life. Indeed, prayer can be her survival lifeline. Pray daily, hourly, or minute-by-minute. Even if you don't feel like praying, pray anyway. It's okay to tell God that you're angry at the circumstances in which you find yourself right now.

Of course, separation and divorce were never part of the plan for your life on your wedding day! Even though your Father in heaven is aware of your pain and confusion and trials, tell him about all these emotions during prayer.

Here is a guide that you can use to include the different components of prayer: adoration, confession, thanksgiving and supplication. Give God the glory for your life and his creation. Confess any sin, remembering that marriage is a two-way street. Thank him for your blessings—yes, you still have some. Pray for your needs—what a long list—as well as those of others.

You can pray anywhere: at the kitchen table, on a deck chair, in the car, in the den—or in the bathroom if your small children create too much noise everywhere else.

You can pray in bed, while taking your daily walk for exercise, when playing the piano or even in the shower. You can pray for a long period of time or for just a few short minutes. Remember that your prayers can be silent or uttered aloud; the language can be very simple or elaborate. Details don't really matter.

You know how pleased you are when your child talks with you about a problem that's on his mind. One divorced woman was thrilled when her teenage son came and asked her opinion about his date for the prom his junior year in high school! The same is true of God. Your heavenly Father wants to hear from you regularly. Commune with him.

*1 Thessalonians 5:17*

*Pray without ceasing.*

Remember to care for your body during this difficult time of your life. You need to stay healthy and avoid illness if possible, because the great stress that you're under makes you more vulnerable to sickness.

Exercise has many potential physical benefits for women—lowered blood pressure, improved joint movement, decreased pulse rate, improved cardiovascular fitness, weight loss and even reduced rates of osteoporosis.

Physical activity also promotes mental health with endorphin release. Walking outside in winter during the snow, in the spring with blooming yellow daffodils, in the warm summer sun and during the fall with colorful leaf splashes is an excellent way to chase away thoughts of depression.

I continue to walk with my neighbor and ask her advice about my children as they adjust to life without their father in the house. And this therapy is free of charge!

Choose whatever form of exercise is appropriate for you. Jogging or vigorous walking is available to almost everyone and riding a bicycle is both fun and healthy. Another option is an aerobics class, offered at recreational centers or at many churches for reduced rates.

A great form of exercise for anger management, along with physical fitness, is kick-boxing. Or if you have health limitations, chair stretching might be a wonderful option for you to look into.

Just do something to get moving! This is not only a great habit to establish now but could be setting a pattern for life-long fitness.

*1 Corinthians 6:19–20*

*Or do you not know that your body is a temple of the Holy Spirit within you, which you have from God, and that you are not your own? For you were bought with a price; therefore glorify God in your body.*

Most women enter into a period of separation and divorce with many financial concerns. There seems to be less money available for everyday living expenses, much less any luxuries such as travel or new furniture for the house. This is a source of intense worry for many women who are separated. Do you sometimes feel as though you can't even afford to go to the grocery store?

It's important to carefully manage the resources that God has entrusted to you. Make a list of all your household expenses. Pray about your budget, asking God for assistance and seeking his will for the money you have. Remember that you don't need to make extravagant purchases at this particular time.

Buying to make you feel better temporarily will only make you feel worse when those bills begin to mount—so stick to your budget!

If you receive child support payments from your husband, use the money wisely. Try to go out to eat only once a week; it's much cheaper in terms of money, calories and fat grams to eat at home. Purchase what your children need—not designer clothes and expensive tennis shoes.

Don't be afraid to tell your children that you can't afford a particular purchase, but try to avoid talking about money constantly. Gladly accept financial assistance from your family members if it is offered; this may be the Lord providing for you during this time of need. And don't forget to thank your father, brother or aunt for such generosity.

Trust God to care for you. He wants only the best for you and your family.

*Matthew 6:25–26*

*"Therefore I tell you, do not worry about your life, what you will eat or what you will drink, or about your body, what you will wear. Is not life more than food, and the body more than clothing? Look at the birds of the air; they neither sow nor reap nor gather into barns, and yet your heavenly Father feeds them. Are you not of more value than they?"*

Are you angry because of the circumstances of your separation or divorce? Are you angry with your husband, yourself, your children or your family? How is your anger affecting you?

Anger is a normal and natural human emotion, and you may indeed be mad about your husband's actions and your marital state. This is certainly understandable and most expected; you wouldn't be human if you were elated about your separation.

Remember, however, that you cannot control another person's actions. Yes, you can pray for another person and his actions, but you can only control your own.

Therefore, you have choices. You can let your anger consume your body and your spirit to the point of causing illness or extreme bitterness, or you can surrender your anger to God. It may take a very long time before you are able to completely give your anger to God, but as a Christian woman you can move in that direction.

How can you deal with your anger on a daily basis? Talk to God, a trusted friend. You may also choose to talk to your pastor, a Christian counselor, aloud to yourself, or scream outside—but not at your children. Or pedal your bicycle really fast and let the wind hit you in the face, listen to loud music, dig in the garden dirt, jog, dance, go to a kick-boxing class, or hit a punching bag at the gym.

Keep a journal, and use this as an outlet for your feelings. During times of crisis in my life, I might play the piano for hours. One woman, after a very bitter divorce, learned to play the trumpet and would sit on her front porch, blowing loud tunes as a release for her anger. Find a constructive outlet for your anger, and give it to God.

*Matthew 5:22*

*But I say to you that if you are angry with a brother or sister, you will be liable to judgment.*

A new day is stretching out before you, and you can stretch along with it. Think a good thought! Before you get out of bed, commit this day to God and give him thanks for five specific things. Smile. Then take a deep breath. Hold it for five seconds and then release.

Rid yourself of the tensions and concerns of yesterday, while remembering that the first year after separation is the hardest. You're taking this journey one day at a time with the Lord's help, and you were able to survive yesterday. Now today is a blank page that is full of potential.

What will you do today? What do you want to accomplish? Are you going to make a written or mental list? You simply may choose to let the day unfold as it goes along. Will you play with your children? Go to work? Take a nap? Pay bills? Read a book? Drink a cup of hot tea? Serve God? Cook supper or go out to eat? Sing together as a family? You have many choices to make.

Mornings are times of renewal; they're perfect times to feel refreshed and decide anew to make Jesus the Lord of your life.

Be glad for another new beginning, because this is indeed a day that the Lord has made. You will never have this particular day again, so make the most of it!

*Lamentations 3:22–23*

*The steadfast love of the Lord never ceases,*
*his mercies never come to an end; they are new*
*every morning; great is your faithfulness.*

During times of separation and divorce, most children live with their mothers. Therefore, single mothers often have more stresses of daily life than single fathers living apart from their children. But, as a mother, you also have immense joys that are not available to an absentee parent. Rejoice in each moment you can spend with your children.

Have some *fun* with your children every day. Almost all children like warm homemade cookies straight from the oven, and baking is a great activity that you can do together. Go on a picnic and count the number of ants you see, take a nature walk in your neighborhood, or go to a nearby park. Read books together.

Pop popcorn in a pan on the top of the stove with only a small amount of oil and leave the lid off—the popcorn will zip straight up in the air! Watch a movie together or play a piano duet. Talk with your children and let them see you're still a family. Smile. There is enough sadness in your life without always walking around with a frown on your face. Joy is contagious—if you smile, your children will often return that grin. Play a board game together, no matter what the ages of your children might be.

Go out for an ice cream cone, even in the cold of winter. Attend fun activities for the family at your church. Remember that life will get better. You, and therefore your children, will slowly work through the hurt and anger and pain of separation or divorce. Time is a great healer, and those smiles can become more frequent and much wider.

*Psalm 127:3*

*Sons are indeed a heritage from the Lord,*
*the fruit of the womb a reward.*

What is your focus in life right now? Are you focused on yourself and your feelings of anger, bitterness or depression? Are you concerned about your children or your finances? Are you plotting revenge against your husband? Are you focused on the past or the future?

Our focus, as women of God, should not be placed solely on any one of the above. Instead, our primary focus should be on the Lord. Our Christian beliefs will determine our motivations, daily actions, thoughts, priorities—and, consequently, our entire lives. We worship God in both our words and our actions every day. God is jealous, and he should be at the top of our priority list.

The Lord can bear our burdens, lift us up in times of trouble and infuse us with joy. He can strengthen us to live another day as a separated or divorced woman, comfort us through our tears and point us to times of gladness. God can make the good times better and the bad times bearable.

Give your life completely to God. Focus on him and you will find that he can supply your every need.

*Hebrews 12:2*

*Looking to Jesus the pioneer and perfecter of our faith, who for the sake of the joy that was set before him endured the cross, disregarding its shame, and has taken his seat at the right hand of the throne of God.*

Are you filled with doubt? Will your children be okay without their father in the house? Do you doubt their academic abilities without two parents to assist them in their homework? Can you be their spiritual guide?

Are you a doubter with regard to your abilities around the house? Do you doubt whether you can mow the yard, fix leaky toilets, prune the hedges, unclog a hair-filled drain, repair broken dishes or fix a broken appliance?

Can you do all the cooking and cleaning, make major purchases alone, work on a dripping faucet, change a flat tire, replace fuses, change the oil in your car, hammer a nail or run a weed eater? Do you doubt your wage-earning abilities? Can you make your house payment? Do you doubt whether your family will assist you during this incredibly difficult time of your life, and do you doubt your friends?

We all suffer from doubt, especially during life's storms. That is a natural human response and a completely normal one.

A central question to ask during separation or divorce is, "Do I doubt God and his powers?" Remember that God is always in charge. Lean on the arm of the Lord. He will not let you down. He is all-knowing, all-powerful and working on your behalf right now to provide solutions for your situation.

*Mark 9:24*

*Immediately the father of the child cried out,*
*"I believe; help my unbelief!"*

Separation and divorce are usually accompanied by spiritual, social, emotional and even physical pains.

A Christian woman may believe that divorce is biblically wrong but have no choice in the matter if her husband leaves the family. This can cause extreme spiritual discomfort.

If you find yourself in this situation, consult with your pastor because he can give you invaluable advice and guidance. Likewise, a newly separated woman may experience social pain because she has no single friends. She may be hesitant to go anywhere on her own.

Separated for only one week, one woman received some very helpful advice from her aunt before venturing to a high school football game alone to see her child in the marching band. "Go on to the game and you'll find somebody to sit with. Just don't sit home alone!" Wise words. She met new friends, while finding that old friends came to her rescue just by sitting with her and saying nothing about her present circumstances.

Emotional pain is often very deep during separation. As a victim of infidelity, a woman might be deeply wounded and often wonder if she can ever trust another man. Cry, talk with a friend, love your children, and visit your family members. Emotional recovery and healing take a long time, so you shouldn't expect to "get better" in one month.

Physical pain and aches are frequently present during this incredibly difficult time. It is said that a person can die from a broken heart. Women during the separation process often become ill due to the immense strain that their bodies are undergoing.

Recognize that God can heal all your pain and that he is the great physician.

*Matthew 9:12*

*"Those who are well have no need of a physician, but those who are sick."*

Do you miss having your husband's hugs? We all need physical touch. After being married for a number of years, it's natural to miss those hugs and kisses. You may also fondly remember and yearn for back rubs in the bed, spooning with your husband in the bed, and sex. Recognize this void in your life and claim it as such; don't deny that you have these needs.

What can you do to compensate for this loss? Hug your children daily, and you'll get hugs in return. Also hug work colleagues—appropriate ones only—neighbors, friends, your brother, sister, father, mother and other family members.

Tell people that you greatly miss hugs and that you need them to hug you, and they will most likely to be glad to reciprocate. If you can afford it, indulge in a half-hour massage at a local spa. Request this as a birthday gift if possible, because a massage will work wonders for you—as you enjoy the touches and rubs while being unbelievably pampered.

Sleep with an extra pillow or a big stuffed teddy bear for company, while you avoid sex outside of marriage. Your children desperately need you to show them God's example of morality during this time of separation, and they don't need the extra confusion of a poor role model from you.

My young daughter wanted to sleep with me during the very painful early separation period, and I took advantage of any back rubs that she wanted to give me. Then I would rub her back softly with my fingernails, and she really enjoyed this gift from me as well. Remember to tell God of your need for hugs, and you may be surprised at his solutions.

*1 John 4:7*

*Beloved, let us love one another, because love is from God; everyone who loves is born of God and knows God.*

How do your parents feel about your separation or divorce? Chances are, they are supportive of you because your mother and father dearly love you. They hurt because you're hurting and in pain, and they probably wish they could take your pain away so that you wouldn't have to suffer. Be glad that you have their support, and then thank God for your parents.

Talk to them. If you've always had a close relationship with your parents, draw on that resource now. You don't have to share every detail with them—and you probably shouldn't—but make them aware of your life circumstances. Don't hide the truth from them. When I needed an ear to listen to me cry at 1:00 a.m., my parents were always the best people available to help.

If you are estranged from your parents, this may be a time to mend fences. Extend your arm to them and pray that they will come to your side.

Your parents can become positive Christian role models for your children as well. All children need male examples, and their grandfather may be an ideal person for this job.

Involve your parents in your family life in any way possible. Invite Grandma and Grandpa over for supper, ask them out to the local cafeteria for supper, encourage them to play with your children or invite them to attend a school play featuring your child.

Also call them on the phone, send birthday cards to them, include them in holiday plans and attend church with your parents.

Parents are a gift from God.

*Exodus 20:12*

*Honor your father and your mother,*
*so that your days may be long in the land*
*that the Lord your God is giving you.*

You are teaching your children about God with your words and actions every single day—both intentionally and unintentionally. Talk with your daughter about God's help during this difficult time of separation; share with her any answered prayers that you have had.

Make a conscious effort to say a blessing before each meal and say bedtime prayers together. Pray together about specific needs, such as a child's spelling test or safe car travel. Establish the habit of attending church weekly, and encourage her to participate in children and youth activities there.

You can lead your son or daughter to a personal relationship with the Lord, even while going through a divorce. Love and teach your children with the words you choose to use and with an absence of certain words. Make every effort to avoid harsh bitter words about your husband's actions. Your children don't need to hear negative comments about his behaviors; he will always be their father and they should be able to love him.

It is possible for your children to love their parents without loving all of their actions, and you should try to convey this to them. Ask God to control your tongue, especially in this area. Yes, this can be quite an enormous challenge, but God can handle even this hurdle!

Pray for your children. Specifically pray that they will draw closer to the Lord during this difficult time, instead of blaming God for their father's absence. When friends in your church and neighborhood ask what they can do to help during marital separation, ask them to pray for your children's spiritual growth.

Commit your children to the Lord in every way.

*1 Samuel 1:27*
*"For this child I prayed; and the Lord has granted me the petition that I made to him."*

Cry, and then cry some more; those tears are therapeutic. They can be a release for all the feelings that you have bottled up inside you from the past months, or maybe even years. You probably have feelings of grief at the loss of your marriage, your past memories, and your future dreams of being together as a family.

Or you may feel intense rage and rejection due to your husband's actions. So let your tears flow. They can help wash away your negative feelings, help you to feel renewed and help you sleep.

Don't rely on chemical aids unless medically necessary, because they can dull your senses to the point of not feeling some emotions. Always keep tissues in your car and your pocketbook because small events, such as "your song" on the radio, can unleash an avalanche of tears.

Just pull the car over to the side of the road and have a good cry if this happens. You may even need to pack extra mascara (waterproof, of course) and lipstick for these emergencies. You should eliminate eyeliner from your makeup routine during your separation, because your tears will just wash it into your eyes and cause you to cry even more!

It's okay to let your children see you cry, because they need to know that you're human. Your children might be very sad at the prospect of divorce because they were probably hoping for an immediate reconciliation of their parents. Remember to give them permission to cry, too. Make a special point to let your sons know that they have a right to cry and don't have to be stoic.

Don't be afraid or ashamed to cry, either alone or with your children.

*John 11:35*

*Jesus began to weep.*

Is there any joy in your daily existence? If not, then look around and find some reasons for a joy-filled life. Literally list your blessings—write them down on a piece of paper—God's love, your life, children, work, church, friends, parents, in-laws, aunts, uncles, sisters, brothers, cousins and grandparents.

You could add neighbors, your home, food to eat, a car to drive, a Bible to read, music, your former marriage and possible reconciliation. There are others—a beautiful sunset, a colorful sunrise, your husband's involvement with the children, sunshine, the ability to exercise and starry skies at night for gazing.

Even more—nature's beauty, your work, choices in life, your health and even a new recipe for that yummy chicken pie that you prepared for supper. How about the opportunity to witness to your children during this separation? You can be joyful that you can show them God's way in life. What a tremendous blessing this can be!

Always remember to be glad in the Lord's love. God cares for you in every detail of life, whether it is providing an extra $10 to treat your children to a sandwich for supper at a fast food restaurant or giving you a full night's sleep when your mind is full to the point of overflowing. He loves you and your entire family, and this is an incredible reason to be joyful.

Rejoice in the Lord!

*Psalm 98:8*

*Let the floods clap their hands;*
*let the hills sing together for joy.*

What are you doing in response to your husband's actions? Are you so bitter that you also want to have an extramarital affair? Do you want to leave home because you're overwhelmed with the responsibilities of single parenthood?

Do you feel justified in plotting revenge? Are you telling everyone about your husband's behaviors? Some women admit to having wished for their former husband's death in an automobile accident, while others have secretly hoped for his bankruptcy. However, we are all aware that these aren't model Christian thoughts.

Instead, follow the example of Jesus. It is important for your own mental and spiritual health, as well as that of your children, that you practice what you preach. If you claim to be a Christian woman who loves the Lord, you won't have an affair of retaliation, you won't leave your children out of sheer desperation, you won't plan revenge and you won't hope for your husband's demise. Instead, treat your husband and your children in the manner that you want to be treated.

Maintain an atmosphere of openness and honesty in your home, and your children will feel that they can come to you to discuss any problem they have. And you can share your own concerns with your children. If you're completely overwhelmed with the house and yard work, assign them chores such as cleaning the toilet or mowing the grass. Likewise, strive to treat your husband with respect.

You never know if you may be able to reconcile through joint counseling, and you may make this impossible if your actions are consistent with an attitude of bitterness. Ask the Holy Spirit to control your life; God can help you to practice the Golden Rule.

*Luke 6:31*

*Do to others as you would have them do to you.*

What are you saying to your children about their father? And how do you treat your husband when he comes to your home to visit with your two daughters?

Assure your children of your love for them, and tell them that you want them to have a relationship with their father—if this is at all possible. Such assurances can greatly relieve them, as they may have an ungrounded fear that you will keep them from their dad.

They probably feel very conflicted, torn and confused due to the marital separation. Repeatedly stress to your children that you want them to have your maternal love, their father's love and God's love. This may be very difficult or even impossible for you at the present time, but your children do need their father's love if he is able to give it.

Your children may feel awkward around their father and sometimes may want to avoid spending time with him. Encourage them to do simple things like going out for an ice cream cone. It is crucial for children to honor their parents.

Allow your godly influence to permeate your home, words and actions toward your husband—along with his relationship with the children. Pray for him as the father of your children. This prayer may be an incredibly difficult one to utter—in light of the pain of separation—but ask God for help and the Holy Spirit will assist and intercede for you as you pray. One particular woman said, upon separation, that her children were her husband's only link to reality in his new life apart from their family. Therefore, she insisted that he assume some carpooling duties so that he would, at the very least, see his children once each week.

Try to treat your husband with respect, while refusing to tolerate any form of abuse.

*James 4:11*

*Do not speak evil against one another,*
*brothers and sisters.*

How do your in-laws feel about your separation and impending divorce? They are most likely very saddened by the circumstances of your family's life at the present time. They quite naturally love their son, want to support their grandchildren and are probably confused about their feelings toward you.

How do you feel about your in-laws? Are you convinced that they are the big marital troublemakers and blame them for your separation? Were they controlling during your marriage, or did you have a good relationship with them? Just remember, especially now, that you are the mother of their grandchildren.

Try to maintain open communications with your in-laws. Be honest with them, but avoid belittling their son in their presence. Try to set an example for your children, as you continue to make every effort to continue with past holiday or birthday traditions and as you encourage your in-laws to visit their grandchildren. Avoid using your children as a bargaining chip, and don't attempt to keep your children from them unless the situation is very extreme or harmful.

Call your mother-in-law on the phone and ask for a special recipe; this may open doors of communication with her. Then invite her to come to your daughter's piano recital or your son's Scout ceremony, and thank her afterward for coming.

Pray for God's guidance and patience in your dealings with your mother-in-law and father-in-law. This may be a good opportunity to use some humor! You also can be a Christian witness to them as they see you continuing to be a godly mother to their grandchildren.

*Proverbs 17:17*

*Kinsfolk are born to share adversity.*

How do you feel at the end of your day? Are you exhausted, content, energized, creative, loving, short-tempered, patient or tolerant? Are you giving, selfish, enthusiastic, depleted, angry, joyful, sad or happy? Are you satisfied or dissatisfied with what you've accomplished on this particular day?

To a large measure, your satisfaction with your day has to do with your relationship with God. If you have remained with him all day, you'll be much happier than if you have strayed from his will as you know it.

God wants you to care for your children; ask for his help to find the energy to cook for them, clean your home, play with them and witness to them. Also, ask the Lord for time to simply relax with your children. Weekend evenings could be a wonderful time to sit together and watch television or play a board game—with the phone turned off to avoid all those interruptions! God also wants you to be productive at work. Pray for a clear mind free of worry and distraction, in order that you can accomplish what is laid before you at the office. You can then be satisfied at the end of the day.

God wants you to take care of yourself, too. Do something good—just for you—every day. This may include finding 10 minutes to sit and read a book, making time for a quick 15-minute power nap or calling a friend on the phone to talk for a while. In the evening, reflect on your day.

Have you walked with God? Are you weary and ready to fall into bed after a day with your children and work? Did you do some little thing for yourself? If so, then smile and sleep well. If not, there's always tomorrow.

*Matthew 25:21*

*"'Well done, good and faithful servant!'"* NIV

Where can you get enough strength to keep going?

How can you possibly take care of everything that is on your "to do" list for today—children, meals, house, yard work, emotional upheaval, tears, work, laundry and sleep (if you're lucky)? All of life's many, many chores can be completely overwhelming at times!

You need to turn to God early each and every morning to ask for his strength during marital separation and during your entire life.

He and he alone can give you the sustenance to keep going. Admit your powerlessness to the Lord and ask for help. Give to God all your concerns, joys, praises and prayer requests.

When you feel weak—and you may frequently feel weak during separation from your husband—examine your priorities and your source of power. You can do almost nothing on your own, but ask Christ to give you strength. The Lord has an unending supply of power, which is yours for the taking. Jesus Christ can help you not only to survive, but to thrive!

*Philippians 4:13*

*I can do all things through him who strengthens me.*

Examine your priorities in life, and reinforce your decision to be a disciple of Christ. Allow God to use you as he sees fit.

In order to fully commit your heart to God, you need to establish a quiet time with him every day—a point in your busy day to read your Bible and pray. The hour of the day is your decision; some people prefer an early morning devotional while others read the Word and study in the evening hours.

Deliberately begin to spend time with the Master, and start today. One very busy woman with four toddlers had to be incredibly creative in order to find a moment or two. She often retreated to the bathroom with her Bible in hand so that she could be alone talking to the Lord! Read the Bible in order to discover God's will for your life, and then ask him for help with daily decisions for your family. If you're truly under Christ's control, then you can bear fruit for him as you become aware of his plans for you. If, on the other hand, you're so busy seeking guidance from other people and never taking time to read the Bible, you can never discover God's true purposes for you.

Put Christ at the center of your life during your separation and divorce and you will continue to grow as his child.

*Mark 1:35*

*In the morning, while it was still very dark, he got up and went out to a deserted place, and there he prayed.*

God loves you and cares for you.

God also loves your children and wants to comfort them during this terribly difficult time of hurt and pain in their young lives.

God, the only God, the one true God who created the universe and all that is in it, loves you. Take a moment to absorb the awesome truth of that statement. Reflecting on that truth can always comfort us and help us to endure whatever trial may come our way on a certain day.

His love is perfect and complete, and at times, it is almost impossible to comprehend. You may feel small and seemingly insignificant in the world, but God does love you. He wants the best for you, watches over you, guides you, helps you with every decision, and is in control of your life. Still yourself and quietly accept this wonderful gift. He loves you so much that he gave his son Jesus to die for you.

Thank God today for his wonderful love that surrounds you and bask in the warmth of his love.

*John 3:16*

*"For God so loved the world that he gave his only Son, so that everyone who believes in him may not perish but may have eternal life."*

Are you often flooded with memories of your life with your husband? Did you attend the senior high school prom together or college football games? Do you remember your wedding day, the first time you made love, the births of your children, and building your first home—or going to the grocery store for the first time as a married couple to buy all the household food staples and spending oodles of money?

How about your first paycheck as a married woman, your daughter's first word, that special song, your son's first step, preparing a special meal for your first wedding anniversary dinner or a wonderful vacation together? Do you remember your first kiss? Are your memories sweet or bittersweet? Allow yourself to remember these special events and treasure the happy thoughts. Such remembrances are natural, and they will probably surface very often during upcoming years in your life. Enjoy these good times and don't neglect to share them with your children, because they need good memories of your family together.

Likewise, you cannot completely block out painful memories. You may be assaulted by unfortunate thoughts of substance abuse, domestic violence, addiction or infidelity. Sometimes these memories can literally cause you to have a physical ache in the pit of your stomach, or they can trigger an extremely angry reaction. And you may just have to endure the memory until it passes, while trusting that the feelings will most surely get better with time.

Continue to take life one day at a time, smile at good memories, and be assured that God will help you to survive what could be horribly unpleasant trips down memory lane.

*Ephesians 1:16*

*I do not cease to give thanks for you
as I remember you in my prayers.*

You are probably tired from doing at least 2,000 things each day. In fact, you might be downright exhausted! Each morning you get yourself out of bed, get your children up, prepare breakfast, think about your marriage, try to smile, get ready for work, make your bed and get everybody out the door to officially begin the day.

Then you go to work, run errands at lunch instead of eating, check for any telephone messages, work through the afternoon, go to the grocery store on the way home, grab a quick glass of water to drink and then drive your daughter to her piano lesson. Then you cook supper, sweep the kitchen floor, return any phone messages, eat with your children, wash two loads of laundry and ask the children to fold the clothes and put them away.

In the middle of the laundry, you tutor your daughter in algebra and assist your son with the rhythm on a band musical piece he is learning. You remind your children to do their chores—taking out the trash and feeding the dog. Finally you get everybody to bed and sit down to catch a breath before reading your Bible.

It's no wonder that you're fatigued beyond belief!

Finally you collapse in the bed, but your mind is running at such a furious pace because you're worrying about your marriage and can't sleep. Ask God for rest. Give this need to him, and he will supply you with much-needed physical rest so that you can continue to care for yourself and your children.

God is in charge. He is able and will handle this most basic physical need.

*Matthew 11:28*

*"Come to me, all you that are weary and are carrying heavy burdens, and I will give you rest."*

Rest in the Lord, and you will find true rest.

Spiritual wrestling and indecision can take a tremendous emotional toll, and only God can help in this area. Do you sometimes blame God for the messy state of your marriage? Do you surrender your marital separation to the Lord, only to act like a yo-yo, retrieve it and then continue to worry about it? Your human side may often creep in, as you think that you know best how to fix a particular problem.

A Christian approach is to commit your entire being to God. The arm of the Lord is strong and able to withstand any problem. God wants you to trust him, obey him, give your burdens to him and then leave them with him.

Trust that he is already taking care of your problems in a far better way than you could alone, and thank him for this. Remember that God loves you immensely. The Lord God has a special plan concerning your marriage and family; pray that his will be done and then commit your family to him.

Your Father wants to care for you.

*Matthew 11:29*

*"Take my yoke upon you, and learn from me; for I am gentle and humble in heart, and you will find rest for your souls."*

What do you value in life? What do you treasure? Do you value money, a big house, a brand-new car, impressions of power and prestige, a promotion at work, accumulation of stocks and bonds, exotic vacations, fine jewelry or expensive clothing?

Perhaps you value reading the current bestselling novel (which might be X-rated), buying more and more stuff, having plastic surgery to remove wrinkles or owning 35 pairs of shoes.

Or do you treasure your family, your volunteer work in the community, your church family, friendships, motherhood, and your relationship with God? Maybe you also hope to someday reconcile with your spouse. Take an inventory of how you spend your time. This analysis will reveal precisely what you value most and what your treasures are.

As a Christian woman, you should not concentrate only on earthly possessions but on heavenly attributes. When you consider the entire span of history, you are on the earth for such a short period of time.

Things of God will last, whereas the latest fashion clothing will quickly come and go.

*Matthew 6:19–21*

*"Do not store up for yourselves treasures on earth, where moth and rust consume and where thieves break in and steal; but store up for yourselves treasures in heaven, where neither moth nor rust consumes and where thieves do not break in and steal. For where your treasure is, there your heart will be also."*

Music can be so therapeutic and comforting to a hurting soul. What is your favorite music for listening—classical, rock, contemporary Christian, oldies, easy listening, gospel or swing? Whatever type of music you prefer, listen to it often because it will soothe some pain.

Sing along and your mood will instantly improve. Dance, either alone or with your son or daughter, and you'll begin to smile. You just can't help it. Listen to loud music if you're angry. Turn the volume up, and this might exorcise some of the ache in your heart.

During my separation, I often played my car radio at full tilt with the windows open while strumming my fingers to the rhythm of oldies music. It helped!

Make some music. Playing a Beethoven sonata on the piano can serve as an incredible release of tension on a day when you're riding that emotional roller coaster. Find a hymn book and play some old favorites; they can give you such a lift.

Sing something—even a television commercial jingle. Blowing a trumpet or trombone while tapping your foot to the beat can also help to chase away those pervasive sad feelings. How about blowing into a kazoo?

Sing those hymns at church; your voice may be drowned out by other more beautiful voices around you if you have only bathroom shower singing abilities, but it doesn't matter. Sing anyway; make that joyful noise!

If your children are musicians, enjoy the sounds that they make. It's wonderful to hear your son or daughter play a tune on the piano or even to hear them screech those beginning pieces on a violin.

Let music help your heart be happy again.


*Psalm 100:1*

*Make a joyful noise to the Lord, all the earth.*

Friends can help you survive a marital separation and divorce.

You may need someone to talk with about your husband's infidelity, substance abuse or pornography addiction. Just having a trusted friend for ventilation can keep you sane. Remember to choose carefully with whom you share confidential details, or your whole neighborhood will know all the information that you wanted to keep private. True friends will let you call them and talk at any hour of the day or night. My standard question to my neighbor, who listened to hours of intimate details of my life, was, "Is the psychiatrist in?"

If her answer was in the affirmative, I knew that she was then free to talk with me for a solid 30 minutes, and I could tell her anything and everything. Her friendship was—and still is—invaluable! Do you need an ear to hear about your loneliness, or do you simply need a hug? A friend can help.

A friend can go out to eat breakfast or lunch with you as a companion or sit with you at the kitchen table for a cup of hot tea as you cry tears of sadness. Or she can offer advice on helping your children to cope.

During my separation, I developed female friendships that I had ignored for ages. One Friday night three of us got together for salad and cheese tortellini. We talked for five hours about our dreams, broken dreams, children, church, hopes, husbands and lives in general. The food and fellowship kept me going throughout the entire subsequent week, and I still treasure the friendship of these wonderful Christian women.

You may have a trusted friend in your neighborhood, at church, in your child's school or at work. Talk with her, thank her for her gift of time and then thank God for friends.

*Proverbs 17:17*

*A friend loves at all times.*

Mopping a kitchen floor can be a form of therapy during this time of separation. It is possible to think through problems even while washing the supper dishes. Talking aloud to yourself is not only permitted, but encouraged while dusting and vacuuming. "Venting" to the air is a good thing. Talk to God.

Housework enables you to keep busy and think. You can plan the next outing with your children as you clean the bathtub, and it is possible to review your household budget while sweeping the hall. How about planning the supper menu as you scrub the kitchen sink?

Talking out loud, silent thinking, crying, whistling, singing and praying are activities that are perfect companions with your multitude of household chores.

When separation follows months or years of marital turmoil, you may find that there is a very long list of chores to be done. You can get free mental therapy while crossing many items off your to-do list. How about putting up a coat rack that has been sitting in the garage for months? You can wash dust boards that haven't been touched in three years. Or how about cleaning out your bedroom closet and getting rid of your old clothes by donating to a local charity?

Housework provides plenty of opportunity for satisfaction, because you can easily see the fruits of your labor. Gratification is immediate when you can once again see through the bay window in the den without looking through all of those smudge marks.

You can clean your home, both physically and spiritually, and claim it as your own.

*Leviticus 16:30*

*For on this day atonement shall be made for you, to cleanse you; from all your sins you shall be clean before the Lord.*

Are you lonely during separation?

You probably are. After many years of marriage, it's normal to be lonely during specific times of the day, such as: When you roll out of the bed in the morning and there is no one to say good morning. Coming home from work to an empty house. When there is no adult to discuss the course of the day (Remember the phrase, "How was work, honey?"). When the children are in bed and there is no adult present for conversation. When your husband is not there to tell you good night. Going to bed and sleeping alone.

You will also feel alone during holiday periods, so be prepared for a fresh ache of your heart. Call a friend or sister on your birthday and take your children out to eat at a fancy restaurant. Make plans to do something special for yourself on your wedding anniversary.

Let yourself feel lonely; there is no reason whatsoever to deny your pain. You must experience the pain and grief in order to have true healing and recovery, but try not to dwell on your loneliness for hours and hours.

Instead, surround yourself with people that you love—your children, parents, friends, siblings, church family, neighbors and work colleagues. Pets are also wonder companions when you're lonely. You may also find that you enjoy your own company. Read a book, sit and think, plan that dream vacation, take a walk, listen to music, or sing.

Remember that the Lord is with you constantly. You are never truly alone when you have him by your side.

*Matthew 28:20*

*"And remember, I am with you always,*
*to the end of the age."*

Gossip can get out of control. Remember the game you played as a child when everyone sat in a circle, the leader whispered one sentence to the person on her right, and then it was whispered from person to person until it got back to the leader once again? Invariably, the final sentence was light years away from its humble beginnings.

Gossip about marital problems—communication issues, adultery, domestic violence, abandonment, addictions, drug use, pornography, alcohol abuse —just gets increasingly distorted and exaggerated as it is repeated. Make every effort to avoid spreading gossip about your family situation, and don't share all of those juicy details with every neighbor on the street.

A standard response when someone asks a question concerning your marital separation might be something like, "This is very personal and painful. Please pray for our family." Have this phrase memorized and on the tip of your tongue, as people can be quite nosy at times. However, it is also important to avoid telling lies.

Don't lie to your children about the reason for your husband's departure, but tell them only the facts without additional emotional embellishment.

Any necessary details will most certainly be revealed as time marches on. Likewise, if an in-law or other family member asks a specific question of you and indicates that she is aware of personal details, simply nod your head without being untruthful.

Be comforted with the knowledge that God knows the truth. And other significant people in your life will know details of your separation when you decide that the timing is right. You are in control of this situation.

*James 3:6*

*And the tongue is a fire.*

Grief is a process and it takes time. In fact, grieving for a dissolved marriage can take a very, very long time. Allow yourself to grieve and don't be ashamed of it.

You're probably grieving for many past memories, future family plans, the loss of a "together" family, your dreams, your children's life without a father on an everyday basis and even the loss of anticipated family vacations together. You may also be grieving for other losses—financial security, attending family reunions as a unit, romantic evenings with your husband, celebration of a 25th wedding anniversary and even sitting together as a family in church.

Grief has many stages, but they are not concrete. Your feelings will ebb and flow. They may come and go as you move through grief's many different forms.

Shock and denial, anger, depression, bargaining and acceptance are some of the standard pieces of the grief process. You may be the type of woman to march through each stage quickly, or the process may take many months or even years.

Remember that the stages are fluid, and you may be in denial and angry at the same time. There is no master schedule for grief work. Simply recognize what is happening in your life and ask God to steer you through this separation from your husband.

Most importantly, realize that it is entirely normal and appropriate to grieve for this tremendous loss.

*Genesis 37:34*

*Then Jacob tore his garments, and put sackcloth on his loins, and mourned for his son many days.*

Denial is a defense mechanism that protects you. You may not be ready to admit to yourself or anyone else that your husband is planning to leave your home or is already gone; you may be totally denying that your marriage really is in trouble. That's okay—don't push it. And don't allow anyone else to push you, either.

Denial actually prevents you from feeling incredible amounts of pain when you're not ready for this particular assault. This stage of grief maintains the status quo. You may be afraid to discover the complete truth about your husband's adultery or his drug addiction. You may be covering any evidence of domestic violence with makeup, or you may be unable at this point to search for any more bottles of alcohol.

It is certainly possible to believe that things will get better, even in the light of verbal, emotional or physical abuse that has been ongoing for years.

You may be asking yourself, *Why me? Why my family?* You're still in shock that your marriage is on the edge of collapse, and you're having a difficult time believing that this is truly happening. After all, you love your husband!

Denial allows you to continue your life as it has been, and it may be God's way of helping you to cope in the present time. Perhaps your husband has just recently left you and your children.

Denial of the reality of marital separation may help you to believe that he will come back tomorrow—or next week at the absolute latest. And you believe that everything will immediately be "fixed" when he returns.

Denial can be quite helpful to you in the short term.

*Luke 22:34*

*Jesus said, "I tell you, Peter, the cock will not crow this day, until you have denied three times that you know me."*

Anger is usually a very recognizable form of grief processing. Arguments with your husband may have begun before your separation, or they may have escalated to full swing for the first time after he moved away from home.

You're probably mad at the entire situation—angry with him, angry with yourself for turning a blind eye for weeks or months or years while hoping for improvement, angry at abandonment, angry at single motherhood or angry at "failed" joint counseling.

Loud outbursts at the children, short tempers, gossip with friends, focusing exclusively on yourself, rising blood pressure and inward fuming are clear indications that anger is present. You usually know when you're mad! But remember that anger has a purpose. It can cleanse you of remaining doubt and can have a very cathartic effect. However, sometimes you may think that you have your anger under control, only to be suddenly and unexpectedly seized by intensely angry feelings toward your spouse. At such times, you may feel as if your anger has taken over your life. It is quite easy for anger to become self-destructive.

Claim your anger for what it is, a very normal human emotion, but ask God for control. He is big enough to handle it, and he will provide coping mechanisms, such as exercise or music therapy or a counselor.

Don't give in to your anger, because God has a far better plan for your life. Ask God for a forgiving spirit.

*Ephesians 4:26*

*Be angry but do not sin;*
*do not let the sun go down on your anger.*

Sadness at such great losses in your life is natural. It's almost expected that you will enter into some form of depression in light of the tremendous upheaval in your life. Some signs of depression include sleeplessness or sleeping more than usual, continuous crying, overeating, eating nothing or an inability to concentrate.

Be aware of your emotional state during your separation and divorce proceedings. Recognize that some depression is a normal part of grief, but notice if your sadness gets more profound. Do you stay in bed all day and cry, only hoping to eventually get up when your children get home from school? Have you gained five pounds in one week from overeating?

Or have you lost ten pounds in two weeks because your stomach simply cannot accept food? Are you completely overwhelmed at work and unable to accomplish even small tasks due to scattered concentration? If you are concerned about increasing depression, consult a medical professional. If you are depressed and the idea of suicide ever enters your head, tell someone *immediately* and pray to God for help—never ignore such thoughts!

On the other hand, if you have occasional tears but are able to carry on with the usual activities of life, you may be experiencing the normal depression associated with grieving. Be alert to what your body and mind are telling you.

Guilt about your role in the marital separation may also be playing a big role in your sadness. You may wonder: *Could I have forgiven him just one more time? What else could I have done to keep our family together? Is this my fault because of something I did or didn't do?*

Read from the Psalms as an antidote for depression.

*Psalm 42:6*

*My soul is cast down within me.*

After a while you are no longer in denial that your marriage is in trouble, and after the passing of a few months, you're probably able to handle your anger a bit better. Perhaps you are still very sad and have some days that are tear-filled. In addition to some residual feelings of depression, you may also notice that you have some bargaining thoughts drift into your mind.

Do any of these thoughts sound familiar to you? *If I just lose these extra 25 pounds, he'll love me. Bring him back home, God, and I'll go to church every Sunday for the rest of my life. If I just love him more, we can reconcile. I'll be a better lover and he will be more satisfied. I'll clean the house better so he won't get angry and hit me. If I control the children more, he won't use drugs.*

You may bargain silently with yourself, aloud with your children, verbally with your husband or prayerfully with God. You may still want an intact family because you feel that is God's ultimate will—and you may be willing to do almost anything to make that happen, including making some promises to yourself and others.

Most bargaining is simply a way to make you feel as though you have some control over your marital situation. However, in reality, you may have very little control over your husband's infidelity, abandonment, domestic violence, abuse of alcohol or drug use.

But you most certainly do have control of your own actions. Pray to God the following, the only bargain you will ever truly need—"Lord, be my God and I will be your child."

*Proverbs 19:21*

*The human mind may devise many plans, but it is the purpose of the Lord that will be established.*

You may finally arrive at some form of acceptance several months—or even years—after separation and divorce.

Acceptance may be defined differently on each day of the week. On Monday, you may be relieved that your heart doesn't flip flop when your husband picks your children up to take them out to supper. And on Tuesday, acceptance is defined as an absence of anger.

Wednesday brings relief that certain behaviors are forever out of your house. Thursday may define acceptance as not hoping that your husband will call to talk with the children so that you can hear his voice on the telephone. When Friday arrives, you can mention the word "forgiveness" in your prayers.

On Saturday you no longer have a burning need to tell your closest friend another ugly detail about the extramarital affair. Finally, while sitting in church on Sunday, you smile very broadly while thanking God both for peace in your life and for sitting in the pew with your son and daughter.

Even in the midst of acceptance, you may feel angry at times and still deny some of the pain of separation. Grief work does occasionally take two steps forward and one step backward, and that's okay.

Pray for God's blessings and love to be heaped on you daily as you struggle with an unwanted breaking of your family unit. Remember that you're dealing here with accepting the loss of a marriage and detaching yourself from your mate.

God can supply strength as you grieve for such an incredible loss.

*Psalm 131:2*

*But I have calmed and quieted my soul,*
*like a weaned child with its mother; my soul*
*is like the weaned child that is with me.*

What words can you think of to describe God?

Good. Steadfast. Present. Faithful. Giving. Powerful. In control. Uplifting. Forgiving. Loving. Most High. Refuge. King. Judge. Loyal. Wonderful. Almighty. Strong. True. Beautiful. Father. Spirit. Able. Holy. Source. Fortress. Infinite. Lord. Trinity. Saviour. Ruler. Comforter. Peace. Majestic. Awesome. Blessed. Pure. Glorious. Righteous. Victorious. Creator. Great. Living. Grace. Peace. Only. Wise. Always. Immortal. Splendor. One. Healer. Exalted. Light. Provider. Mighty. Master. Best. Sacrificial. Everlasting. Omnipotent. Supreme. Perfect. All.

Worship God and praise his name.

*Psalm 99:5*

*Extol the Lord our God; worship*
*at his footstool. Holy is he!*

What gifts do you possess?

Are you a gifted gardener, even helping those summer geraniums to bloom in the middle of February? Is writing your strength, using your spare time to jot a note of sympathy or encouragement to a friend? How about singing, offering up your beautiful voice in testimony to the Lord in church when asked? Do you consider your loving maternal attributes one of your strongest gifts? Your greatest gift may still be that of a loving and giving wife.

Maybe you are the best volunteer in the neighborhood, addressing envelopes for charity or asking for donations for medical causes. You may be the best homework assistant your fourth-grade child could ever have. Can you cook a wonderful chicken and broccoli casserole or an awesome chocolate pound cake with cream cheese icing? Is encouragement an extra-special gift of yours? Have you ever been nominated for the teacher of the year in the school system? You just might be the most gentle and caring nurse working at the local hospital. Have you ever thought of yourself as the best church secretary that has ever existed? Some women are phenomenal housekeepers and attack the chore of housework with a song on their lips. Do you light up an entire room when your smile?

Search yourself. Identify some of your hidden talents and gifts from God.

*Matthew 13:12*

*"For to those who have, more will be given, and they will have an abundance; but from those who have nothing, even what they have will be taken away."*

What spiritual gifts do you possess?

God gives gifts to us in order to build his church on earth. It is important to realize that all spiritual gifts come from God and that they're not of our own making. And it is also important to realize that they are still present even in the midst of the ache, pain and anger associated with marital separation. God does give each of us different gifts and we can use them for God's glory, and not merely for our own purposes.

If you are a natural teacher, continue with your ministry of teaching the children's kindergarten Sunday School class when possible. You may be a witness to a child or her family even in the middle of your turmoil. Persevere with leading the children's choir at church; it will be good therapy for you as you praise God even when hurting. Continue with exhortation; encourage the young adult in your church congregation who comes to you with a problem of her own while perhaps being unaware of your own struggles. By all means, fulfill your monetary obligation to the church and give proportionate to your income as you always have.

Your spiritual gifts of compassion and cheerfulness speak volumes to Christians and non-Christians around you at church, home, work and play. The gift of healing is special indeed and should be used for God's glory and in his service.

God will reveal your spiritual gifts to you if you only ask.

*1 Corinthians 12:4–6*

*Now there are varieties of gifts, but the same Spirit;
and there are varieties of services, but the same Lord;
and there are varieties of activities, but is the same
God who activates all of them in everyone.*

In the midst of marital separation, it's easy to feel confined by life's obligations. You may work in order to provide for your family, cook supper at night for you and your children, wash load after load of dirty laundry, continue in cleaning dirty bathrooms and mow the yard. In addition, you continue to struggle emotionally.

Reflect on how many times you've asked yourself the following questions: *Should I let him come back if he wants to return to our family? Can I endure any more verbal, emotional or physical abuse and continue to exist as God's child? What Christian example am I setting for my children if he continues in an adulterous situation within the bounds of our marriage?* These questions may gnaw at you and make you feel as though they are 50-pound weights constantly dragging you down.

Recognize that God can take these concerns of yours, because he has very broad shoulders for handling burdens. Follow Christ and remain in the Word so that you can be free from such confining thoughts and behavior patterns. Give all your burdens to God, and let him work this out because he knows what is best for you.

Have you noticed that you feel the most liberated that you have in years because your husband's torments are no longer a daily occurrence? Have you broken free from his oppression?

God wants you to grow as a Christian and does not want you to be defeated. Freedom to follow God and his commandments is absolute freedom.

*John 8:31–32*

*Then Jesus said to the Jews who had believed in him, "If you continue in my word, you are truly my disciples; and you will know the truth, and the truth will make you free."*

Did you eat breakfast today? You may have been so busy packing the children's school lunches and hurrying out the door that you completely forgot about feeding yourself. What did you have for supper last night—fast food again or a more nutritious meal?

Take care of yourself. You're under stress right now during your separation, and what you eat can make you stronger or deplete you. If you eat only junk food, you may feel like junk. Eating well does not have to be very costly, and you don't have to cook a six-course dinner each night. Every morning, remember to eat breakfast. If this is not your habit, start now.

Eat some protein to get you going in the morning —egg, cheese, yogurt—and put some healthy carbo-hydrates with it. You will notice a huge difference in your energy level and thinking ability.

Make yourself eat lunch instead of running errands for your family. You can quickly put together a turkey and cheese sandwich, or eat leftover soup from last night's dinner. If you eat a snack in the afternoon at work or when you get home, be sure that it's a healthy one. A candy bar and cola every now and then is okay, but don't plan on these calories keeping you going until your evening meal.

Cook supper. If you don't have money or time to be a gourmet chef, try soup served over rice for your children along with fresh fruit. Even grilled cheese sandwiches with carrot sticks and milk can make a meal in a pinch. And remember that you can get added benefits of family fun if your children peel those carrots and cook in the kitchen with you. Try a new recipe from a magazine occasionally, and you may even discover a hidden talent!

As we nourish our bodies, God's Word provides nourishment for our souls.

*Jeremiah 15:16*

*Your words were found, and I ate them, and your words became to me a joy and the delight of my heart; for I am called by your name, O Lord, God of hosts.*

Do you feel stressed, burned out or fried to a crisp? Has your hair turned gray from a lack of caring for yourself or being cared for by others? Or, are you actually losing a handful of hair in the bathtub drain every day? Of course you're stressed at this point in your life!

Well, do something about it. Smile, "vent" to a friend, maintain your weight, pet your dog, call a friend, walk, read a book, take a bubble bath or give yourself a manicure. Yes, you deserve it. No, you didn't deserve abuse or abandonment, but you do deserve a manicure. Don't continue to be a victim.

Make a to-do list, avoid procrastination, laugh out loud, sing a Christmas carol two months late, get a new haircut, decorate your house for Valentine's Day or buy a pair of sexy shoes. Even though you don't feel sexy now, you might later with God's blessing. Take slow deep breaths, pray, eat some popcorn, rub some fragrant body lotion on your hands and arms or soak in the tub for 20 minutes while listening to music and burning candles.

Give yourself a pedicure and paint those toenails flaming red. This can be your middle-of-the-winter secret under your shoes. Walk in the rain or sing in the shower.

Pray some more and smile some more.

You could find a hobby you like—cross-stitch, painting, reading, cooking, knitting or stenciling. Have some fun and play for 10 minutes each day, as play is a great way to decrease your stress level. Simply unwind and be good to yourself.

*Proverbs 17:22*

*A cheerful heart is a good medicine, but a downcast spirit dries up the bones.*

Are you in a hurry for an end to this marital separation? You may find that you're in a rush for successful counseling with your husband to lead to reconciliation. Or you may find the thought of living with him again to be deplorable and catch yourself crossing the days off your calendar until a divorce might become legal.

We are often trying to speed things along without regard to God's intervention. Do you have a plan for your life that you're ready to put into place without consulting God? It's so easy to decide what we want and then ask for God's seal of approval.

God is in charge, and he has a master plan for your marriage and your life.

His timing is perfect, and we must always remember to seek his will and wait on him. If you push headfirst into what you want or what you think is best for you, often the end result is total disaster and not the good that God intends for you.

Be still and listen to God. He may ask you to wait longer, or he may provide an immediate answer. His certain promise of strength will help you to endure the difficulties associated with separation and divorce.

Wait. Wait on God.

*Isaiah 40:31*

*But those who wait for the Lord shall renew their strength, they shall mount up with wings like eagles, they shall run and not be weary, they shall walk and not faint.*

You may be feeling very nostalgic on this Valentine's Day. Perhaps you are missing your husband and crying. Did you find an old Valentine card that had been stuck in a drawer? Go ahead and be sad for part of the day but then try to think some positive thoughts.

Instead of moping around the house all day, make a list of everybody that you love on this Valentine's Day during your time of separation from your husband. Write these names down so that you can have a visual reminder of everybody that you love.

Do you still love your husband? Then go ahead and put him on your list. Include your children, mother, father, sisters, brothers, grandmother, grandfather, uncles, aunts and cousins. Your in-laws may also be included—mother-in-law, father-in-law, sister-in-law and brother-in-law.

Maybe you have a very dear Christian friend who has comforted you during this terribly awful thing called separation. Definitely include her on your list of loved ones. Next, make a list of people who love you. God's name should top your list, as his love is perfect and complete. Bask in the love that your children shower on you, and return that love with hugs and smiles. Have your parents been unwavering in their support of you? Then list their names in capital letters.

Include other family members, friends, co-workers, neighbors, your pastor and church members. Now take several long minutes to examine these lists. You love and are loved.

Happy Valentine's Day!

*1 Corinthians 13:7*

*It [love] bears all things, believes all things, hopes all things, endures all things.*

Do you want to get back at your husband for hurting you? All too often a woman will have a sexual affair with another man as a form of retaliation against her husband for the pain he has inflicted with infidelity. Or perhaps she'll begin to drink large quantities of alcohol herself as a way to get back at her husband for the destruction that his alcoholism has caused in the family. Sometimes a woman will physically strike her husband after he has hit her or their children.

Maybe you want to yell insults at your husband after enduring months and years of verbal abuse, which have left you emotionally scarred and empty.

One woman was so devastated by her husband's adultery that she had a physical affair with another man almost immediately after her husband left their family home. About eight weeks later, she discovered that she was pregnant and was unsure who the father of the baby might have been. Even 20 years later, she regrets her retaliation behaviors and tells other women to avoid her negative example.

Jesus Christ taught his disciples to show mercy and think positively instead of focusing on harming others. It is indeed human to want to retaliate against your husband, but it not Christ-like. It is incredibly difficult to take the initiative to do something good when you are left in a path of destruction from a failed marriage.

Once again, pray and ask for God's help; you cannot overcome retaliatory temptations by yourself. Ask God to control your actions, and bring them in line with his commandments. Pray for the ability to demonstrate merciful behavior through the Holy Spirit's guidance.

*Matthew 7:12*

*"In everything do to others as you would have them do to you; for this is the law and the prophets."*

You'll have many important choices to make during your time of separation from your husband. Will you stay in your home? Or are you going to sell the house for financial and emotional reasons? Do you plan to go back to work or discontinue working? Will you increase your work hours from part time to full time? Who will have custody of the children? Is your husband able to have the children for weekend visitation? Will you continue to abide in Christ? Or will you abandon God and blame him for the demise of your marriage?

If possible, delay some major decisions for several months, or even a year, while you take time to think and truly assess your situation. Your children might benefit from the stability of remaining in their home if you can financially afford to remain there. The absence of their father is a huge adjustment, and the familiarity of their own bedrooms may help to comfort them. Attending the same school and playing with the neighborhood children who have been their friends for years could also make them feel more secure.

Choose your work schedule carefully, as your children will most surely need your presence during the marital separation. They need to be assured that you won't leave them, often a huge unspoken fear of children in the midst of marital upheaval.

Our biggest choice as women of separation is whether to lean on the Lord. What we choose can forever alter the remainder of our lives. Choose to abide in Christ.

*John 15:16*

*"You did not choose me but I chose you. And I appointed you to go and bear fruit, fruit that will last, so that the Father will give you whatever you ask him in my name."*

Are you a Christian? If you are, praise God and continue to live your life according to his Word. God's ways are true, holy, pure and good. But the ways of the world are often the exact opposite—false, vile, impure and bad.

Living in Christ is a way of life. Christianity guides your thoughts, desires and actions. If controlled by Christ, your behavior will reflect God's love. But being a Christian does not guarantee a life free of trouble! You're well aware of this fact, being in the middle of separation from your husband.

You never planned for your family to be torn apart, but some actions are beyond your control. Even though Christianity does not protect us from the trials of life, your faith can sustain you and help you to ultimately respond in a positive manner.

If you have not accepted Christ into your heart, read your Bible and consult a pastor of a nearby Christian church. Jesus was born to die on the cross for your sins and he rose victoriously from the dead. God loves you freely and abundantly. His love through Christ is a gift that you cannot earn or buy, but it is yours for the taking.

In order to become a Christian, you simply have to accept his offer and believe in Christ. It will change your own life as well as those of your children and grandchildren for the better and forever. Your reward is eternal life!

*1 Corinthians 15:3–4*

*For I handed on to you as of first importance what I in turn had received: that Christ died for our sins in accordance with the scriptures, and that he was buried, and that he was raised on the third day in accordance with the scriptures.*

Read some books written by Christian authors during your separation. Go scavenge your local Christian bookstore. If money is in short supply you can borrow a book from your church or public library or ask a friend for a book loan.

There are books available on every topic imaginable related to marriage, separation and divorce. But be careful what you choose, because many books are secular while claiming to be written from a Christian viewpoint. They promote a "do what feels good" philosophy, while steering clear of God's commands. Find a book about nurturing relationships, those dealing with children and marriage.

You can locate a book discussing children of divorce and suggestions for handling sensitive topics. By all means, read a book about growing as a Christian, as separation is an ideal time to deepen your relationship with Christ.

Do you like to read novels? Locate one penned by a Christian woman, sit in your favorite easy chair with a cup of hot tea and devour it. It can be a wonderful diversion for your busy mind.

How about a book of inspiration? Many Christian bookstores feature short pieces that will lift you emotionally and give you some much-needed hope. Have several on hand, and take heart from the experiences of others.

And, of course, remember to read your Bible. As a Christian, you cannot know what God expects from you unless you partake of the Word on a daily basis.

*Deuteronomy 17:19*

*It shall remain with him and he shall read in it all
the days of his life, so that he may learn to fear
the Lord his God, diligently observing all the
words of this law and these statutes.*

What is your greatest fear? Is it cancer, financial ruin due to limited monetary resources, or your children liking your husband's girlfriend? Are you fearful of your son becoming an alcoholic like his father or your daughter becoming promiscuous? Are you afraid of continued domestic violence, depression or losing your job?

Two months after separation from my husband, a water leak developed when an upstairs toilet clogged. Our house was 15 years old at the time, with an assortment of aging issues. I was able to use a plunger to unclog the mess, and was feeling quite proud of myself due to extremely limited handyman abilities. However, that pride was very short-lived, since my daughter immediately yelled up the stairs and informed me that water was dripping into the kitchen through the ceiling. I ran down the stairs and saw water pouring onto the floor!

I called my father, who came over and cut a hole in the ceiling for the five or six gallons of water to drain so that the ceiling wouldn't cave in. What a mess—buckets and towels were everywhere.

Of course, I was seeing dollar signs before my eyes through my tears of frustration. At that moment, the phone rang and a friend from my Sunday School class issued a dinner party invitation. I told her about the mess, and her husband suggested that I call a plumber in our church.

The plumber came over the next day, quickly diagnosed the problem, and repaired the problem by lifting the toilet from the floor and replacing the seal. He flatly refused any payment—he wouldn't even accept money for the parts.

God is big enough to handle all our fears, even those of homeowner and toilet repairs!

*Genesis 15:1*

*After these things the word of the Lord came to Abram in a vision, "Do not be afraid, Abram, I am your shield; your reward shall be very great."*

It's very easy to complain during marital separation and divorce. Grumbling about bad luck, finances, custody arrangements, home upkeep, single parenting, fatigue, loneliness and stress are common for women in these circumstances. Are you tired of making decisions alone that you previously made jointly with your husband? Perhaps you're just stuck in a pattern of constant whining and complaining.

Women in the midst of marital difficulties will often complain to everybody—family members, friends, co-workers, children, neighbors and church members. They've even been known to share their life's circumstances with strangers in the grocery store checkout line!

What are your alternatives to constant griping?

Complain to one chosen friend who has a big heart, sing loudly, smile or make a very conscious decision to "kill with kindness." If you are always complaining, your Christian witness will not be very strong. Your children and others could get a false impression of Jesus Christ and the gospel. And this terrible habit can eventually lead to depression, both for you and your children.

Be careful and cautious. Ask God to help you, especially to stop complaining—an action which will then allow the world to see Christ in you.

*Philippians 2:14–15*

*Do all things without murmuring and arguing, so that you may be blameless and innocent, children of God without blemish in the midst of a crooked and perverse generation, in which you shine like stars in the world.*

Have you found yourself uttering an occasional curse word during separation from your husband? This sometimes happens, especially when you're particularly angry or frustrated—or tired.

Try to guard against this behavior. Ask God for help, because it may be impossible for you to eliminate this very common behavior without divine guidance.

Foul language, cursing and vulgar speech have absolutely no place in a Christian's vocabulary, and these behaviors definitely do not reflect God's presence in our lives.

One friend whose husband was an abusive alcoholic developed the unfortunate habit of cursing as a way of dealing with her frustration at her marital situation.

She became dismayed when one of her young daughters told her to "quit talking dirty," and told her that her Sunday School teacher had told them not to say "bad words." You cannot praise God when coarse language is spewing forth from your mouth.

Make a decision this very day to clean up your speech, and then do so with heavenly help.

*Ephesians 5:4*

*Entirely out of place is obscene, silly, and vulgar talk; but instead, let there be thanksgiving.*

If you're like most separated women, you're short of money. Often a woman in these circumstances will find herself working one full-time job and another part-time job in order to provide the basics for her family. Money, or the lack of it, may always be on your mind as very few women are better off financially after separation than beforehand.

Be wise and seek the counsel of a competent attorney who will assist you in making sure that you get a fair financial settlement from your husband. It is crucial that you locate legal counsel and not simply trust your husband to "do the right thing." A separation and property settlement agreement that you reach with your husband during this time will determine your personal long-term financial future, as well as that of your children. Remember that he is legally obligated to monetarily support his children, so be persistent and work toward an agreement that provides the very best for your family.

Have you ever noticed that you tend to lean more on God and ask for help when circumstances are bad? When times are lean, as in your marital separation, you may think that you need God more than when your life is cruising forward at maximum speed. When you are stable financially, you may think that you are okay without the Lord in your life. The truth is that you need God every single day of your life. He always cares for you.

Do your part toward providing for your family, make certain that your husband provides his portion, and leave the rest to God. Do not dwell exclusively on money. Instead, let God receive your attention because he cares for you and wants to provide for your family. Try to focus on this certainty rather than the uncertainty of day-to-day finances.

*Luke 1:53*

*He has filled the hungry with good things,*
*and sent the rich away empty.*

Just as you are grieving during separation, so also are your children. They grieve for the loss of their father, for past memories, for future plans, for the safety and security of their family that now seem to be gone and for your pain and tears that they see.

Respect the feelings of your children, talk about them and tell them that all their feelings are acceptable. Don't admonish them with statements such as, "You shouldn't feel that way." Expressing emotions is not a sign of weakness; instead, expressions of grief can help your children to deal with their immense sorrow at the separation of their parents.

You may see evidence of the same stages of grief in your children as yourself—shock and denial, anger, depression, bargaining and acceptance. Again, these stages will come and go as time goes on.

Interestingly, older children almost seem to grieve more than those who are younger. Perhaps they're able to verbalize their feelings more freely and display them more openly. A toddler may not fully understand what is happening to Mom and Dad, but an adolescent may fully comprehend the consequences of certain actions. An 18 year-old daughter will have more family history and memories over which to lament than a preschooler, although preschoolers may incorporate the loss in their personality development. Don't discount the grief work that a much older child may need to work through. Even a 30 year-old who is married with children of his own will be greatly affected by his own parents' separation and divorce.

You can help your children grieve.

*2 Samuel 1:11–12*

*Then David took hold of his clothes and tore them; and all the men who were with him did the same. They mourned and wept, and fasted until evening for Saul and for his son Jonathan, and for the army of the Lord and for the house of Israel, because they had fallen by the sword.*

## February 24  Children's Grief: Shock and Denial

Your children may totally deny that their parents are separated, because acknowledgment of this fact hurts them entirely too much.

They may hide the separation from their friends. They may not want to talk about their father's absence from the home, or they may talk about his returning on a daily basis. A teenager who is in high school may be more willing to talk than a preteen in junior high. Children in junior high school may even refuse to go to a counselor. Talking about parental separation may just be too painful and make them feel as if they are betraying their father or mother. It is quite common for such denial to continue for many months.

If your child moves past complete denial and finds a friend to talk with, encourage this bond. One woman's daughter didn't want to talk with her mom about her dad living somewhere else, but she felt comfortable talking with one of her girlfriends. Great! The mom thanked God that she had found an outlet. Give your child time, and she may open up to you or her father as well.

Don't force your children to talk about the separation, but let them know that you are always available to do so. They may still be in complete shock that their father is no longer living with them, and they just may not be able to believe what's happening. Remember that denial is helpful and protective to children just as it is for you, since they may not be ready to deal with this loss. Therefore, don't strip your child of this valuable defense mechanism.

Always answer their questions truthfully, and they will talk and process their feelings when they are ready.

*Matthew 26:69–70*

*Now Peter was sitting outside in the courtyard. A servant-girl came to him and said, "You also were with Jesus the Galilean." But he denied it before all of them, saying, "I do not know what you are talking about."*

You will notice signs that your children are angry, as the markers can be very obvious.

Perhaps your son refuses a birthday gift from his father, or your daughter slams the door and goes to the playroom to watch television alone. Tears and foot stomping are frequent, and your children may even tell you that they hate you or their father. Allow them to be angry.

They may direct their signs of anger toward you because, after all, you're the available parent most of the time. They are angry at their dad for leaving, for his alcoholism, for his domestic violence or for his adultery. Your children may be angry at you for "throwing him out," for tolerating undesirable behaviors or for failing to "fix it." You may catch all the angry behaviors, simply because you are at home with them.

Act as a sounding board and let your children talk if they will. Tolerate some door slamming, but draw the line where you think it should be drawn. After all, remember that you are the parent. Recognize that your children are hurt and angry; acknowledge that these behaviors are normal to a certain degree, but don't allow them to spiral out of control.

Direct your children's anger appropriately. Encourage them to exercise, play the guitar, bang loudly on the piano or talk to a friend. You can provide them with a journal for recording their feelings.

Discourage your teenage son from driving the car when he's angry and reinforce the fact that it is inappropriate to hit another person. One woman provided a punching bag in the basement as an outlet for her child's anger.

*Mark 3:5*

*He looked around at them with anger; he was grieved at their hardness of heart and said to the man, "Stretch out your hand." He stretched it out, and his hand was restored.*

As your children grieve for the loss of their intact family and the daily presence of their father, some mild depression will inevitably follow. It is a very normal part of grief work.

Signs of depression in children include the obvious —crying, an inability to sleep, sleeping constantly, overeating or under eating. Be alert to clues of worsening depression. Does your teenage son come home from school every afternoon and go straight to bed? Is your daughter putting on extra weight from comforting herself with food, or is she starving herself in an effort to control the family situation?

Another hint of depression in children may include difficulty with concentration. Perhaps your son's grades are dropping due to his continuing distraction about his home and family situation. Or maybe your daughter completely forgot that she made a commitment to babysit for the neighbors on Saturday night for two consecutive weekends.

Be alert for signs of social withdrawal in your children. If your daughter drops out of all extra-curricular activities, you need to investigate further. Does your son stay in his room for the entire Sunday afternoon and listen to music on his CD player instead of interacting with the family? Has your child quit her part-time job at the grocery store?

Recognize that some depression is normal. However, if you see obvious signs that it is worsening, consult a professional. And if your child ever mentions the possibility of suicide, seek help immediately and do *not* just assume that this is a passing whim.

Watch your children for signs of depression.

*Psalm 42:5–6*

*Why are you cast down, O my soul, and why are you disquieted within me? Hope in God; for I shall again praise him, my help and my God.*

Your children may make many bargains in the hope of reuniting their mother and father. They may silently promise God to attend church every Sunday for the remainder of their lives if their family can be together once again. Or you may notice that your daughter, who is usually extremely messy, begins to make her bed every single morning and suddenly keeps her room very neat. Your son may suddenly offer to take out the trash every day without being prompted, or he may suddenly begin studying for hours each night in an attempt to bring home a straight-A report card. A child may also practice her piano piece without being asked in order to prepare for a recital that is still many weeks away.

Bargaining is another predictable stage of grief for your children, just as it is for you. You may also occasionally notice there is still some denial, anger or depression in the midst of their bargaining offers. Keep in mind that grief stages are very fluid.

You might see that your children are on their best behavior. They may fold laundry, walk the dog, feed the fish or set the table for supper voluntarily. Enjoy these pleasant surprises, but recognize that these may be misguided efforts at controlling their unraveling family.

Reassure your children repeatedly that your separation from their father is not their fault. Children may automatically assume that they're to blame, and may bargain to undo any wrongdoing that they perceived to have caused the rift.

Continually stress that they are not the cause of a marital breakup, and this may reduce some of their obvious bargaining behaviors.

*Psalm 66:13–14*

*I will come into your house with burnt offerings; I will pay you my vows, those that my lips uttered and my mouth promised when I was in trouble.*

It may be many, many years before your children fully accept separation and divorce. It is normal and very natural for your children to want a reunion of their parents. Therefore, acceptance may be much longer in coming to them than to you.

Also stop to consider that you probably knew about their father's addictions, abuse or alcoholism long before they did. You had more than likely done some anticipatory grief work during the long process of discovery, but your children didn't have this head start on grief.

Don't expect your children to come to terms with separation after a few months. They have many issues to ponder, cry, decide, pray and act. Give them time and space and don't attempt to rush their adjustment. But most certainly set boundaries because all children need them.

As a mother, you may be grieving anew when you see your children struggle with their own pain. Don't be afraid to let your children know that you care, and tell them every single day that you love them. Hug your son and daughter. When in doubt about what course of action to pursue, it is always appropriate to pray and love.

Your children will follow your lead. If you continue to deny marital trouble or let your anger infect your attitude after several months of separation, they will do the same. If you display open hatred toward your husband, they will mimic that behavior as well.

But if you slowly move toward acceptance of divorce and enjoy the fellowship of other believers while seeking God's will for your life, your children may ultimately see that as behavior to be copied.

*Philippians 4:19*

*And my God will fully satisfy every need of yours according to his riches in glory in Christ Jesus.*

Leap for joy as you look around and acknowledge God's many provisions in life!

Leap with smiles in your heart as you reflect on your children, who bring immense happiness to your life. Your daughter's hugs and your son's life choices warm your heart.

Leap with gratitude because of a work colleague whom you acknowledge to be "the best secretary ever." Has she been a trusted confidante who has patiently listened during the trials of your marriage and separation?

Leap with delight when you think about a special friendship with your walking partner whom you meet at the park each morning for a two-mile walk.

Smile as you think about the girlfriend who goes with you to watch a romantic movie when you need a good cry. Grin as you remember a cousin who treats you to lunch every other month and always pays the bill, because he is aware of your tight finances.

Leap with contentment when reflecting on your family's support through the previous few years of marital change. My parents, sister and brothers have fiercely supported my children and me through both good times and bad.

Finally, leap for more joy while thanking God for his great love, comfort and protection for your family.

*Nehemiah 8:10*

*"The joy of the Lord is your strength."*

What do you gain as a separated woman through fellowship with other believers?

What benefits do your children receive by attending your local church? Love, a shoulder to cry on, Bible study, smiles, unconditional acceptance, understanding, shared tears, friendship, prayer, encouragement and sharing.

Your community church represents Christ's body here on earth. It becomes much easier to follow God's commands when you have life in him, and one wonderful way to live in the Lord is through fellowship with true believers in the Word. God wants us to participate in church activities in order that we may be built up and that we may build others. Love is a strong message to the whole world that you are marked as a disciple of Jesus.

Christian friends can help to guide you if you steer far from God's known path, by gently reminding you of a better way. You can grow as a believer by fellowshipping with others.

Three months after separation, I was feeling very alone when a church member invited me to a dinner party. I was hesitant to attend since I would be the only unattached adult there. The usual arrangement would have been to have couples sitting together at the sides of the table, with the host and hostess sitting in the two arm chairs at the table's end. But to my great delight and immense relief, the host sat the pairs down each side of the table and then removed his end chair. He proceeded to sit beside me as my partner in order to make me feel more included.

This is Christian fellowship and love in action.

*Hebrews 10:24–25*

*And let us consider how to provoke one another to love and good deeds, not neglecting to meet together, as is the habit of some, but encouraging one another, and all the more as you see the Day approaching.*

Is your husband blaming you for marital failure? Perhaps he tells you repeatedly that his alcoholism, drug use, domestic violence or addiction is your fault.

You are most surely not to blame for your husband's actions, as the Bible assures us that we can resist temptation by asking God for strength. Of course, no marriage is perfect and you should accept responsibility for your part of poor communication patterns or other problems. You, a Christian woman, should indeed acknowledge your responsibility for any wrong actions and ask God for forgiveness. But you may find that your husband continues to blame you for *his* behaviors instead of assuming responsibility for them.

He may tell you that he was powerless, or he may claim that every other man in town is doing the same thing. Your husband may state that he was totally helpless to avoid hitting you and the children, that he only abused you while he was under the influence of alcohol, or that he was pressured into thoughts of online pornography addiction by someone else. "Nobody's perfect" is a standard reason given for certain behaviors.

It is very common for a wife to temporarily shoulder the blame for a husband's actions since she may desperately want to keep her family together. However, God tells you that you do not have to accept blame for your husband's choices. We are each responsible for our own individual choices.

*James 1:14–15*

*But one is tempted by one's own desire, being lured and enticed by it; then, when that desire has conceived, it gives birth to sin, and that sin, when it is fully grown, gives birth to death.*

Your children need your love during this critical time in their lives—perhaps more than ever before. Never be afraid to tell your children and demonstrate to them that you love them.

"I love you."

Those three words can have a magic effect on children whose parents have separated. Your son and daughter might wonder if you still love them, since they may have heard you and your husband say that you don't love each other anymore.

Reassure your children and utter those magical words on a daily basis. You can tell your son that you love him even if he is a senior in high school. As your daughter goes out to school in the morning, tell her that you love her and will be thinking about her during the day. It takes only two or three seconds to repeat the phrase, but the effects will linger all day long.

In addition, *show* your children that you love them. Hug them and cook their favorite supper of grilled tenderloin with macaroni and cheese. Play a board game like Monopoly with them, which can promote togetherness since it can take hours and hours. Give your small son a back rub in the bed at night or read a book to him. Comb your daughter's hair or paint her fingernails.

Your time is a precious gift to your children, so try to give it liberally. When you display your love to your children, you are showing them God's love in action.

*John 15:9–10*

*"As the Father has loved me, so I have loved you; abide in my love. If you keep my commandments, you will abide in my love, just as I have kept my Father's commandments and abide in his love."*

Pray for your children every single day—or every single hour.

Pray that they will abide in God, and that they will draw near to God as a source of strength during their parents' separation and divorce.

Trust that your son will lean on God and that his Christian faith will mature. Make intercession to God for his comfort in this confusing time and pray for his healing. Also pray for him to be able to forgive in order that he will not grow to be a bitter man in years to come. Continue praying that he will learn godly ways of behavior from appropriate role models, in order that he can be a Christian husband and father as he gets older. Believe that God will help him to love his father. Give your son to God.

Also commit your daughter to the Lord. Pray for her Christian growth as you make petition to God that he will strengthen her. Specifically pray for her recovery from any wounds that she may have incurred. Ask God to imprint Christian beliefs in her soul, and pray that she recognize right from wrong. Let your daily prayer be one of her knowledge of God and his power.

Pray that God will control your children's entire lives—thoughts, beliefs, behavior and examples to others. Pray that God will also comfort your children during this time of heartache and give them true peace and joy.

*Psalm 6:9*

*The Lord has heard my supplication;*
*the Lord accepts my prayer.*

Guard and protect your children from harm and wrong actions. Children, no matter if they are three years old or thirty-three years old, tend to trust their parents. That's just their nature. Both you and your husband are influencing your children through your behavior.

Often you may be put in a position of having to protect your children. If your husband is abusing alcohol or illegal recreational drugs, it is your responsibility as their mother to protect them from being in his presence during these times of known use. If they visit with their father and report drunken episodes to you, quickly act to prevent this from happening again.

One mother of a young preschooler reported that her husband left their child unattended during a weekend visit in order to go out to dinner with his adult friends. She took swift action to protect her daughter and act as her child's advocate.

Maybe your husband is involved in an adulterous situation. Make your desires clearly known to him concerning Christian nurturing of your children. If your children question you, simply state the truth without verbally assaulting their father.

Do everything within your power to keep your children away from a battering father. Their very lives may depend on you as you guard them from harm.

*Matthew 18:6*

*"If any of you put a stumbling block before one of these little ones who believe in me, it would be better for you if a great millstone were fastened around your neck and you were drowned in the depth of the sea."*

What kind words did you say to your children yesterday? What unkind words? Verbal comments can either build your children up or tear them down. Practice kind and uplifting phrases and repeat them to your children.

Try a minimum of one per day. Great! Way to go! Super! You tried really hard! Fantastic job! Awesome! Well done! You're important! You mean so much to me! Incredible! Nice! I'm so proud of you! Thanks! Terrific! You're such a joy! You made my day! Outstanding! You're special!

Don't give praise to your son or daughter so routinely that it becomes empty of meaning. Instead, give true praise when it is due—for a good report card, taking out the trash, going to bed on time, doing homework without being told or setting the table for supper.

Praise them for making their beds, cleaning their rooms on Saturday morning or playing quietly when you have a headache. Other times for appropriate praise could include—walking the dog, feeding the fish, playing with his younger sister or helping her brother with homework.

Remember that courteous and respectful speech can have lifelong positive influences on children. We all bloom with sprinkles of praise. Likewise, verbal assaults and stings can result in a negative self-image that a child can carry through his or her entire life.

Your words to your children are a witness for Christ.

*Colossians 4:6*

*Let your speech always be gracious,
seasoned with salt, so that you may know
how you ought to answer everyone.*

Are you troubled?

Perhaps your list of troubles includes aging parents, a broken heart, fear of ever loving another man and being wounded again, hurting children or an angry son.

You may also be troubled by wanting to lose 15 pounds, too much housework, physical illness such as diabetes, chronic physical pain, depression or a job that you dislike intensely.

We are reminded in the Bible that there might be a specific purpose in our suffering. Troubles can help us look to eternal life, rather than focusing exclusively on our earthly existence. Big problems can also keep us humble and help us to look anew at Christ's suffering on the cross.

How do you handle your troubles? Do you complain and make everyone else around you as miserable as you might be? Or do you try to smile and try to serve as an example of God's strength?

Any affliction that we encounter during separation, reconciliation or divorce can serve as a wonderful opportunity to draw closer to the Lord through constant prayer and leaning entirely on him.

*2 Corinthians 4:17*

*For this slight momentary affliction is preparing us for an eternal weight of glory beyond all measure.*

You may feel like giving up! All this effort that you're putting forth may just not seem worth it. You're sick and tired of arguing over a separation agreement, frustrated with trying to make financial ends meet, never having a moment to call your own and just plain tired from lack of sleep. Do you have dark circles of worry under your eyes? Have you gotten a head full of gray hair during your separation and divorce proceedings?

It would be so very easy to quit—your marital problems are enormous, and joint counseling is a huge effort. You might be searching in vain for that light at the end of the tunnel. Instead of throwing in the towel, allow the Holy Spirit to strengthen you.

Decide once again to serve Christ and look beyond the pain of today. Just put one foot in front of the other and keep marching. You are focusing on a great reward of eternal life at the finish line. What a wonderful assurance!

A friend was at a very low point about six months after separation from her husband. Tears were frequent, and she wanted her husband to return to their family in spite of incredible heartbreak. One day she got on her knees and asked God yet again for the strength to carry on. That afternoon when she took her daughter to a piano lesson, the teacher gave her a book on the power of prayer and surrender to God. This act spoke volumes in terms of friendship, God's timing and divine intervention at just the moment she needed it.

You also are being strengthened, even now, by Christ's power. And remember that this power is available to you every moment of every day.

*2 Corinthians 4:16*

*So we do not lose heart.*
*Even though our outer nature is wasting away,*
*our inner nature is being renewed day by day.*

Many women are helped by finding a Christian counselor and talking freely. Venting all your anger, pent-up feelings, frustration and screams can be wonderfully therapeutic. She will be available for listening without judging, and you may even find that she becomes a new friend.

Make an appointment to go every week, and you will find that talking with her often helps you limit the number of other people to whom you need to talk.

It is crucial that you locate a counselor who is a Christian. Non-Christian counselors often advocate an approach of a "feel good" philosophy. For example, she may encourage you to just quit working on marital problems and date someone else even though you are still legally married to your husband. A Christian counselor, on the other hand, will listen and assist you in seeking God's will for your life.

An experienced counselor will help you laugh and cry. She can draw on her previous contacts to steer you through separation and can recommend resources such as divorce support groups at local churches.

A counselor may assist you in broadening your vision of marriage in a way that will encourage you on your journey. She can serve as a much-needed source of strength for you.

Seeking Christian counsel is not a sign of weakness; there is no need to be ashamed. Rather, it is a sign of strength to ask for help instead of blindly plundering ahead in a thick fog. Listen to any ideas that your counselor may propose, and then make your own decisions with God's help.

Wait for God.

*Proverbs 15:22*

*Without counsel, plans go wrong,*
*but with many advisers they succeed.*

There is another type of counselor available to you as a Christian woman. This counselor is perfect, powerful, and comforting—the Holy Spirit. The Spirit of God came to care for the disciples after Jesus departed, and this Spirit is still present with us today.

The Holy Spirit functions as a counselor, comforter and helper. Stop for just a moment and digest that truth. God sent a counselor in the form of the Holy Spirit to comfort you. Wow! If you've ever needed comforting, now is probably the time. The Spirit is also an advocate—one who works on behalf of another.

The Holy Spirit is real, powerful and working for you in your separation at this exact moment in time. Claim this power and use it every day in your life.

Have you ever cried into your pillow at night? Do you hurt from the hair on top of your head to the end of your toenails, over your husband's departure from your family? Have you agonized over seeing him scream at your children while they cower in the corner of the den? It is the Holy Spirit who can give you peace in these situations. This Supreme Counselor can comfort you while you are in your bed alone uttering a prayer of help.

Jesus promised us the Holy Spirit, and then went further to assure us that the Holy Spirit would stay with us forever. Therefore you can always call on this Counselor for help and comfort. Remember to teach your children that they also have this most powerful resource available to them. What true peace the presence of the Comforter can be.

*John 14:16*

*"And I will ask the Father, and he will give*
*you another Advocate, to be with you forever."*

What activity makes you happy? What do you like to do? I like to read to my daughter, ride my bicycle, curl up with a good book, play the piano, sing, go bowling, watch old movies from the library and window shop at the mall.

I like to throw the Frisbee with my son and daughter, bake cookies, paint my toenails bright red, drink a cup of hot tea, talk to my sister on the phone for an hour, talk to God aloud, laugh loudly and play a card game with my children.

Also on my list of favorite things to do are laughing with my children at selected comic strips, taking care of my home, drinking flavored coffee, going to aerobics class, writing and giving my daughter a back rub before getting one from her.

I like to call my neighbor to talk on the phone, sit in front of the fire, plan a dream vacation, look at the stars at night, see a pretty sunset, take a bubble bath, go for a walk with a friend and try a new recipe.

I also enjoy planting bulbs that will come up in the spring, telling my children that I love them, going to church activities, praying for people I know who are hurting, bouncing a small rubber ball that will go really high, encouraging my children and dreaming about the future.

I relish going to work, rocking in my favorite chair, having quiet time to think, dancing, looking at family pictures and going to a block party where I get to talk with all my neighbors.

Know yourself.

Make your own lists. You are unique. God means for you to enjoy all of these activities that he provides.

*Proverbs 23:15*

*My child, if your heart is wise, my heart too will be glad.*

Put on the armor of God every day to defend yourself and your children from Satan's worldly influences. Don't just put on a selected piece of armor; the Bible instructs us in the book of Ephesians to put on the *whole* armor of God. That instruction tells you to don every single piece each day.

As a Christian believer, you are subjected to many of Satan's powerful schemes. And you need all the protection available to you, especially during this vulnerable time of divorce. Satan is active in vicious attacks on Christian families and churches.

It's important to remember that the struggle can be a daily one. You don't conquer influences once and then continue to march through life with no further problems.

Rather, you should constantly be on guard for unwanted influences in the life of your family. What worldly influences might you have been exposed to during your marriage? Adultery, gambling, pornography addiction, use of illegal recreational drugs, excessive use of alcohol or domestic violence could be on your list.

You have godly weapons, and you can use them to have a joyful and strong life in the Lord. Paul describes the armor of God in detail—the belt, breastplate, shoes, shield, helmet and sword. Get fully dressed each morning and be a true Christian warrior.

*Ephesians 6:11–12*

*Put on the whole armor of God, so that you may be able to stand against the wiles of the devil. For our struggle is not against enemies of blood and flesh, but against the rulers, against the authorities, against the cosmic powers of this present darkness, against the spiritual forces of evil in the heavenly places.*

Mentally slip a belt of truth around your waist every day. Fasten that belt and leave it around your body securely, because you don't want it to be loose enough to fall off. God has already revealed to you his ways of pure truth. Do not allow your husband to tell you that his battering is a result of your actions, such as failing to take out the trash.

Such a statement is the opposite of truth. It is merely a rationalization for undesirable behaviors. Neither is it true that our heavenly Father excuses behaviors such as gambling or pornography addictions. God does not intend for you to be a slave to anything apart from him.

Pray that God will help you discern the truth in your daily walk. Lies can often sound like the truth, so be alert and stay on your guard. Women in separation and divorce are incredibly vulnerable from many perspectives—emotional, social, financial, and spiritual—and it is often quite difficult to see clearly.

Don't tolerate statements from others who try to tell you that God is false, and just a figment of your imagination. Instead, enjoy life fully knowing that you are in God's truth and not the lies of Satan.

Under God's strength, you can discover his perfect truths for your life.

*Ephesians 6:14*

*Stand therefore, and fasten the belt of truth around your waist.*

You know right from wrong, and God's word supplies the answer whenever there may be doubt in your mind. Put a breastplate of righteousness on as you dress for work in the morning. This breastplate covers your heart so be careful that it is secure. Your heart rules your emotions, your level of trust and your actions.

If you're wearing God's righteous laws and his seal of approval on your chest, you will be able to ward off dark actions. Satan is actively attacking and planting seeds of doubt in your mind. *Am I doing the right thing? What should I do about child custody? Would my husband change if he came home one more time? Where in the world will I get enough money to make my house payment without my husband's income? Can I guide my children?* Still your mind, for you know what is right.

A breastplate of righteousness is absolutely not a license for you to adopt a "holier than thou" attitude. God does not intend for you to judge others and consider them to be inferior to you, so be careful to guard against such an attitude. We all have areas of imperfection in our lives.

God will protect your heart. Remember that God loves you and sent Christ to die for you. If you are living for God, you are always in the right.

*Ephesians 6:14*

*And put on the breastplate of righteousness.*

Remember your shoes as you dress each morning. God wants you to wear those shoes—whatever size or style or color—as you proclaim the gospel of Christ. There is no better news to share with another human being than the love of God as poured through his Son.

Complete truth, peace, hope, love, joy and guidance for everyday living are available to Christians through God's word.

Remember that you have an obligation to share the gospel with others, and that your example of godly living can be evident even while separated from your husband. As you tie your shoes, you can be ready to carry God's words of peace as you walk through your day. This task can be overwhelming, as there are many opportunities to witness that we sometimes waste.

Satan wants you to be overwhelmed to the point of giving up—too many people, too many rejections or too many other obstacles. Continue to endure. Every person needs to hear of God's love through your actions and words.

Your husband, children, parents, in-laws, siblings, cousins, grandparents, neighbors, friends and co-workers all may be seeking God. They are likely to have an internal longing for their Creator that they may not yet fully understand.

One separated woman adopted the practice of praying before eating when she took her small children out to a restaurant for dinner. What a powerful statement! People will hear the gospel from you in verbal and nonverbal ways. You are always a witness. Pray to God that you can be a positive force for him.

*Ephesians 6:15*

*As shoes for your feet put on whatever will
make you ready to proclaim the gospel of peace.*

You may feel as though you are under attack on many fronts during separation from your husband. Are you being tempted by some circumstance in your life? Have you endured one setback after another as you attempt to gain some financial stability? Perhaps you've been a victim of unkind gossip about your own behavior. Has someone insulted your abilities as a mother? Are you so incredibly angry at your husband that you sometimes want to strike him?

If so, gladly put on your shield of faith to protect yourself from the tools of Satan. You can be safe as a Christian woman as long as you have your faith in God.

The soldier's shield that Paul referred to in the book of Ephesians was large and made of leather. It was often soaked in water to fireproof it; therefore, any fiery darts were unable to harm the soldier.

Likewise, a shield of faith is essential during your spiritual warfare. Mentally visualize this marvelous shield and know that you can live victoriously in Christ with this fantastic protection. It truly helps you to be invincible through God, no matter what tempting dart may come your way.

God promises to be your shield and is committed to you. All you have to do is take the shield of faith in your hand, and victory is possible.

*Ephesians 6:16*

*With all of these, take the shield of faith,*
*with which you will be able to quench*
*all the flaming arrows of the evil one.*

Have you ever doubted your salvation? Indeed, Satan wants you to doubt God and Christ. Does God love you? Can he forgive you? Can he forgive your husband? Can he possibly heal your family?

Satan, always present, wants you to turn away from God as you struggle with marital separation and divorce. Gossip, bitterness, hatred, lies, wickedness, an affair of retaliation and giving up on God are possibilities that may be planted in your mind.

The devil is able to provide you with an easy excuse or rationalization for any behavior, and he wants you to believe that there will be no consequences for any choice you make.

However, if you put on the helmet of salvation as you dress each morning you will be better equipped to protect your human mind from doubting God.

Such a helmet is a wonderfully strong defensive weapon and is a sure one for your regular use. A helmet can guard a soldier's head from physical attack. Likewise, the spiritual helmet that Paul referred to can truly guard your mind from seeds of doubt placed there.

Ask God for exactly this kind of protection, and he will abundantly provide it. Mentally, place the helmet of salvation on your head in a very intentional and methodical manner and claim God's protection in the area of doubt.

You don't need to question your heavenly Father, who is by your side every day to support and reassure you as your faith grows. Instead, trust that God is working in your behalf right now as he accomplishes his purposes for your family through you.

*Ephesians 6:17*

*Take the helmet of salvation.*

A sword is an offensive weapon for use in a battle. So take that sword in your hand and get to work! Ward off the possibility of attacks before you are even aware of them by immersing yourself in God's Word.

The Bible can give you hope, peace, strength and joy as you discern God's plan for daily living. Do you remember when your son pretended that he was a warrior during his toddler years?

He may have had a plastic sword that he used as he went outside to fight all the imaginary "demons and dragons" coming his way. Likewise, a daily habit of Bible reading and praying for God's will is one of the very best weapons for use against immoral or impure life choices.

When you're tempted by the ways of this world, your best ally is the truth of the Bible.

When in doubt as to whether or not to participate in extramarital sexual activities in order to relieve this very real stress, consult God's Word. The answer is clear.

If you are yearning to tell your husband every hurtful thought on your mind, read a passage in the New Testament. You will find the solution there as God talks to you and gives instruction.

The sword of the Spirit is the powerful Word of God, the Bible. It can help you to resist Satan. It is the final piece of armor to use every day, and it will help you to stand true to God in the midst of all the storms of separation that you are enduring.

*Ephesians 6:17*

*[Take] the sword of the Spirit, which is the word of God.*

Giggle! Laugh! Smile! Guffaw!

It's true that laughter is good for the soul. Rent an old comedy movie from the local video store and watch it with your children. There are many from which to choose, but be careful that it is appropriately rated for the entire family. Don't hold anything back—pop some popcorn, pour soft drinks and laugh yourself silly. Just let all those tears of laughter roll down your cheeks. They will be a welcome relief and a wonderful contrast to all your sad tears that you've surely been crying recently. Allow yourself to laugh so hard that you slap your knee and rock back and forth on the sofa. Let your children see that you can still have a good time.

Laugh at yourself. Perhaps you tried a new recipe which turned out to be horrible. I tried to cook chicken and dumplings shortly after separation, and they were a *disaster*. My son sat quietly at the supper table and picked over the dumplings, which were tough, bland and incredibly chewy. My daughter thought they were just wonderful and kept eating. I concluded that she was either starving or fearful of hurting my feelings. So I decided to laugh my way through this "doughy" situation, by admitting that I thought they were terrible and that I would throw the recipe in the trash can. Then we all got a big laugh out of my attempt to cook this classic Southern dish. I declared that I'd never cook chicken and dumplings again!

Laugh at a joke and encourage your children to tell jokes at the supper table. Or enjoy the comic strips together. Some of them provide daily doses of uproar and laughter, since the ones about teenagers often hit really close to home.

*Proverbs 15:30*

*The light of the eyes rejoices the heart,*
*and good news refreshes the body.*

Can any good come out of the trials and tribulations that you are enduring? Or is this just going to get worse and worse?

As Christians, we're sure to face trials but the book of James assures us that it is possible to profit from them. You can learn more about yourself, draw closer to God, develop new friendships, find a sense of self-discipline and grow closer to your children during marital separation.

When one door is closed, God will open another one for you. God is growing you into a mature Christian and assisting you in becoming more like his Son as he guides you through the hardships you face. We're not given a promise of God's protection from pain, but we are given a promise that he will help us through pain and suffering. He most surely will not abandon you.

Ask God to help you solve problems and look for creative solutions. Perhaps your greatest trial this week has been dealing with a preteen daughter who is crying at the absence of her father, but blaming her tears on her algebra homework.

Take a deep breath, pray for your daughter, pray for your tolerance and ask God to show you what to do. One woman encountered just this very difficulty. As a solution, she raided the money jug with all her spare pennies, and she was able to have a special mother-daughter lunch one Saturday afternoon. It was great fun sitting in the restaurant while talking about "girl things" and their outing seemed to defuse some stress. They discovered that they could have lots of fun, even in the middle of family trials.

God can show you his great love during your trials and use them for his ultimate glory.

*James 1:2–4*

*My brothers and sisters, whenever you face trials of any kind, consider it nothing but joy, because you know that the testing of your faith produces endurance, and let endurance have its full effect, so that you may be mature and complete, lacking in nothing.*

Do you miss having sex with your husband? This may be a source of tremendous frustration and anxiety for you, as it is for very many women during separation and divorce. Remember that these feelings of deprivation are normal!

God gave you the gift of sexuality, and it should not be ignored. Sex between two married people is a wonderful way to communicate love and maintain closeness that may not be achieved in any other way. Snuggling, hugs, kisses, back rubs and sex are an integral part of marriage.

Therefore, you probably miss physical touch, especially if you had been married for many years. Be assured that there are many creative solutions to this problem. First of all, ask God in prayer every day to help you control your urges, because asking for help does indeed work miracles in this arena. Secondly, talk to other separated people, your female friends and your counselor for advice.

Third, you may have a close confidante such a sister with whom you could share more intimate details about sexual frustration. Last, seek guidance from your pastor. He can be a great source of comfort as he prays with you while acknowledging this very human need. Simply talking about sex can be a wonderful outlet.

The Holy Spirit is working to transform you into Christ's image, and God's ultimate plan is one of self-control as you deal with sexual pressures.

*1 Thessalonians 4:3–5*

*For this is the will of God, your sanctification: that you abstain from fornication; that each one of you know how to control your own body in holiness and honor, not with lustful passion, like the Gentiles who do not know God.*

Are you working toward reconciliation in your marriage, or are you just minutes away from signing the final divorce decree? Never take separation from your spouse lightly, but instead remember that a separation or "cooling off" period may be a new beginning for your marriage. Separation may not be the end, but the start of something new and good in the Lord's eyes. You and your spouse may be able to heal from hurt and grief inflicted upon each other during years of marriage.

Divorce can be very destructive and hurtful to everyone involved, and God intended that marriage be a commitment to last your entire lifetime.

Seek guidance from your pastor, an individual counselor, or a joint marriage counselor. If at all possible, try to reconcile in order that your marriage might be restored. However, some behaviors such as abandonment, abuse, adultery or addictions may leave you with no choice other than ending the marriage. God loves you, protects you, wants you to grow as his child, and does not intend for you to be a doormat.

Make every possible effort to help your marriage grow stronger, and you will be able to look back with a clear conscience years down the road. And do not intentionally inflict upon your husband the degree of hurt and pain which you may have received from him.

Commit your marriage and family to God and remember that he is in charge. God has good plans for you and he will direct you concerning separation, reconciliation or divorce.

*Malachi 2:16*

*For I hate divorce, says the Lord, the God of Israel,*
*and covering one's garment with violence,*
*says the Lord of hosts. So take heed to*
*yourselves and do not be faithless.*

Are you sad and down in the dumps? Missing your husband terribly and a bit depressed?

Then go outside and take a look at everything that God created for your enjoyment, and your mood will probably improve. God's creation truly is intricate, awesome and fantastic.

Look at the wide blue sky, big white swirling clouds, bright warm sunshine, green grass, giant oak trees, a thin crescent moon, majestic mountains with rolling hills or squirrels eating the sunflower seeds you put on the deck this morning. Enjoy the view of a rabbit in the woods, a creek in the back yard, the ocean waves lapping the sand at the beach, a bird's nest, a blue jay drinking at your bird bath or an awesome sunrise loaded with pink colors.

More of God's creation that may uplift you include cool rain, dark clouds, mud puddles, interestingly shaped rocks, yellow daffodils blooming, a purple crocus or yellow pansies with dark purple faces. Do you see leaves blowing in the wind, pink tulips, your black cat rubbing up against your leg, a neighborhood dog barking like crazy at your cat, creepy bugs, a gloriously beautiful sunset, a full moon and shining stars?

Search for even more—fog, evergreen cedars, snow falling, holly trees with red berries, a burning fire for marshmallow roasting, the unpleasant odor from a skunk, white blooms from a flowering pear tree, pink flowers on a cherry tree, bare trees whose leaves have yet to sprout, mint leaves or a rosemary plant.

If your home is still under ice and snow, just imagine the summer colors—red petunias, soft green grass, pink geraniums, cool white candy tuft, purple verbena, wildly colorful zinnias and green leaves on every tree on your street.

Enjoy God's goodness in nature, and allow it to help your heart to sing.

*Psalm 19:1*

*The heavens are telling the glory of God;*
*and the firmament proclaims his handiwork.*

Healing from a physical wound or disease can take a long, long time. Surgery, medications, physical therapy, as well as long-term rehabilitation may be indicated on the physician's plan of care.

Likewise, healing from a broken marriage will probably take many years. You shouldn't expect to recover from abandonment, infidelity, alcoholism or drug abuse in a few months. Your pain may be very deep, perhaps piercing at certain moments. More likely than not, you continue to grieve for the loss of your marriage and your family togetherness.

Some days you might feel strong, while on other days you simply cry for hours. All of these feelings are normal for a grieving Christian woman who is separated from her husband. Don't deny your feelings, which can vary wildly from one day to the next.

Rather, take some advice from a friend of mine whose wife left him after 15 years of marriage to live with another man. "The only way through this thing is straight through. Let yourself hurt and cry, because that's part of the healing process. Don't fight it. Just go through the middle of the pain," he told me on many occasions as I blubbered into the telephone.

Ask God—the ultimate source of healing—for help. Also recognize that he gives you the gift of time. No magic timetable exists for a woman to quit loving her husband, who may have wounded her to an incredible degree. You might continue to think about him on a regular basis. Just keep going one day at a time and trust that healing will happen on God's timetable.

*Luke 8:47*

*When the woman saw that she could not remain hidden, she came trembling; and falling down before him, she declared in the presence of all the people why she had touched him, and how she had been immediately healed.*

It's easy to take care of everyone but yourself in a stressful situation—and what you're living through right now definitely qualifies as stressful!

You may have been a caregiver for so long that you truly don't have any idea of how to care for yourself. Stop and ponder that possibility for a moment. Does it apply to you?

One way to care for you is to be less of a perfectionist. You don't have to have a spotless house, because the dirt will be there next month for a cleaning opportunity.

Don't stress out about having a house that could be featured in a magazine. Rule number one—if it's not dirty, don't clean it. Run the dishwasher only when it's full. Wash only full loads of laundry. This also helps with the water and electric bills. And don't worry about changing the bed sheets every single week.

You could have a hen party and talk with your girlfriends—cook, laugh and cry together.

Take a bubble bath. Soak in the tub for 20 minutes while candles are dancing light patterns all around your bathroom. Simply close your eyes and relax.

Slow down. You don't have to clean the bathrooms, dust and vacuum all in one day. Grocery shopping can be a leisurely experience as you look at new and different foods to cook. Read a book in three weeks instead of quickly devouring it and then wondering what you read. Schedule some time into your day just to sit still and think. Also schedule some prayer time. God wants you to talk with him, and he wants to talk to you.

Go for a walk. Walk briskly or stroll leisurely if that is what your mood dictates today. Take deep slow breaths and release the tension of the past week as you learn to care for yourself.

*1 Timothy 4:4*

*For everything created by God is good, and nothing is to be rejected, provided it is received with thanksgiving.*

Have you noticed that you're extremely sad and teary during your periods of peak hormone activity? Maybe you feel incredible urges of rage as your hormones zing during ovulation and during the days immediately preceding your menstrual period.

If this is the case, take heart because you're not alone! Let yourself cry and become moody.

Don't fight it, or the feelings may intensify to the point where they become unmanageable. Just break down, have a good cry and then wipe your eyes. And if you need to cry again in an hour, let the tears run one more time.

It is very normal for you to re-live emotional events during hormonal surges. Expect this and try to be prepared. For example, you shouldn't plan to teach an all-day workshop three days before your period is to begin. Neither should you lead the Sunday School lesson through your tears.

Instead, stock your car and your pocketbook with tissues and warn your girlfriend that you may need her listening ear more than usual if you are going to survive these wild hormone swings. Also, plan to exercise regularly as an antidote to stress.

Fortunately, you can take heart and be assured that the passage of time will help these horrible mood swings to abate somewhat. Do not hesitate to seek your doctor's advice if this becomes too overwhelming.

You will not always feel like a wild woman who is under the complete control of her hormones. Pray, and know that God can handle even female hormones.

*Psalm 22:8*

*"Commit your cause to the Lord; let him deliver—*
*let him rescue the one in whom he delights!"*

Maybe you're feeling guilty because you are separated from your husband; you may feel in your heart that divorce is against your Christian beliefs. You may wonder if there was something more that you could have done that would have prevented such a drastic step in your marriage.

Or perhaps well-meaning friends have added to your sense of guilt by verbally expressing their disapproval at your marital dissolution. Such comments can sting and add to your pain, and they are totally unnecessary.

In situations such as these, have your standard answer ready: "Our family is hurting. Please pray for us." Of course, friends will hear gossip and may witness certain behavior, but only you and your husband know all of the details.

Guilt can paralyze a Christian woman in your situation. Naturally, you wonder if you committed any unpardonable act that your husband considered unforgivable.

However, remember that God forgives any sin if confessed. And reassure yourself that you acted with good intentions and put your whole being into salvaging your marriage before separation.

Acknowledge any unconfessed sin to God and then allow this confession to bring you closer to Christ. Any guilty feelings that you harbor shouldn't act as a barrier between you and God, because he does not want any guilt to cripple you or make you fear him.

*Psalm 19:12–13*

*But who can detect their errors? Clear me from hidden faults. Keep back your servant also from the insolent; do not let them have dominion over me. Then I shall be blameless, and innocent of great transgression.*

Your children have many fears right now. They may talk about them, or they may be very hesitant to tell you their concerns because they don't want to hurt you.

Maybe your son is afraid of your hurt and pain, as he has seen tears on many occasions while you mourn the loss of your marriage. He may be fearful that you will never be reunited with his father. Another very common fear for children is abandonment by the remaining parent—sickness or death on your part.

Is he afraid that you will remarry in a few years and he will have to deal with a stepfather? He may worry about repeating his father's mistakes of abuse or alcoholism that divided his family. Or his fear may even be that you'll be alone when he goes to college next year. He may wonder if you even have enough money to send him to college now.

Your daughter might be fearful that her daddy doesn't love her anymore, if he now spends more time with his girlfriend than with her. After all, she may now have a changed image of her father from the man she has always known. Your little girl might be afraid that he will have other children and forget about her. She might wonder if he will still come to her birthday party next month, or if he will continue to help with her yearly science fair project at school as he has done in years past.

Verbally acknowledge your children's fears as they begin to confide in you. Don't force the issue however, because talking about their concerns right now might be too painful for them. Just be there and ask the Lord to give you guidance when the opportunity to talk presents itself.

Christ is the cure for fear.

*Mark 6:50*

*For they all saw him and were terrified.*
*But immediately he spoke to them and said,*
*"Take heart, it is I; do not be afraid."*

Have you lost your self-identify? It is possible that you have been totally immersed in your husband for all the years of marriage to the point of neglecting your inner self? You may have adopted his friends, hobbies, spending habits and entire lifestyle.

Separation from your husband can be an ideal time for self-discovery. Take time to remember who you were as a single woman. Did you like to exercise or were you a couch potato?

Did you cook grilled cheese sandwiches and tomato soup for a fancy meal, or was grilled salmon and a Caesar salad more to your liking? What did you do with your leisure time? Did you attend Bible studies with other women? Were you frugal or a big spender? Were you a loner or a socialite?

Talk to God and discover what he wants you to change about your life now. Certainly, a change God wants is for you to place him at the top of your priority list if your husband had been pushed to the number one spot.

Develop yourself with new habits—good habits such as daily Bible reading, a better listening ear, a slower tongue, frequent smiles, hiking in the mountains, regular church attendance, improved nutrition, quiet time with your cat, listening to music or reading a novel.

Or resurrect old habits like having dinner twice a month with your Christian female friends, careful spending to get your finances in order, hugs for your son, praise for your daughter, less television time so you have more think time, and identification with Jesus Christ.

Find out who you are. Chances are that you have many gifts and interests, which might have been ignored for years. Now is a wonderful time to rediscover yourself!

*Romans 13:14*

*Instead, put on the Lord Jesus Christ, and
make no provision for the flesh, to gratify its desires.*

Stop to consider what you may have lost during separation from your husband. A "together family," hugs and kisses, seeing your husband every evening, help with the children and eating supper with your husband at the table.

Other losses could include weekends with your stepchildren, vacations as a unit, a daily father figure in the house, a lover, some financial freedom, dreams of being grandparents together, a handyman around the house, Saturday morning breakfasts together and someone to fix your ailing car.

Even more that may be missed are praying together, someone to give you a back rub in the bed, a smile from your husband right as you wake up, greeting your husband after work with a kiss, "couple times," a spiritual partner and car-pooling assistance to your children's various activities.

There are additional ones such as help with yard work, anniversary celebrations, couple friends for dinner plans, someone to hold your hand, a male role model for your children and dreams of spending the rest of your life together with the first love of your young life.

Allow yourself to ponder and admit all of these losses, because there are many for a separated woman of God. And they are very, very real. Admitting these lost roles and dreams is a part of grief, healing and recovery.

As always, admit these to God. Tell him verbally and nonverbally of your great losses and grief. God is always there for you and he does not care if you tell him the same thing day after day. Thank him for his faithfulness in the face of all that you have lost.

*Psalm 55:22*

*Cast your burden on the Lord, and he will sustain you;*
*he will never permit the righteous to be moved.*

Now stop to consider what you may have gained during separation from your husband. Potential gains include total reliance on God, more moments with your children, peace, additional time with the Word and less laundry to wash.

More gains could be time to develop female friendships, more smiles, less dependence on medication to get through your day, improved communication with your parents and humming or singing as you do your housework.

Even more gains are a greatly reduced stress level, a new family unit, sleep, innovative ways to make financial ends meet, truth, different and positive relationships with your children and new vacations as a smaller family.

Other gains that you may have seen since separating from your husband are spiritual growth for the children, less anxiety, new friendships, innovative holiday celebrations, improved communication with your children, children's smiles, self-insight and better role models for your children.

Finally, gains might include a better relationship with your in-laws, siblings helping each other with homework and absolute trust in God to provide for your unknown future.

Examine your gains, as you did your losses. Then thank God for all these gains and his promise to continue to guide you through separation and divorce.

*Psalm 48:14*

*That this is God, our God forever and ever.*
*He will be our guide forever.*

Do you feel foolish for believing in your husband time and time again? Maybe you were certain, deep in your heart, that he would stop his alcohol abuse or keep his promise to stop hitting you. Did he go through a recovery program for drug abuse and claim to be drug-free?

Perhaps your husband declared to you that the Internet affair with his secretary was over and that it would never happen again. Did he come home after inexplicably abandoning you and the children for six months and profess a forever commitment to his family? You probably believed his many promises, only to be let down several times over.

And you were hoping with each promise for a life change, only to find yourself devastated one more time.

There's nothing wrong with hoping and believing in possibilities, so hold your head high and try to quit feeling foolish. You wanted your family to be together if possible, and that is an honorable desire of a godly woman's heart.

It doesn't matter if all of your neighbors knew of his extramarital affair before you did or if your counselor warned you that his pattern of repeated physical abuse would continue.

A true fool is someone who rejects God and his laws. In contrast, you are a wise Christian woman who believes in God and is working to please him.

*Psalm 14:1*

*Fools say in their hearts, "There is no God."*
*They are corrupt, they do abominable deeds;*
*there is no one who does good.*

Who is a wise woman? The opposite of a fool, a wise woman is one who seeks God and his will for her life.

A sure foundation for a wise Christian woman is a strong faith in the power of God, which will influence her thoughts, attitude, and actions. If you are truly wise, you are striving to please God on an everyday basis. However, simply knowing about God without allowing him into your life can be an empty faith, yielding little in the long run. God can teach us about his will for our lives if we will only ask.

One woman, married to an abusive alcoholic man for 15 years, had two beautiful daughters who were four and six years old. Her husband lost his job just as she was ready to file for divorce and end the nightmare of constantly fearing for the safety of her daughters. She realized that she would be forfeiting any child-support monies if she filed for divorce while her husband had no income. Therefore, she turned to God for an answer and received one—wait. This strong Christian woman endured two more weeks with her husband, while shielding her daughters from their father's wrath, and waited for his unemployment income to begin. Shortly thereafter, her husband secured a well-paying position that afforded this woman and her children financial security. Asking God's direction and waiting were wise moves.

Seek God and ask for his wisdom.

*Psalm 14:2*

*The Lord looks down from heaven on humankind to see if there are any who are wise, who seek after God.*

Many women have found comfort by lighting a candle every day and enjoying its warmth and aroma. I like to light a candle when cooking supper in the kitchen and while reading in my favorite chair in the den.

You can light a candle while taking a long hot soaking bubble bath, when you're helping your children with homework at the kitchen table and during your evening meal.

Candles often can make you smile and give a sense of calm, as the flicker from the wick creates interesting shadows and dances around. The shape, color, size or fragrance of the candle really doesn't matter because it is simply meant to be enjoyed and give light.

Occasionally, a candle can even light the way in the event of a power outage. Likewise, you are meant to give light as a Christian and show others the way to God.

Your shape, color, size or fragrance doesn't matter either. Don't hide your witness simply because of your marital situation. Instead, live for Christ and show others the Lord in your life.

Let your light point others to Christ's truth.

*Matthew 5:14–16*

*"You are the light of the world. A city built on a hill cannot be hid. No one after lighting a lamp puts it under the bushel basket, but on the lampstand, and it gives light to all in the house. In the same way, let your light shine before others, so that they may see your good works and give glory to your Father in heaven."*

Be bold and ask for God's blessing.

God *wants* to bless you—your family, home, health, work, travel, marriage, separation and children. He desires infinitely more for us than we can even comprehend.

In fact, he wants to pour his boundless goodness on us every single day. Stop for a moment and consider that glorious concept!

Think about everything that God has done for you in the past, and then realize that it cannot compare with what he has in mind for your future. This assurance was very comforting to a friend in my neighborhood after her husband abandoned her family. There were many weeks in her early separation period when she didn't even have money to buy groceries for her children. But she continued on one day at a time, eventually sorting out her life with the Lord's help. She realized that God was blessing her through financial assistance from her mother and father. He also blessed her through other offers of help with yard work from Christian friends. And God further blessed her with free baby-sitting offers from her neighbors when began working at a job for the first time in twenty years; she had been a stay-at-home mom since her children were small. Wow! She received all this after asking God to bless her and her family.

God is able to abundantly supply all that you need, if you pray and ask.

1 Chronicles 4:10

*Jabez called on the God of Israel, saying, "Oh that you would bless me and enlarge my border, and that your hand might be with me, and that you would keep me from hurt and harm!" And God granted what he asked.*

You probably have a to-do list at work that helps guide your daily activities. More than likely, you feel a sense of accomplishment each time you complete a chore and cross it off your list.

Make a to-do list at home as well. It could be a daily or weekly list. You may often be confused and not know which way to turn, especially in the early weeks of separation. However, a list can keep you organized and looking forward.

Write down things such as dental, medical and counseling appointments for yourself and your children. Also include errands like dropping off clothes at the cleaners, picking up pictures being developed at the drug store, making a deposit at the bank and shopping for groceries.

And don't forget your exercise class, volunteering one evening at your daughter's elementary school, Bible study at church, your son's soccer practice or your daughter's cheerleading tryout.

A list can serve as a guide so that you don't forget as much when your mind is clouded with emotional issues surrounding marriage. It can let you visualize what you accomplished during a terribly busy day, and this list can even keep you from booking two appointments at the same time.

A daily to-do list can give you a goal and a sense of direction. It can also keep you from getting sidetracked and can prevent feelings of being totally overwhelmed with all that you have to do in your life as a separated woman.

*Proverbs 4:25*

*Let your eyes look directly forward,*
*and your gaze be straight before you.*

Your wedding anniversary day will probably be very difficult for you, so prepare yourself a few days beforehand. Make plans with your friends or family to do something special or different, and be with people you love.

Also ask God to help you make it through this particular day as you may be flooded with memories, both pleasant and unpleasant. If you've always celebrated your anniversary with dinner and a movie, you may choose to avoid this established routine now.

Instead, go on a hike with your Sunday School friends. Or plan a picnic to the park with your children. How about something totally different like planting a tree in your front yard? Or painting your bedroom a new shade of blue? You could also have your parents over and grill cheeseburgers on your back deck.

Let yourself have some time of sadness on this eventful day.

You will probably shed some tears as you remember your wedding day and all the dreams that may now be broken. You may experience feelings of rage on this day at your husband's continued addictions or abandonment. Or you may also fondly remember many family milestones. And that's okay because your entire marriage probably wasn't as bad as the few months preceding separation.

On the other hand, if you are continuing in joint counseling with your spouse in an effort to reconcile your marriage, you might consider spending the evening with him. This will depend entirely on your current life circumstances.

Whatever you do on your wedding anniversary, thank God for your marital union because you married your husband out of your love for him and for the Lord. If possible, don't allow your current situation make you regret your entire marriage.

*Ecclesiastes 3:1*

*For everything there is a season, and a
time for every matter under heaven.*

The period of time surrounding six months of marital separation is often very turbulent and emotionally charged for a woman. Therefore, be prepared for an avalanche of feelings.

About six months after separation from your husband, you may begin to forget some of the hurt and pain in the marriage and begin to dwell on the more positive aspects. Perhaps you're choosing to temporarily suppress all the pain associated with his alcoholism and physical abuse. Instead, you're remembering your wonderful honeymoon and the first house that the two of you built together. Right now you're sick and tired of not having help around the house, so you may actually yearn for your husband to come back home. Indeed, his return may be all that you think about night and day. It is quite normal to strongly desire reconciliation with your spouse during this time. You are *unbelievably* vulnerable to your husband's emotional overtures right now, so be careful to guard your heart and pray for God's guidance every single day.

You need to make decisions based on God's leadership instead of your emotional gut feelings. If God is leading you and your husband to him and there are signs of true repentance in your marriage, follow the Lord's leading. However, if the opposite is true, you may be wise to resist all urges to reunite at this point. You may not need to re-enter your marriage at the present time. Instead, pray passionately.

When one woman was at this emotionally-laden six-month point of separation, she approached her pastor for counsel and he suggested that she wait to see if her husband's words of regret were sincere.

Sadly, she discovered that his profession was hollow and reconciliation was not possible at that particular time. God was leading her.

*Jude 1:20*

*But you, beloved, build yourselves up on your most holy faith; pray in the Holy Spirit.*

Keeping a journal of your feelings, emotions and actions can be extremely valuable during marital separation. A written record can be wonderfully therapeutic for you as you quietly vent any anger and pent-up rage.

It can be a reminder of specific events that are unfolding in your life right now. Writing down troubling thoughts can be healing in itself. A journal can also serve as evidence in a court of law if that becomes necessary at some point in the future.

So find something to write on—a tablet of blank paper, a borrowed composition book from your child's school supplies, your computer screen, a fancy bound journal or individual sheets of typing paper.

Begin to write today. You can write in many fashions—poetry, simple lists, elaborate prose, questions or phrases of a few words. Choose which form works best for you or change from one entry to the next.

Write on a daily, weekly or monthly basis. And if you're like most women, you will want to keep your writings in a private and confidential place.

Make a note about how you feel each day. Are you angry, sad, prayerful, teary, happy, relieved, peaceful, wishful, hopeful, resigned, mad or joyful? Also include special events such as going to a new exercise class, a counseling session for yourself or your child, going to lunch with a friend, talking with your husband about college selection for your daughter, a church women's retreat or planning a vacation.

Of course, be sure to include things both beautiful and bizarre that happen in your life during your separation and divorce.

Periodically review your writings, reflect on them and learn from them.

*Jeremiah 36: 2*

*Take a scroll and write on it all the words that*
*I have spoken to you against Israel and Judah.*

Your prayer life has probably increased since you separated from your husband. You may find that you talk to the Father several times throughout your day because, after all, you have many needs and concerns right now. Your prayers can take many forms, and may often be even one sentence utterances as you sail through your many tasks of the day. Be glad that you have the privilege of openly praying any time of the day. What a blessing this link to God can be!

When one woman discovered her husband's infidelity, she began to earnestly pray for marital healing. She prayed this prayer every day for two months. Once it became obvious that healing was not going to happen as her husband was continuing with his behaviors, she began to pray differently. She initially asked God for strength—strength to be able to discover all the truths in her marriage and strength to be able to withstand all that was happening.

Next, she boldly asked God for hope—hope in him and his Word, in the future, for her children and that all of her marital mess could somehow get better, even if it meant separation. Then she prayed to God for joy. She was so despondent over marital failure that she had been depressed, and smiles were hard to come by. So she asked God to infuse her with his joy. Finally, she prayed for peace. God's peace is supreme—the very best possible.

God abundantly answered these prayer requests. He has granted this godly woman strength, hope, joy and peace. She continues to ask for these four blessings regularly. Keeping a prayer journal lets you clearly see how God answers your prayers.

*Philippians 4:6–7*

*Do not worry about anything, but in everything by prayer and supplication with thanksgiving let your requests be made known to God. And the peace of God, which surpasses all understanding, will guard your hearts and your minds in Christ Jesus.*

Letting go is a process which does not happen overnight. You are letting go of your marriage, much of your past and some future dreams. There is a lot of work to do!

How is it possible to let go of a vow that you made to God, to your husband and to yourself on your wedding day? The only way to accomplish this monumental task is one day at a time with God's help. The old phrase, "Let go and let God," is quite appropriate in this situation.

If your husband persists in domestic violence, alcoholism or drug abuse that endanger his family, let go and surrender the entire situation to God. Your heavenly Father can handle even this, and you must let him.

Give it to God, and let go of your marriage if the circumstances demand it. Yes, it will be difficult—painful, sad and lonely.

But once you begin to heal with God's help, you can look forward to a future that is full of spiritual hope—and joy, calm, peace, love and happiness.

Don't hurry up the process of letting go.

You must experience each stage of grief and let yourself feel all the emotions associated with letting go in order to properly recover and heal. Go slowly, enjoy your children, have some fun when you can, enjoy your solitude and pray often.

God will help you to let go.

*Psalm 34:18*

*The Lord is near to the brokenhearted,*
*and saves the crushed in spirit.*

Easter is a phenomenal time of rebirth, a season when the entire earth springs back to life. Cherry trees sprout pink blossoms, grass turns from winter's gray-brown to vibrant green, yellow daffodils push their way into the world once again and red tulips come out of hiding.

Spring can be a wonderful time for you to begin again. Just as you can visually see God's handiwork in nature, you can imagine his handiwork in your future life.

Your marriage may be restored through the Lord or it may dissolve permanently. Your life will be improved through God's peace and truth as will the lives of your children. They will be able to see God's joy and serenity in your life and realize that they can begin again as well. Indeed, it is possible to have a family rebirth.

Begin a new Easter tradition, one that is different from anything you've ever done. One newly single mother in my church took her three teenagers on a ten-mile biking trail. The children loved seeing their mother happy and realizing that they could still be a family—a different family with different numbers and shapes, but still a family.

The best part of the Easter season is the rebirth that God gave us through his Son. What a gift—the death of Jesus on the cross, followed by his resurrection! Consciously incorporate the glorious hope of Easter into celebrations at home and church, instead of merely visiting the Easter bunny at the local mall.

Joyously and openly tell your children of Jesus' resurrection and our amazing hope through him.

*Matthew 28: 5–6*

*But the angel said to the women, "Do not be afraid; I know that you are looking for Jesus who was crucified. He is not here; for he has been raised, as he said."*

Do you have some shrubbery that has grown out of control? If so, go find your pruning shears and get to work! Spring is an ideal time for some therapeutic yard work.

I had some large holly bushes in a side yard that had grown to the size of giant trees after separation. They literally looked like a mass of jungle vines and I had a huge challenge before me. One Saturday morning I enlisted the help of a neighbor, and we sawed and hacked on those branches for three continuous hours in order to reshape the five plants. The holly shrubs truly had tripled from their original size, growing at all kinds of weird angles. We pruned short and long branches, living and dead. We were very proud of our work after it was all completed, and I was looking forward to new growth in just a few short weeks.

During the pruning venture, I was reminded of the familiar Bible passage below and a recent Sunday School lesson. A woman in my class had commented, "The more you prune, the closer you are to the Source." I thought at the time of the lesson that this was a profoundly true statement and it led me to examine my life. What does God need to prune in our lives? It might be emphasis on possessions, gossip, misplaced priorities, worry, thoughts of revenge and wrong focus.

We all need to let the Gardener work in our lives every day. We can surrender all that we have and all that we are to the Lord and watch what he clears away in order that we can, indeed, grow closer to the Source. As separated or divorced Christian women, we can continue to allow God to prune our lives so that we can be productive and bear fruit for him.

*John 15:1–2*

*"I am the true vine, and my Father is the vinegrower.*
*He removes every branch in me that bears no fruit.*
*Every branch that bears fruit he prunes to*
*make it bear more fruit."*

Do you feel as though you've lost your mind since you separated from your husband? If so, you have lots of company.

Your daughter may be talking about her school day, then ask your opinion about an algebra problem when all of a sudden, you realize that you have no earthly idea what she is saying. After all, you weren't even thinking about algebra. You were deciding what nutritious meal you could quickly throw together for supper in 15 minutes.

Or you may get to the grocery store, have your cart full and get ready to write a check for your $85 weekly bill. You search your pocketbook three times, only to discover that your checkbook is nowhere to be found. You were absolutely positive that you took it with you!

One woman called her neighbor two days after her husband left home. She was living with her two teenage daughters, who had been quite shocked to discover that their father was having an affair. This poor woman reported to her neighbor that she was having rectal bleeding again, a problem that had required some medical treatment just the previous year. She was distraught at the thought of having possible medical complications to compound her marital separation. Her neighbor calmly questioned her if she might be having her menstrual period, which was exactly the case. She said she felt so stupid, but that she just couldn't think clearly. In a calm manner, her neighbor laughed lovingly and reassured her that she was just "in a mental fugue."

It is normal to be absent-minded when your life undergoes tremendous upheaval. Rely on God and trust that your mental clarity will slowly but surely improve.

*Proverbs 3:5*

*Trust in the Lord with all your heart,*
*and do not rely on your own insight.*

Are you a busy woman who cannot take time out to seek God? Perhaps you're so busy with everyday life that you never actually stop or be still.

Turn off the CD player, television or radio and enjoy the stillness of the moment. Make a habit of riding in your car in total silence. We all enjoy music, but if you're constantly bombarded with tunes and news, you just can't think. Let your children see an example of stillness as you glorify God in times of quiet. Satan wants you to be constantly busy so that you cannot give your time to God. Listen to that still small voice inside, the conscience given to you by God. What is God revealing to you—about him and about yourself?

You may discover a new truth about your Father in heaven, see his grace or view a problem from an entirely different angle. Perhaps you're able to thank God for taking care of you during separation. During such a quiet still moment, one woman acknowledged that it was the Lord who directly supplied that volunteer from her church to come and put a trap in her attic. There was a rat up there, running around and scaring her with noises when she was lying in the bed alone at night. She was frightened to tackle that problem alone and she gave the credit to God above during a quiet moment in her car.

If you are concentrating on God during those moments of stillness, it is impossible to concentrate on marital problems. Feelings of anger about verbal abuse and worry about paying the bills can completely destroy you, but you can focus on God's goodness instead. Don't put all of your attention on these earthly matters. Instead, be still and listen to God.

*Psalm 37:7*

*Be still before the Lord, and wait patiently for him;*
*do not fret over those who prosper in their way,*
*over those who carry out evil devices.*

Have you prepared your tax return?

April 15th is a day of the year that many people dread—a day of settling monetary balances with the Internal Revenue Service.

You may have a few friends who willingly pay everything that they owe to the IRS. But you probably know of far more people who will try every deduction, both legal and illegal, in order to avoid paying additional money to the government. Failure to pay your fair share of taxes can result in harsh financial penalties, and actually is contrary to God's teaching. Remember that you have both a moral and legal obligation to pay those taxes, as painful as it may be to your checkbook.

Questionable shortcuts and nonpayment of taxes due may be tempting, especially during a time of separation when your money is incredibly tight. It is certainly acceptable to take every legal deduction, but avoid cheating on your tax return. Pray that God will help you to steer clear of this real temptation. It may be wise to seek expert help in completing your documents, even though your husband may have always handled it himself.

Even the act of paying your fair share of taxes can be a powerful Christian witness to your belief in the Lord.

*Luke 20:22, 25*

*"Is it lawful for us to pay taxes to the emperor, or not?"*
*He said to them, "Then give to the emperor the things that*
*are the emperor's, and to God the things that are God's."*

Are you going to continue tithing to your church during separation? This can be a turning point for you—total dependence on God instead of relying on your own strength and devices.

For many women who are separated and divorced, money may be in short supply. But God demands and deserves our first and our best. Sacrificial giving involves analysis of your income, evaluating everything that God has given to you, deciding what proportion of your income to give to church and other ministries and then trusting the Lord to provide.

One friend who was recently separated established the habit of writing her check to the church each month for the amount of $300. It was a huge financial stretch for her, but she considered it just another one of her monthly bills that she was obligated to pay. However, during one horrid month, she was faced with an unusual stack of bills. Her teenage son's large car insurance bill was due, along with a life insurance premium and a gutter repair bill. She was totally overwhelmed and at the point of tears when she realized that she had no money left to pay her tithe. Shaking her head in frustration and trusting God, she wrote a check to the church for $300 and hoped that it would be a long time in making its way to her bank. The very next day, her bank statement arrived in the mail and she sat down to balance her checkbook. To her complete shock, she discovered that she had made a subtraction error in her checkbook, and she had more money in her account than she thought— exactly $300 more in the account! No more, no less.

This was no coincidence. God is in control of every facet of life.

*2 Corinthians 8:12*

*For if the eagerness is there, the gift is acceptable according to what one has—not according to what one does not have.*

Are you longing for someone to take you in his arms and reassure you that all is well? If you're like most separated and divorced women, you need some comforting.

You may turn to a neighbor, a close friend, a dear friend at church, pastor, your child, mother, sister, brother, father or a work colleague for comfort. And they can indeed provide some wonderful help and reassurance during separation.

The best and most abiding comfort, however, comes from the Lord. His constant presence is an assurance that he will never leave you, even in the midst of all your hurt and pain. When you scream in anger over another ugly event, when you feel like you can't continue for one more day, and when you are so tired that you don't even want to take care of yourself or your children anymore, he is there.

God will never abandon you, because he loves you and cares for you in a far better way than anyone on the earth.

Ponder and consider that God loves you to an even greater degree than your parents—his is an extraordinary amount of love. And that wonderful source never ends. Pray for God's comfort and he will provide it abundantly.

*2 Thessalonians 2:16–17*

*Now may our Lord Jesus Christ himself and God our Father, who loved us and through grace gave us eternal comfort and good hope, comfort your hearts and strengthen them in every good work and word.*

Do you feel as though you have been abused in your marriage? Perhaps you were a victim of ongoing verbal taunts or domestic violence, and your self-esteem may be non-existent due to such treatment.

Did you forgive a marital affair once you discovered the truth, only to have the adultery continue? Maybe your husband incurred thousands of dollars of debt and left you financially destitute when he abandoned you and the children.

God intends for a wife to submit to her husband and follow his leadership in a Christian relationship, but he never intended for you to become a doormat and suffer abuses. Rather, the Father has a better plan for your life that involves willing submission to Him alone. After all, you are God's child and he wants only the best for you. God also planned for a husband to care for his wife and submit to *His* will.

Such a marital relationship is one of mutual love and respect, as well as strong love for the Lord. A Christian marriage exists when both spouses have a strong union with Christ and willingly obey God because of their love for Him.

Likewise, God desires husbands and wives to love each other and lovingly submit to each other as they are concerned with one another's happiness.

*Ephesians 5:21–24*

*Be subject to one another out of reverence for Christ. Wives, be subject to your husband as you are to the Lord. For the husband is the head of the wife just as Christ is the head of the church, the body of which he is the Savior. Just as the church is subject to Christ, so also wives ought to be, in everything, to their husbands.*

Perhaps you still love your husband and desire reconciliation. Great!

Do you continue to cry each night into your pillow and wish he was there with you? Does your heart still lurch when he comes to see the children? Do you have a woman's intuition that you are meant to remain married to him? Maybe you hope that he will call the children so you can have an excuse to talk to him on the telephone each night. Has God shown you that you should continue in your marital relationship and try again?

Then pour your whole being into the possible salvage of your marriage. Don't be ashamed of your feelings of love. Instead pray constantly, seek God's will, attend joint counseling meetings and go to individual counseling sessions. Ask your husband to eat a meal at your home with you and the children if this is appropriate, consult him about necessary home repairs to make him feel included in the family or attend your children's school functions together. Consult your pastor, read and study your Bible and ask others to pray for your marriage to be reconciled.

After all, God intended marriage to last for a lifetime. That is his expressed will, and this can be your goal as a Christian woman if at all possible. It just may be that your separation will be an entirely new beginning in your marriage.

*Ephesians 5:31–33*

*"For this reason a man will leave his father and mother and be joined to his wife, and the two will become one flesh." This is a great mystery, and I am applying it to Christ and the church. Each of you, however, should love his wife as himself, and a wife should respect her husband.*

Are you mad at your husband for his past or present behaviors? You may continue to feel indescribable rage at his actions toward you and the children. Chances are, you have frequent flashbacks and re-live moments of excruciating pain in your marriage.

Were threats issued in your marriage? Do you still remember incidents of domestic violence? Perhaps you have feared for your daughter's safety as she rode in a car with her father after he had consumed alcohol.

You may cringe each time you drive by the hotel where your husband had an afternoon fling with his secretary. How is your husband's current behavior? Does he see your children on a regular basis? Is he making an effort to attend their school functions? Maybe he continues to drink heavily and endanger others when he drives a car. Or he might persist in his financial recklessness, leaving little money for alimony or child support obligations.

It is normal to recall events, even if incredibly painful. And as time goes on, your sharp pain will begin to dull and you may be more in control of your feelings. Remember that it was not God who let you down or disappointed you.

Time and the Lord's healing can help you remember certain moments in your marriage without quite so much bitterness and anger.

Ask God to help you find a constructive outlet for those mad and angry feelings.

*Jonah 4:1–2*

*But this was very displeasing to Jonah,*
*and he became angry. He prayed to the Lord.*

If you don't find an outlet for continued anger and let those feelings fester, you may grow to actually hate your husband. Therefore, be careful with your emotions spinning out of control.

It has been said, "He who angers you, controls you." As godly women, we want to be controlled only by God. Marital separation and divorce are a breeding ground for patterns of anger and hatred, but there is a very big difference between hating a person and hating an action. Perhaps it is that contrast that the Ecclesiastes author was addressing in the verse below. It is quite acceptable for you to dislike hurtful behaviors because it is important to differentiate between right and wrong.

Remember that God still loves your husband, as he loves us all. God is able to help you avoid hating your spouse. Hatred has many negative consequences, such as actions of revenge and wishing harm to come to your former husband. It can cause rebellion in your heart—rebellion against God's perfect ways and his perfect timing for your life. Hatred can blind you to your own sins, such as gossip or gluttony, and can lead to depression and despair. Hatred can also cause you to become obsessed with your husband. Are you so busy hating him that you can't think of anything or anyone else? If you are so focused on your husband, you can't focus on God and his wonderful plan for your life.

Ask God to manage any feelings of hatred you have.

*Ecclesiastes 3:8*

*A time to love, and a time to hate;*
*a time for war, and a time for peace.*

Keeping up appearances can be a full-time job and frequently, as human beings, we judge another person by her appearance.

How do you appear to the outside world? Do you spend hours at the gym working out every week in order to maintain that hourglass figure? Is there room in your budget for a manicure and pedicure twice a month? What do you wear? Do you go to the salon to have your hair styled each week? There is nothing inherently wrong with these individual habits, because God wants us to be healthy with moderate amounts of exercise. And he probably wants us to be reasonably attractive and happy about how we look. But we should remember that these are simply outward appearances and we shouldn't make this the dominant focus in our lives. Appearances by themselves do not reveal much about true values because we are all going to grow older, get several wrinkles, probably gain a few pounds and get some gray hair.

God has a different standard—one of inner beauty. It is possible for a person to be deceptive—physically attractive but living outside of God's will. Your focus, as a separated or divorced Christian woman, can be on developing lasting inner qualities.

Your character, faith and relationship with the Lord are far more important than weight or dress size. God knows the true appearance of your heart.

*1 Samuel 16:7*

*But the Lord said to Samuel, "Do not look on his appearance or on the height of his stature, because I have rejected him; for the Lord does not see as mortals see; they look on the outward appearance, but the Lord looks on the heart."*

The very name of our Father in heaven implies that he is jealous of anything that we place above him in terms of loyalty. He is God, not a "god" but the only one true God of all.

Therefore, separation and divorce are ideal times to assess your priorities. Do you value money or your position at work more highly than you ought? What other gods are present in your life—your house, husband, children, friendships with other women, shopping for new clothes or leisure activities? God expects to be at the very top of that list.

As women, we should not place possible reconciliation with our husband or marriage counseling before our relationship with the Lord God. Neither should we be so consumed with earning a salary to pay every bill in our desk drawer that we let this creep into the number one position on our priority list.

Worship God only, not earthly things. Inventory your time, and you will very quickly realize what you value. Spend your time with God and you will begin to value this relationship more than anything else on the entire earth.

God demands your complete devotion, and in turn, he will bless you abundantly as a child of his.

*Exodus 20:3, 5*

*You shall have no other gods before me.*
*You shall not bow down to them or worship them;*
*for I the Lord your God am a jealous God, punishing*
*children for the iniquity of parents, to the third and*
*the fourth generation of those who reject me.*

If only you had been more attentive to your husband, or recognized the signs of adultery before it continued for many years. If only you had sought premarital counseling to identify some emotional problems early in the relationship with your husband.

If only you had fewer children, or more children. If only you were aware of his alcohol problems years earlier, or had been a better lover. If only you had separated from your husband the first time you discovered his pornography addiction, or had a perfect hourglass figure.

If only you were more patient and loving, or had prayed on a daily basis for marital rescue. If only you were a more mature Christian, or were younger and prettier. If only you had a college education in order to get a better job, or had a less controlling personality.

If only you had argued less, or had identified your husband's addiction to street drugs before it destroyed your family.

Quit beating yourself up over past problems, because you can't do anything about them now. The "if onlys" can lead to self-doubt, self-recrimination and misdirected self-reliance. Nobody on this earth is perfect.

And God forgives anything and everything if we confess it to him, completely repent of wrongdoing and change our behavior. Confession of any sins opens the path of love and communication with our Father, and fellowship with God leads to supreme joy in this earthly life. Look forward and not backward.

*1 John 1:9*

*If we confess our sins, he who is faithful and just will forgive us our sins and cleanse us from all unrighteousness.*

It is normal to experience a honeymoon period during the early weeks of separation. You may feel relieved not to have massive amounts of alcohol in your home any longer. Or perhaps you now are thrilled that adultery is not continuing under your roof.

Maybe you smile all day long just knowing that you don't have to listen to any more verbally abusive comments about your appearance or housekeeping. Now you can rest better because you no longer are a partner, even an unwilling one, in Internet pornography.

Are you breathing easier because your husband is not home to gamble away all of your retirement money through his addiction?

During times such as these, you may feel as though the weight of the world has been removed from your shoulders. These feelings of freedom are a gift from God, so go ahead and enjoy these days and weeks of a honeymoon period. Sweep your kitchen floor to remind you that you are cleaning up your life.

Smile, breathe deeply and go outside to enjoy a sunny day while sitting on your front steps. Embrace all the new possibilities in your life. You don't have to plan out the remainder of your life at this moment.

Simply relax, take a breath, relish these good days and be thankful for them. Offer prayers of gratitude to God for bringing you to this point in life.

*Psalm 52:9*

*I will thank you forever, because of what you
have done. In the presence of the faithful
I will proclaim your name, for it is good.*

Even though your life is chaotic, you may be in the right place right now—the very place God wants you to be.

You may be alone in a long-term marriage, separated or divorced. Perhaps at this point you are contemplating marital separation due to circumstances beyond your control. You may be hurting, somewhat depressed, and wondering how in the world you can move forward. On the other hand, you may be recovering and happy, while planning for marital reconciliation. Either way, rest assured that God is in control.

As a Christian woman, you have surrendered your entire life and very being to God. You know that he is planning something wonderful for you— something better than you can even imagine at this point in separation. But it is God's plan, so it must be wonderful.

Therefore, you are right where you need to be. You have prayed about your marriage, your separation, your divorce. In addition, you have waited for God's leading. You continue to pray every day or every hour, and you know that he continues to guide you each step of the way. He cares about you and about every minute detail of your present situation. So allow yourself to hurt, cry a bit if you are somewhat depressed and wonder what will happen next week. Then let yourself move forward one day at a time, learn to smile again and ask God to help you figure out a long-term plan for your life.

Just rest assured that, with divine intervention, you will move from this right place right now to an even better place in the Lord.

*Psalm 47:7*

*For God is the king of all the earth;*
*sing praises with a psalm.*

God is able to take tragedy and the worst circumstances in life, and use them for good and for his glory.

Yes, God can even use drug addiction, gambling, adultery, abandonment, domestic violence or verbal abuse and bring good out of it. It is indeed possible for something wonderful to emerge from all these ashes! Some short-term good may already be evident if you are separated from some painful, hurtful behaviors. Of course, it is difficult and you probably continue to mourn the loss of future dreams. But think of what goodness God is planning for you on a long-term basis.

If you are reconciled with your husband, your marriage will be better than it has ever been—full of love, faith and trust. And you can work as a married couple for the Lord in ways that he reveals to you.

If you are divorced, God will show you that what he has in mind will most certainly be better than what you may have endured in the latter stages of marriage. He may show you a plan to be an active Christian single woman.

Your challenge, as a Christian woman in separation, is to trust God and wait for him to bring good out of the circumstances of your life. Pray every day for patience to wait on God and see what wonderful good he will work in your life and those of your children.

God will triumph to bring about his will.

*Genesis 50:20*

*Even though you intended to do harm to me,*
*God intended it for good, in order to preserve*
*a numerous people, as he is doing today.*

Do you have faith that God can and will prevail in your life? Do you believe that he will accomplish his purposes in and through you? In your marriage, separation or divorce? As a married or single woman? In your role as a single mother?

Faith in God is an amazing concept. Perhaps you can remember your toddler's arguments and questions about this, because he couldn't see God and couldn't touch him. Your son or daughter may have asked how you knew God was real. During a painful separation or divorce, it is common to have had some of these same doubts yourself; you may have wondered if God exists and if he really cares about your hurt and loneliness.

It is precisely at this point—when faith in God is called into question—that your faith has an opportunity to stretch and grow. Examine your past life. Perhaps, God gave you parents who loved and cared for you, and he guarded you through your tumultuous teen years to adulthood. God provided a mate for you on your wedding day that you loved with all your heart. He provided blessings of children, and may have even provided you with the strength to be the parent of a special needs child. God provided the endurance to "tough out" the very difficult parts of your marriage. Step back for a moment and just marvel at what he has already done in your life.

This wonderful past dims in comparison to what God can accomplish in the future if you have faith in him. Faith in self, spouse, children, education, work or money is not what will yield positive results.

But faith in the Lord can most assuredly bring new and glorious results in both your present and future life.

*Hebrews 11:1*

*Now faith is the assurance of things hoped for, the conviction of things not seen.*

What problems have you encountered on an everyday basis since separation or divorce? If you're like most women, the list is quite lengthy.

Your daughter is frustrated with history homework, there are ants in the kitchen, your bicycle has a flat tire, the garage door opener broke and the bolt rolled away to some unknown dark corner, the dog urinated on the clean carpet, or the car is almost out of gas when you have a big trip planned for work starting very early tomorrow morning. You volunteered to teach a portion of a Bible study at church before discovering that now there is very little preparation time, your teenage son stayed out past his curfew, or you don't have time to cook supper before having to hustle out the door to a PTA meeting.

You've probably become frustrated because your husband is not home to help out with the simple daily chores of life, such as assisting with a child's homework. Do you sometimes feel like screaming?

Instead, try to pray and smile. And then get to work attacking those problems. Take ten minutes to calmly offer homework help and put out garlic cloves to send the ants running back outside. Next, assign your son the chore of finding a bolt to repair the garage door opener and use some stain remover to clean that spot on the carpet. Do it!

Don't procrastinate or just assume that those everyday little problems will go away.

Instead, they will likely multiply and get worse. Yes, it is maddening because you can't ask your husband for help with something as simple as going to fill the gas tank in the car. So, it is okay to let out a small scream as you ask God to help with even these daily concerns.

*Psalm 46:1*

*God is our refuge and strength,*
*a very present help in trouble.*

A friend once said that it takes six months of time during separation and divorce to grieve for each five years of marriage. For a marriage of 20 years, therefore, a woman can expect to mourn for a minimum of two years according to her advice. Another acquaintance advised just to survive the first year after separation—her assurance was that it would get much better after that point. Yet another woman said that the rule of thumb is three years; she warned of total misery for at least that long before it would be possible for any wife to "get over him."

The time frame for working through marital separation and divorce is individual, and no single guideline applies in every situation. But letting go is a slow process that does get better with the passage of time. For example, separation from your husband is generally easier at one year when compared with the first month after his departure. There are many reasons for this improvement.

Distance is a big plus, and growth as an individual can now be possible. Maybe you're gaining confidence in your ability to perform simple chores around the house, and are less frustrated by the everyday annoyances of life.

Gaining strength through God and having his assurance that you will survive with divine help is a huge boost to a woman who is separated.

So believe that things will continue to improve and get better. God is helping you every day not only to survive—but to *thrive*!

*Psalm 32:7*

*You are a hiding place for me; you preserve me from trouble; you surround me with glad cries of deliverance.*

What is going on in your daily life? Are you working for your own glory, or are you working to please God?

You can show your love for God and please him in various ways. Perhaps the primary and most important way to please God is to know him. Simply know him by spending time in God's Word, talking with him and giving your all to him with total joy.

Other means to please God include praying, focusing on him instead of your daily issues of life, asking God to keep you pure, being a loving mother, working toward reconciliation in your marriage (if that's possible), having a consistent family Bible devotional time and attending church regularly. Other ways of displaying your devotion to the Master may include filling your mind with eternal thoughts, reading Christian literature, caring for your body appropriately, clearly identifying sin and eliminating it from your life, guiding your children to the Lord, praying for your children and smiling.

Abiding in God's will in every known area of your life—even in a simple choice of recreation or clothing —pleases God. Obedience and service are inherent in giving pleasure to the Lord. Naturally, sometimes it's difficult to obey, because obedience might not be what we really want to do at any given moment in time. But it is absolutely the best path for our lives.

As a Christian, you can take great joy in pleasing God in everything you do.

*Psalm 40:8*

*"I delight to do your will, O my God;*
*your law is within my heart."*

Is your life uncertain and a jumble of unknowns?

What about your future? Do you think you will remain married to your current husband, divorce him, marry another man or remain single? Can you continue to grow in the Lord and put your trust in him despite feelings of being overwhelmed at the moment? Do you believe in your heart that your children will continue to grow in God, love both you and their father and be joyful community citizens? Do you even believe that anything good is possible at this point in your life?

We don't know the future, and it can be very uncertain. And God very intentionally planned it this way. Perhaps if we knew everything that was going to happen in the coming years, we might be completely overjoyed or completely overburdened. Imagine that you could know what's in store for your future. If you were aware that one of your parents would become very ill or that you would divorce your husband, you might feel as if you couldn't face the coming months and years. On the other hand, if you knew for certain that God would lead you to a particular Christian man for remarriage, you might not be willing to wait for that special man.

God is in control of what will happen—to you, your husband, children, siblings, parents, in-laws and friends. Our only true certainty is eternal life through belief in Christ.

Give your life, marriage, children, work, home, flowers and weeds to God. It is all his anyway; he just wants us to acknowledge this fact and turn our entire existences over to him. Rest in God, work in God and trust in God. He will wonderfully surprise you in the midst of uncertainty with an assurance of his certain love for you.

*John 14:1*

*"Do not let your hearts be troubled.*
*Believe in God, believe also in me."*

It is well-known that many women in the process of separation and divorce comfort themselves through food. Mashed potatoes with butter and gravy, cookies and milk, or a huge piece of chocolate cake can temporarily relieve feelings of loneliness or sadness.

But the relief is only temporary and continued binging on unhealthy foods is a poor way to handle stress. Let yourself eat one sweet thing a day, instead of three or four, and know that it's okay to treat yourself occasionally.

Go on and eat that thin piece of chocolate cheesecake! Weigh yourself often if overeating is a problem for you. Make every effort to keep your weight under control, since gaining ten pounds in one month will simply make you feel more sad and depressed. You will also be a good example to your children with respect to their health if you keep your weight in the normal range.

Go outside and take a walk, clean the kitchen sink, or pull weeds from your flower garden if you feel the urge to binge. One woman found that the desire to eat a whole bag of barbecue potato chips usually went away in ten minutes if she didn't yield to the temptation. She just needed an interim activity to occupy her time and mind, along with a peppermint to suck. Pray to God, because he is able to help you resist that warm giant-sized chocolate chip cookie when you walk by the cookie factory at the mall.

God wants us to care for our bodies, his temples. Overeating to the point of being unhealthy is an example of defiling the Lord's dwelling place. Ask the Holy Spirit for daily or hourly help with overeating, and he will provide.

*1 Corinthians 6:20*

*For you were bought with a price;*
*therefore glorify God in your body.*

Many women under marital stress neglect their bodies by undereating and losing massive amounts of weight. Sometimes a woman will insist that this is the only area of her life that she is able to control, and undereating then becomes a serious health problem. Don't set a goal of fitting into a size 6 dress to attract men, as you have many other priorities at the present time. Consult a weight chart if you are truly uncertain what a healthy weight is for your height and body type.

Starvation can lead to chronic diseases, and this is not in God's plan for your life. God is concerned for your physical as well as spiritual health, and he wants you to eat well. A balanced diet has many advantages during separation—giving you enough energy to cope with life's many demands as a separated woman, avoiding illness, setting an example for your daughters and helping you to generally feel better.

If you have a problem with neglecting your body and severely undereating, keep a food diary to let you truly see your eating patterns. And if you detect a concern, ask God for help as you begin to better care for your body. You may be so sad and despondent that you truly have no appetite for food, or your stomach may be constantly upset due to the emotional trauma that you are undergoing.

Call your medical doctor, dietitian or counselor for assistance if necessary, as anorexia or other eating disorders can result if a pattern of undereating is left untreated. Remember that God wants only the best for you, even during your separation or divorce.

*3 John 1:2*

*Beloved, I pray that all may go well with you
and that you may be in good health,
just as it is well with your soul.*

Walking with God every day, and all day long, can be the greatest joy that a Christian woman will ever know.

One woman in my church, separated from her husband after 5 years of marriage, said that she found more time to spend with God during separation. She openly and joyfully declared, "I just adore God." She discovered additional morning minutes to read her Bible and pray, and she used this time to her advantage in order to grow spiritually and discover what God wanted for her life. Her behavior was such a powerful witness to other women—those with both healthy and troubled marriages.

Taking the time to develop the habit of always abiding with God can yield tremendous blessings of love, gentleness, self-control and strength. If you are in constant communion with God, you will more easily discern his will for your life. His will for small details, such as making a decision about whether to purchase a particular piece of clothing. And his will for large decisions—such as selecting a college with your child.

Walking with God doesn't imply that you are perfect; instead, it means that you truly love and obey God and that you want to love and obey him for the remainder of your life. Love and obedience, as you walk with God, can result in indescribable peace and wonderful blessings for your life.

*Genesis 6:9*

*These are the descendants of Noah.*
*Noah was a righteous man, blameless*
*in his generation; Noah walked with God.*

Do you have a praise band at your church? Perhaps it's led by young people with acoustic guitars and glorious voices who sing uplifting contemporary Christian music as they praise God. The words of the beautiful choruses that they sing at my church are quite moving, and the songs stay with me for days after hearing our praise band.

Do you like to sing hymns? Some of the older ones are so familiar and comforting as you sing them weekly in the worship service. Their messages are usually clear in terms of trusting and obeying God.

If you are happy, sing to God. Praise him with your words, the tunes and the music in your heart. Sing at home, at church, in the car, when you cook supper, as you clean the house, when you pull garden weeds and at work.

And if you're sad and heartbroken over your state of separation or divorce, also sing to God. Your mood will probably instantly lift, and you'll be able to give thanks to God for all he has done in your life in the past. You can be assured that he is giving you strength to survive both the present and the future.

So find opportunities to sing to God and praise his glorious name.

*Ephesians 5:18–20*

*Do not get drunk with wine, for that is debauchery; but be filled with the Spirit, as you sing psalms and hymns and spiritual songs among yourselves, singing and making melody to the Lord in your hearts, giving thanks to God the Father at all times and for everything in the name of our Lord Jesus Christ.*

Are you arguing with your former husband about a separation agreement, child custody, vacations, money, holiday arrangements or visitation? Do you argue with your children about cleaning their rooms, doing homework, taking out the trash, feeding the dog, cleaning out the cat's litter box or their choice of clothing? Are you continuing to argue with your parents about their control over your life as their adult child? Is there an ongoing feud at your office about who should make the morning coffee?

Chances are that you've had these arguments many times before—the very same arguments about the very same things.

Calmly discuss decisions with your husband, if possible. Don't yell at him or bring up past issues in your loudest voice. Instead, try answering softly, and search for peace in your life.

Your former husband won't be able to argue if you answer him in soft tones. Your son can't yell at you if you are kind and loving as you ask him for the third time to take out the trash. Likewise, your daughter probably won't scream again if you answer her accusation with soft words.

Practice the art of answering argumentative words from others with peaceful, firm, calm and quiet words.

*Proverbs 15:1*

*A soft answer turns away wrath,*
*but a harsh word stirs up anger.*

There are some areas of your life in which you need to stand firm—very firm. Recognizing some behaviors may result in separation from your husband, but it is important to obey what God tells you concerning them. Often, just the *naming* of a certain action for what it is can be an important first step.

Unfaithfulness on the part of either spouse has the potential to rip families apart and it hurts everyone involved—husband, wife, children, grandparents, friends, work colleagues, neighbors and even unborn grandchildren. Abandonment of one's family is also wrong and not part of God's will. Spousal battering, child abuse and sexual abuse are deplorable and should never be tolerated; they have no place in a godly family.

What are other areas in which you should stand firm? Untreated alcoholism can destroy families and lead to chronic health problems. Drug abuse is another difficult trial for a family to overcome, but addiction to street drugs and alcohol *can* sometimes be successfully treated. If God leads you to work with your husband through any problem, then proceed through counseling and therapy programs.

Stand firm in other areas of addictions such as gambling and internet pornography. Monetary embezzlement on the part of a spouse in order to finance lifestyle excesses is not a behavior that is pleasing to God. Verbal and emotional abuses are not part of God's will, so make an effort to stand up to these behaviors. Also, never allow blasphemy against the Holy Spirit in your home.

Be firm, recognize behaviors and then act according to God's directives.

*1 Corinthians 15:58*

*Therefore, my beloved, be steadfast, immovable, always excelling in the work of the Lord, because you know that in the Lord your labor is not in vain.*

It is often very difficult to resist the temptation to judge others.

If you have been wronged by someone close to you, it becomes incredibly hard to leave judgment to God. God ultimately knows when people are unjust and unfair, and there will most certainly be a time when everyone is called to account for his or her actions. Naturally, it may be a normal human response for you to judge your husband if you feel hurt. You might even want him to go to sleep while crying into his pillow over losing the people that you think love him the most—his wife and children. Maybe you have already judged his actions to be wrong, and perhaps you reason that God has already passed judgment on him as well.

You will also be asked to account for your own actions when ultimately judged by God. Any possible sins of gossip, thoughts of revenge toward your husband, neglect of your children, gluttony or hatred are also known by your Heavenly Father. God is a fair judge, but also a just one.

The Lord is aware of all behaviors, along with any attempts toward change. God is also knowledgeable of righteous living and that could include handling marital separation in an atmosphere of strength, dignity, courage and grace.

*Psalm 58:10–11*

*The righteous will rejoice when they see vengeance done; they will bathe their feet in the blood of the wicked. People will say, "Surely there is a reward for the righteous; surely there is a God who judges on earth."*

Are you tired—and tired of being tired?

Then call on your family and Christian friends. One woman who was separated called her parents on the telephone at one o'clock in the morning without giving it a second thought. She needed someone to talk with her as she cried about an upcoming 25th wedding anniversary. Her mother was warm and caring, with no regard to the terribly late hour of the night that the call was made. She listened to her daughter scream about her pain, reassured her that she was not to blame for her husband's choices in life and then offered words of love and encouragement.

Another woman called her pastor, crying buckets of tears. Her pastor prayed with her, encouraged her, and listened to her questions about the future. Naturally, since they had talked many times before, he offered her no false reassurance or false hope. But he comforted and assured her, "There will be another chapter in your life." She said that this one sentence alone got her through the next week, which turned out to be a particularly trying one.

Christians are meant to encourage and uplift each other, and you can accept such assistance with many thanks to God. Kind words can make the difference between survival and defeat.

Just as others are building you up during this painful time of divorce, you will be better able to help others some day in the future.

*1 Thessalonians 5:11*

*Therefore encourage one another and
build up each other, as indeed you are doing.*

What have you done on Mother's Day in past years? Maybe you visited your own mother and mother-in-law as a family. Or perhaps your children made breakfast and served you in bed. You may have a special Mother's Day celebration at church that includes participation in a women's choir or a mother's luncheon.

Prepare yourself for this day because it will evoke many memories—memories of the births of children, times with your husband and special mementos that your daughter made in her Sunday School class at church. Maybe you still have a pin or piece of children's jewelry she made just for you on Mother's Day many years ago. Hopefully, many of these remembrances are pleasant. If so, reflect back on them and let yourself smile with gratitude. However, if most of your maternal celebrations have been quite unpleasant in life, try to smile anyway because you can make today a much better Mother's Day.

Count your blessings of your children, biological family and Christian family. Children are gifts from God and motherhood is special. No one else could have given birth to your children or so specially picked your adopted child. You have nursed them from infancy to the present time, and no one else can ever be their mother. Your daughters are unique, because you have made them so. You are teaching them to love, honor and fear the Lord. And you are most certainly showing them how to handle adversity.

So celebrate today with eating burned toast in bed, going to church to worship God, calling your own mother, fellowshipping with other mothers, talking to your sister who just had her first baby and giving thanks to the good Lord that you are a mother.

*Exodus 20:12*

*Honor your father and your mother, so that your days may be long in the land that the Lord your God is giving you.*

Mother's Day can potentially be a very sad day for women who have no children. You may be childless by your own choice, your husband's choice or through no choice at all. You might feel wistful and full of regret today.

One friend who was separated from her husband found Mother's Day to be particularly depressing. She had always wanted children and had married at the age of 38, after openly sharing her enthusiasm for parenthood with her fiancé. They had even picked out names for both a boy and a girl. But after the wedding, her husband revealed that he never wanted children and flatly refused to discuss the matter any further. Of course, this Christian woman was heartbroken and continued to pray for a miraculous change of his heart. But his stubbornness continued for the next few years and at the age of 44, she finally gave up on the idea of ever being a mother. Sadly, her husband abandoned her one year later for a younger woman who was only 25 years old, and then quickly had two children with his new wife. Naturally, my friend was totally devastated.

So if this un-Mother's Day is going to be hard for you, it is important to have a battle plan! Go to lunch with your parents or another family from church, call a friend or go to a movie. Get outside and take a walk, since exercise is a great stress relief. Plant some flowers outside, because digging in the dirt can be wonderfully therapeutic. Swing in your hammock or go to a park and swing. Just find something productive that will fill your hours on this day and help you feel alive.

Above all, thank God for your own mother who gave you birth. And thank her as well.

*Proverbs 1:8*

*Hear, my child, your father's instruction,*
*and do not reject your mother's teaching.*

Do you feel led to pray for others? Many people in your life may need prayer—children, former husband, parents, in-laws, someone in your office who has had a heart attack or a friend who is out of work due to a layoff. Folks at church might also need prayer support —your pastor, church secretary, your child's Sunday School teacher, the financial manager, deacons, the senior high youth minister, associate pastor and a volunteer youth leader.

How does it make you feel when an older woman in your church tells you that she has been praying for your family since your divorce? Knowing that someone is praying for you is very uplifting and can be a huge source of encouragement.

Intercessory prayer—praying for others—can be a big part of your life even in the middle of pain from marital separation. If you focus on others, your own pain can take a backseat for a day or two.

Pray specifically for known needs. If you don't know specifics, pray for spiritual guidance for the person on your list in addition to just asking God to generally "bless John" or "bless Mary." Pray according to scripture. The following verses are a wonderful guide for intercessory prayer.

*Colossians 1:9–10*

*For this reason, since the day we heard it, we have not ceased praying for you and asking that you may be filled with the knowledge of God's will in all spiritual wisdom and understanding, so that you may lead lives worthy of the Lord, fully pleasing to him, as you bear fruit in every good work and as you grow in the knowledge of God.*

Has your former husband told you that his alcoholism is your fault? Did he say that his battering is your responsibility? Did he tell you that his adultery is because of you? Maybe he tells you that his drug habit is because of something you've done. Has he informed you that his homosexuality is due to your character flaw? Perhaps he is blaming you for his need to "find himself."

Your husband's actions are most certainly not your fault. You are not to blame for his behavior—you are just a very convenient excuse for his use.

However, if you temporarily believe that your husband's actions are indeed your fault, rest assured that you are normal. It is quite common for a wife to accept the fault for her husband's actions. She may have been told repeatedly for years that everything wrong in the marriage was her fault. She might have already been suffering from very low self-esteem, so then, naturally, accepted all the blame.

God has given you a sound mind to use to discern marital problems that were your responsibility. Accept responsibility for your own actions, because everyone makes personal choices. Remember that one appropriate Christian method to deal with marital problems is through counseling and prayer—not through blaming.

*James 4:17*

*Anyone, then, who knows the right thing
to do and fails to do it, commits sin.*

You need to reassure your children repeatedly that any marital problems in the family are not their fault. They may feel that they are somehow to blame for the problems that you and your husband had in your relationship, and nothing could be farther from the truth. Their feelings of guilt can haunt their childhood years and then carry over into adulthood. Of course, they are naturally hurt by the separation and might be quite unsure of the future.

Talk with your children openly about the separation, and answer their questions honestly without providing minute details. They don't need to know ugly specifics, but you should directly tell them that existing marital problems are not their fault. You can tell them that their lives will change, but that they don't have to be ruined. Remember to keep the lines of communication open, and assure them that you will not abandon them.

Try to find a Christian counselor with an adolescent emphasis for your teenage son as he deals with your separation, and consider a female counselor for your daughter. They need a safe place to talk about what is going on in their minds. The help of a counselor is crucial for some children, while others refuse to meet with anyone. Just remember to keep the option of a counselor available for the future, in the event that your child refuses to enter into formal counseling now. Pastors are often able to fill this critical need that children have during the painful time when their parents are separated.

Love your children, and keep them close to God as you tell them over and over again that they are not to blame for their parents' actions or for their separation.

*Job 5:8*

*"As for me, I would seek God,*
*and to God I would commit my cause."*

Brace yourself for your first birthday celebration as a separated or divorced woman, or even a woman contemplating separation. It is likely to be difficult and stressful as you remember many previous birthdays.

One friend, whose marriage was on the verge of collapse due to her husband's repeated gambling and financial recklessness, discovered that her husband was making numerous phone calls to place bets on a horse race the morning of her birthday. She was dumbfounded at this continued outrageous behavior, since he had declared personal bankruptcy just the week before. Obviously, her birthday was a very sour day.

Come up with a plan of action for your birthday. One woman went to flip hamburgers for a church picnic and golf tournament on her birthday during the year of marital separation, and discovered that laughing with Christian friends was very therapeutic. Then she went to her parents' house with her children for a picnic in her honor. It was fun and relaxing, and she didn't sit home all day crying and wondering if her husband would call with good wishes.

*Have some fun!* Smile, take a long bubble bath, read a book, sit outside under a tree and look at the clouds, or dance by yourself to music. Call a friend, take a nap, have a long lunch hour at work, take a bike ride, go out to dinner with your children or give yourself a vacation day from work.

If possible, make sure that you remember to call your mother and thank her for all her hard work on the day of your birth many years ago.


*1 John 3:9*

*Those who have been born of God do not sin,
because God's seed abides in them; they cannot
sin, because they have been born of God.*

Your child's first birthday during separation or divorce can be as difficult as yours. A toddler will react differently than a teenager, and each situation is unique. The reasons for your separation or divorce could also affect your child's behavior on that special day.

If you are in counseling with your husband to try and reconcile your marriage, invite him over for cake and ice cream. This invitation may do wonders for your daughter as she sees her parents talking to one another. It is imperative that you both make your child the priority on her birthday.

Even if you are in the throes of an ugly and protracted court battle, remember that this special day is about your child and not about any spousal dislike. So even under the worst of circumstances, try to be civil and get along temporarily for your child's sake. Even in a very tense situation, you may be able to arrange for your son to have some time on his birthday to be alone with his father. Be the adult in the situation, put your son first and drive him to the park to meet his dad.

Above all, show your love toward your child on this special day with words and action. You don't have to purchase the most expensive toy in the store or even have the party at the most popular location in town.

Just be with your child, smile widely, hug freely and reassure him or her of your unconditional love.

And as always, thank God for your child.

*Psalm 139:13*

*For it was you who formed my inward parts; you knit me together in my mother's womb.*

Are you confused and frustrated?

Are you considering separating from your husband? Do you want to give your marriage one more chance? How will the children handle all these adjustments and changes in their lives? Are you interested in joint counseling? Have you already thrown in the towel and made a decision to divorce or are you now in the process of reconciliation? Do you know a reputable attorney who will handle your divorce? Is there enough money in your bank account to pay the attorney? Will you have to sell your house? Are you afraid of being alone? Is there anyone in your life to help you through this very painful, agonizing process called separation and divorce? Are your children asking you to divorce your husband because he has mistreated them so badly? Do you still love your husband and does he still love you?

It is normal to be confused about all these issues, and even more, when you are pondering the possibility of separation and divorce. You may feel as though your head is spinning at five miles per hour as you try to look at every angle of your marriage and family. It is crucial that you take lots of time to pray and let God lead you. Don't make a decision in the heat of the moment that you might regret later.

Surrender all of your decisions to God and claim his great power to steer you toward him. The Lord can clear your mind of confusion. He is able.

*Psalm 29:11*

*May the Lord give strength to his people! May the Lord bless his people with peace!*

During her separation period, a church friend noticed that her posture began to suffer because she felt defeated. Her shoulders frequently slumped under the weight of many burdens that she was carrying—burdens of mental and physical health, the children's psychological adjustment and everyday maintenance of a family. Additional concerns of money, house upkeep and job security added to her mental load.

Once her shoulders began to slump, she felt fat around her waistline—which made her feel even worse. She was miserable. So she looked around at people who exuded self-confidence and noticed that their shoulders were always straight and tall and that they looked forward. This woman decided to give it a try.

What a difference! Simply pulling her shoulders back helped her feel stronger and more self-confident. She felt taller and five pounds lighter since she was using her abdominal muscles, even though they were a bit flabby. Her smile returned as she began to feel better about herself. She also began to talk slower and look other people in the eye instead of assuming a downward glance.

Take an inventory of your posture. Look in a mirror to examine whether your shoulders are square or slumped over. Then make a conscious effort to push your shoulders back, practice smiling, hold your stomach in slightly and look straight ahead. You will notice an immediate difference in your outlook on life.

*Luke 2:52*

*Jesus increased in wisdom and stature, and in favour with God and man.* KJV

You will be rewarded for living a godly life. Most certainly, God is pleased that you are continuing to place your trust in him and that you are persevering. The Lord sees all your actions and is aware of your purity of heart and desire to obey him. Therefore, he will reward you both on earth and in heaven.

Your ultimate reward will be a life in heaven with God—a life without sin or suffering or hurt. As a woman who trusts and believes in God, you know that there is life after death. This assurance can definitely keep you going in the midst of all your pain, troubles and heartbreak.

However, you may be wondering if you will ever be rewarded here on earth. After all, you may have no help with the daily tasks of parenthood and you wonder how you will survive every single day. You probably want some relief, and you probably want it right now! God knows your heart and he is aware of every single trial that you endure.

Recall the many ways that you have already been rewarded for your continued faithfulness on earth. Do you have friends that pray for you, laugh with you on the phone and cry with you? Are your parents supportive? Did your children give you a card on Mother's Day? Do you have a sense of peace and calm? Are you more serene since you have separated from your husband? Are you attending church? These earthly rewards may not be accidents, but plans of God. He is rewarding you right now in both small and large ways while preparing something beyond your comprehension as a future heavenly reward.

*2 Corinthians 4:18*

*Because we look not at what can be seen but at what cannot be seen; for what can be seen is temporary, but what cannot be seen is eternal.*

You may not be particularly joyful right now in light of your marital circumstances and all the discord in your life, but you can be.

Close your eyes and examine true reasons for both joy and grief. Certainly, it is okay to acknowledge that you do have many reasons for unhappiness—anger, pain, in-law problems, money concerns, children who are hurting, upheaval and distrust. You feel betrayed because life isn't turning out the way you had planned. Indeed, it is very easy for a Christian woman who is undergoing separation and divorce to get discouraged; this is normal considering the situation.

Now think of the reasons that you have for joy—life, health, children, belief in God, parents, work, food, friends, Christian fellowship and a good book to read. Think further and you can list others such as peace, music, encouragement from neighbors, strength, a flower garden, siblings and daily exercise.

No matter what the circumstances of your marriage or your divorce are, you can be assured that Christ is with you. And this is the best reason for joy! All the ugliness that often accompanies marital discord cannot separate you from God's love and faithfulness. God's joy is vastly different from a momentary burst associated with an earthly excitement. Your joy can come from internal confidence in God instead of external life forces, and heavenly joy can flow through you.

*Philippians 4:4*

*Rejoice in the Lord always; again I will say, Rejoice.*

What exactly is grace? Grace has been described as undeserved merit, something that cannot be earned but is given freely. God's grace is given to us without charge, wholly unconditionally and is the best gift that we can ever receive.

A pastor once defined grace by the use of an acronym—God's Riches at Christ's Expense. We do indeed have riches beyond our wildest dreams because God loves us and gave Christ to die for us.

Separation and divorce can be weak times for a Christian woman. Therefore, this can also be an ideal time for God's grace to shine through. God is not going to wave a magic wand and immediately restore your marriage, but he can demonstrate his power during this time. Power from the Almighty can give you courage and fortitude to keep going, and you can survive these horrible days with divine help. Turn to God and ask for help instead of relying on your own abilities.

You can probably see many examples of grace here on earth as well. Because of true Christian love, a man from a woman's church came to her house numerous times during separation to help with necessary house repairs. A broken garage door, burst air conditioning pipes and a tree that fell on the roof during a storm were totally outside of her area of expertise. This man willingly gave of his time and energies, not expecting anything in return. Grace in action.

God wants to do more for you than you are able to imagine. In admitting your weakness, you admit God's strength and visualize his grace which is given freely.

*2 Corinthians 12:9*

*But he said to me, "My grace is sufficient for you, for power is made perfect in weakness." So I will boast all the more gladly of my weaknesses, so that the power of Christ may dwell in me.*

Slow down and take a long deep breath. Breathe in through your nose and then slowly exhale through your mouth. Let your shoulders relax. Shake out the tension. Close your eyes, and let all of your worries and concerns become distant problems for the next several minutes.

Imagine that you're at the beach. God provided this wonderful spot in nature for you to enjoy. Visualize the huge waves lapping on the sand and listen for the noise that those waves make as they splash. Also listen for a seagull as it flies overhead. Do you hear anything else in this imaginary world?

Feel the warm sand on the soles of your feet as you walk on the beach. Squish the sand under your feet and between your toes. In your mind, let the warm salty water swirl around your feet as you continue your stroll. Doesn't the sun feel wonderfully warm as it soaks heat into your tired shoulders?

Spread your beach towel out on the sand and lie down for a few minutes. Smile, relax and be glad that you're here. Continue with those slow deep breaths.

It's quiet and peaceful here. You're all alone, talking and listening to God. Your stresses have evaporated and you feel very calm in your momentary mental vacation.

Take this vacation often. When the worries of life crowd you, close your eyes and remember this time. Then you can relax and unwind again in God's creation.

*Psalm 24:1–2*

*The earth is the Lord's and all that is in it, the world, and those who live in it; for he has founded it on the seas, and established it on the rivers.*

The pain associated with betrayal may feel like it's just too much for you to bear. Some days you may experience a true visceral reaction whenever you remember hurtful actions within your marriage. Do you feel as though you just cannot stand the pain any longer?

Then give it to God. The burden of treachery is entirely too difficult for you to carry alone, and God has very wide shoulders. God is always present and can help you in these times of trouble; He loves you and understands your pain. He knows every ugly, intimate detail.

Hurt and heartache can seem even worse when inflicted by a friend. Your marital wounds might pierce to an unbelievable degree. After all, this was the man that you loved deeply and pledged to honor before God. He fathered your children, sat in church with you and planned to retire with you to the mountains. Naturally, you are hurt beyond measure.

Treacherous actions are incredibly painful, and the consequences may have blown your safe and secure world to bits. Allow God to help you pick up the pieces and glue them back together in a fashion that only he knows about right now.

*Psalm 55:12–14*

*It is not enemies who taunt me—I could bear that;*
*it is not adversaries who deal insolently with me—*
*I could hide from them. But it is you, my equal,*
*my companion, my familiar friend, with whom*
*I kept pleasant company; we walked in*
*the house of God with the throng.*

Begin to establish a habit of praising God and praying every day. Many years ago, a pastor encouraged me to grow in my prayer time beyond simply asking God for everything that I had on my list. He urged me to make a list of praises as well as prayer requests each day. His recommendation for my prayer journal was a minimum of five written praises and five prayer concerns for each day.

My praises are sometimes very specific. For example, I have given God praise for my daughter's orchestra concert going well, an exercise class, a good grade on my son's calculus exam and a vacation that I was able to plan.

On other days, my praises might be general. This is particularly true if I'm having a rough day at work or at home. At such times my praises might be for faithful friends, parents, children, work that I enjoy, my Sunday School class and our home.

Likewise, my prayer requests are often quite detailed. For instance, I have written prayer concerns in my journal relating to comfort for a work colleague who struggles with breast cancer treatments, continued job security in the face of budget cuts, my daughter's health issues, my spiritual growth in the area of time management and my son's college choice.

At other times, my prayer concern list is very global. God is aware that I don't always feel like praying, but I try to pray anyway. Such a list might include summer plans, safety for my family, more energy, my personal health and the upcoming school year.

Praise God! And pray to God.

*Psalm 48:1*

*Great is the Lord and greatly to be
praised in the city of our God.*

You will need the advice of a competent attorney to help you navigate all the legal paths associated with separation and divorce. Try to locate an experienced attorney, because he or she will be better able to understand the many issues in your marriage. A legal separation is difficult enough, and you may not want to be your attorney's very first family law client.

It is often very difficult to even consider the mere possibility of divorce, and it might be tempting just to write an informal agreement yourself. However, you most certainly need the advice of an attorney, who will be able to guide you and offer legal counsel in areas with which you might not be familiar.

You might ask your pastor, friends, family members and work colleagues for a recommendation of an attorney. It is certainly fine to listen to any legal advice that these folks may dispense, but you need to seek legal counsel in order to be fully protected under the court system.

If money is a big obstacle, ask the attorney if you can work out a payment plan. Some lawyers will allow you to pay an equal amount each month, so that you aren't faced with a huge legal bill of thousands of dollars all at once.

Pray for help in finding an expert attorney to assist you in protecting your future.

*Proverbs 11:14*

*Where there is no guidance, a nation falls,*
*but in an abundance of counselors there is safety.*

Your experienced attorney will be able to guide you through legal separation. The actual definitions of terms and conditions vary from state to state, and a wise counselor will greatly assist you.

Do not expect to have a signed and final agreement within one week of physical separation from your husband. The entire process could take many weeks, months or even years. Be prepared to develop patience and stamina, because this ordeal may become a matter of long-term endurance. So stick with it, and do not give in just because you are tired of dealing with the convoluted and complex legal system.

You will likely meet with the attorney who will explain all the applicable laws. In essence, a contract of separation and property settlement agreement is a legal binding piece of paper dealing with a number of issues. Property settlement of your home and its contents will be addressed in this document. Dispensation of cars, jewelry, bank accounts, debts, life insurance and retirement plans are also usually considered. Physical child custody, financial child support, alimony, health insurance, college education of children, tax provisions and child visitation are a few more areas included in the agreement. And there are more!

As you can easily see, this agreement can be quite lengthy and it is vitally important to your future as well as that of any children. Give your separation contract much thought and prayer, then let God and your attorney guide you in these matters.

*Proverbs 1:5*

*Let the wise also hear and gain in learning,*
*and the discerning acquire skill.*

If you are a mother, child custody is a vital part of a separation agreement with your husband. Take this issue very, very seriously.

Pray about child custody and seek God's leading. Did your husband help with the children when he lived at home? Perhaps he was always changing diapers, leading family devotions, attending little league baseball games and cheering your daughter at her violin recitals. On the other hand, he may not have been so attentive. Has he ever physically or sexually assaulted your children? Has he avoided seeing them since the separation?

All these issues, along with the reasons for your marital separation, should be considered as child custody is awarded. Legal custody, physical custody and child support will be decided through negotiations and the separation agreement. If you retain primary physical custody of your children, then the issue of visitation by their father becomes a concern.

Keep your children's spiritual, physical, intellectual, emotional and social interests as top priorities. Try to keep anger and hurt out of the picture as much as possible, and allow your children to have as much contact as possible with their father. Paternal love and affection are very important ingredients in the recipe for healthy children, and you need to foster this affection if possible.

*1 Timothy 5:8*

*And whoever does not provide for relatives, and especially for family members, has denied the faith and is worse than an unbeliever.*

Who controls you? During your marriage, you may have been totally controlled by your husband. You may have allowed him to make almost every decision concerning finances, child rearing, working outside the home, purchase of a home, spiritual matters and family togetherness. Of course, your husband was the head of the home, and it was right for you to defer to his leading in certain situations.

Or perhaps you are still controlled by your parents; it can be incredibly difficult to break strong parental reins. They may continue to offer advice about your family and expect you to heed each word of caution that they offer. Naturally, you should honor your father and mother, but you do not have to let them control your every move.

You may even be controlled by your children, as you may cater to their every desire and are out of control as a parent. Your boss or work associates might also control you to a great degree.

What controls you? You might be consumed with the desire to "get ahead" or make more money than your friends. Or you might let a love of power at work control your every move. It is possible to let all the daily chores of home maintenance control you if you feel that it is more important to mow the yard than cuddle with your daughter in bed on a Saturday morning. Love of recreational activities, country club membership, exercise, worldly possessions and travel are other areas of your life that might control you.

As Christian women, we can surrender control of our lives to God and no one else.

*Romans 6:6*

*We know that our old self was crucified with him so that the body of sin might be destroyed, and we might no longer be enslaved to sin.*

Almost every woman who is separated or divorced has a very long worry list. Are you a worrier? Do you stew about life's problems and try to handle them yourself?

Worrying about your marriage and family does absolutely no good. There are no positive benefits to fretting. Being anxious about the present and future does not solve problems, and continued worry actually has some negative consequences. If you worry and obsess all day long about problems, you could develop high blood pressure. Also, you might see a pattern of tension headaches emerging. It is possible to begin neglecting your children due to being self-centered and focusing only on yourself.

Incessant worry is a breeding ground for Satan to gain control of your thoughts and actions. The devil wants you to think and act as though God is unable to handle problems.

Slow down and ponder how your worry affects God. Chronic worrying is an insult to God, since you are telling him by thoughts that he is unable to handle your life's concerns. Your pride may be an obstacle to giving your worries to the Lord, because you might think of yourself as a strong and self-sufficient woman. There is nothing inherently wrong with internal strength, but relying on our own strength instead of God's can be disappointing.

This verse gives us an ideal approach for dealing with worry—prayer. Instead of listing worries time and again in order to arrive at solutions for our marriage, we can pray to God and depend on him.

*Philippians 4:6*

*Do not worry about anything, but in everything by prayer and supplication with thanksgiving let your requests be made known to God.*

Reflect on the many thoughts that enter your mind each day. Are you thinking about God's joy and peace or your family? Because thoughts frequently lead to actions, try to concentrate on things that are good and true. If you are thinking of obeying the Lord, then your actions will naturally follow suit.

However, if you persist in thinking about revenge against your husband, your actions may reflect these impure thoughts. Do you constantly dwell on your marital patterns of anguish? Maybe you are reading books and magazines that are not holy or true to scriptural teaching. What do you watch on television and what movies do you go see with friends?

A friend who was separated from her husband shared that her guide to behavior was to question herself whether she could tell her mother what she was doing. If she could admit her actions to her mom, then she felt that she was in the clear. However, if she was too ashamed of her behavior to tell her own mother about it, then she needed to quit whatever she was doing at the time.

Pray to God and ask him to help rid your mind of impure thoughts and replace these with pure thinking patterns. This may take some work, because you're at a very vulnerable time of upheaval right now, but it can happen. Then your life will be richer and fuller because of having honorable thoughts.

*Philippians 4:8*

*Finally, beloved, whatever is true, whatever is honorable, whatever is just, whatever is pure, whatever is pleasing, whatever is commendable, if there is any excellence and if there is anything worthy of praise, think about these things.*

Everyone has good days and bad days. Everyone also has some euphoric days and some disastrous days. All of these experiences can be greatly exaggerated when you're in the middle of marital separation and divorce or even while contemplating separation. A bad day can very quickly become dismal simply due to current life changes. Likewise, a good day may seem quite euphoric if there is absence of conflict for a few short hours.

Try to remember that feelings of happiness, exhaustion, anger, hope, love, hate and depression are all normal during this thing called separation and divorce. Do you ever feel like you just can't take anymore? Are you ready to quit?

The ultimate power that a Christian has comes from Christ; we have no true power apart from him. Of course, Christ will not immediately deposit $2000 into your checking account to pay for a roof repair. Neither will he instantly make your child stop undesirable behaviors such as lying about school grades. Nor will the Lord undo your son's car wreck from last week. Instead, he is able to accomplish things far better.

Christ will help you to face trials, difficulties, burdens and troubles that seem humanly impossible—like divorce. Wonderful, glorious power is available from the Lord. Jesus Christ will enable you, lift you up, encourage you and keep you going when you are unable to do so under your own power. Call on Jesus. Ask and you will receive. You can survive divorce with Christ's help and strength.

*Isaiah 41:10*

*Do not fear, for I am with you, do not be afraid, for I am your God; I will strengthen you, I will help you, I will uphold you with my victorious right hand.*

Almost every marriage that ends with separation and divorce has an element of verbal abuse involved. Your husband may have verbally abused you for many years. You may have retaliated, inflicting pain as well. Harmful words cannot be retracted and usually have long-lasting effects for everyone involved.

During quiet moments, you might recall some of the cruel comments hurled during your marriage. If your separation is fresh, you probably think about the accusations frequently. This is quite normal, because you've been hurt. A Christian friend once shared some of her husband's verbal stings as she cried and said that she had no self-esteem left. Painful barbs such as, "You just can't do anything right," or "You ruined the children," left her feeling completely defeated and rejected. She wondered aloud if she had any value at all and whether any other man could ever find her attractive, since her husband had left her feeling worthless and demeaned.

Verbal abuse is incredibly traumatic for the victim, whereas the offending party may feel powerful and controlling while intentionally inflicting trauma. The effects of verbal comments linger—even if directed while under the influence of drugs or alcohol.

You don't need to tolerate verbal abuse any longer. You cannot grow as God's child if you are continually demeaned. Instead, be calm, stay rational and seek guidance.

*James 3:8*

*But no one can tame the tongue—a restless evil,*
*full of deadly poison.*

Did your husband constantly insult you when you were married? Is he still attacking you even though you are now divorced? Unfortunately, this is a rather common practice.

Recognize that you can't control another's behavior, but you certainly don't have to participate in it. Remove yourself from his presence when he comes to visit the children if past verbal patterns resume. Simply go into the kitchen and clean up the supper dishes, or go upstairs to your bedroom and take a nap. Sit in your special chair and read your Bible, since the Word of God chases Satan away. If your former husband persists in insulting you, an option might be for you to firmly insist that he pick up the children outside of your home to spend time with them.

One method used to insult a former spouse is the use of a telephone or an answering machine. Actively screen calls and quickly erase any inflammatory messages. God does not intend for you to be insulted and degraded because he wants only good for you.

Naturally, you still cringe if your former husband begins to insult you once more in an effort to justify his behavior. Comments like, "You never could cook a decent meal," or "You were the worst wife and mother in the world," are completely and totally unnecessary. Insults serve no constructive purpose at all and are meant to belittle the victim. Try to never return such words to your husband, no matter how tempting retaliation might be. You will regret those words later.

Christ can help you to turn away from insulting remarks, because he has not abandoned you. God can also help you to resist the inevitable temptation to return an insult toward your ex-husband. Remember that you have his wonderful power and peace.

*John 16:33*

*"I have said this to you, so that in me you may have peace.*
*In the world you face persecution. But take courage;*
*I have conquered the world!"*

"I'm going to take the children away from you."

"You'd better clean this house up, or you'll be sorry."

"Lose weight, or I'll leave you."

"Go back to work, or I'll walk out on you and the kids right now."

"Take me back right this minute, or I'll never give you another penny to support those children."

"Give me your paycheck, or I'll beat it out of you."

"Control those children, or you'll wish you had."

"You're going to regret going to talk to that attorney about a divorce."

"Do what I say, and do it right now."

Threats from another, whether you are married or separated or divorced, can be very frightening. You probably wonder if there is any truth to your husband's threat to remove the children from your home. Sadly, those threats may be an attempt by your husband to exert some control over you, because his life may feel out of control. Label these threats, for the most part, as idle statements about his discontent about his own life. But if you are truly concerned about any continued threats, seek your attorney's advice.

Recognize that God does not want any husband to threaten his wife or children.

*John 7:18*

*Those who speak on their own seek their own glory; but the one who seeks the glory of him who sent him is true, and there is nothing false in him.*

Does your heart simply break to see your husband acting in a threatening manner? Do you cry when you see these changes in him? His behaviors may be completely out of character for him, compared with the man you vowed before God to always love. You might feel positively certain that the man you fell in love with and married would never have behaved in this manner—even for a brief moment.

The man he has now become truly may not be the man you married many years ago. Some men do change and seek a changed life around them as well. "The aliens just kidnapped him. That must have been what happened—he's not the same man at all," a friend joked by way of explanation after her husband left their family. Another acquaintance quipped that "the planets are out of line, just totally out of line."

Your husband may be sick in sin. Spiritual sin is just as devastating—and sometimes more so—as physical illness. God can handle this sickness and he is the only one that can. He can heal us of any disease—physical, emotional, spiritual, social or psychological—if we only ask. However, each person must call on the Lord as his Healer; you cannot do this for your husband no matter how much you may still love him.

God is able.

*Matthew 4:23*

*Jesus went throughout Galilee, teaching in their synagogues and proclaiming the good news of the kingdom and curing every disease and every sickness among the people.*

It is easy to point your finger at another person's problems, while ignoring your own. Remember that each of us has fallen short of the mark of perfection. Indeed, Jesus Christ was the only perfect person to have ever walked on the earth.

Take stock of your life and ask God to reveal any area of hidden sin in your life. Some are probably readily identifiable to any woman whose marriage is in trouble—anger, worry, gossip and lack of trust in God. However, some subtle sins may be lurking that can undermine your relationship with the Lord. Are you constantly judging your former husband? Do you belittle him in front of your children? Do you have misplaced priorities? Have you lost your focus on God?

Examine your daily life and pray about these problem areas. God cares about all our concerns, both large and small. He wants us to ask for his help in eliminating our sinful thoughts and actions.

Gluttony can be a real problem for women with marital problems, and we may overeat to deal with emotional issues. Comfort eating can lead a woman to gain ten pounds. The only way that one friend began to get a handle on this sin was daily surrender to the Lord. She asked for help if she wanted to eat a large piece of chocolate cake right before bedtime. Every single time that she prayed for God to control her eating habits, he provided the strength to endure temptation. And, interestingly enough, each time that she refused to surrender food cravings to the Lord, she went on a junk food binge. Naturally, overeating just made her feel much worse in the long run.

Be careful about judging others and thinking of yourself as above reproach.

*Matthew 7:5*

*"You hypocrite, first take the log out of your own eye,
and then you will see clearly to take the speck
out of your neighbor's eye."*

Would you like to see the kingdom of God right now? Do you imagine it to be synonymous with your concept of heaven, with streets lined with gold? Do you envision his kingdom to be one of peace and love? You might like to see such a kingdom where marriages flourish and life is perfect.

Then look no further. The kingdom of God is already in your heart if you are a Christian woman who loves and obeys the Lord. Even when you're unhappy with your personal life and your marriage has ended on a sour note, you can still be a member of this glorious kingdom. However, God's kingdom is not synonymous with utopia, because he has not promised us a life free of pain and trouble.

God's kingdom is not a physical area with a fence and gate to let certain people in and keep others out. The kingdom of God is not a specific church either, no matter how large that new fellowship hall might be. Likewise, the existence of special programs in your church or community does not constitute his kingdom.

Rather, his kingdom starts when God's Spirit enters your heart as a woman who loves him. The kingdom of God is evident when you let the Holy Spirit actively work in your life. Then the fruit of the spirit will be visibly active in your life and in the relationships that you pursue.

*Luke 17:20–21*

*Once Jesus was asked by the Pharisees when the kingdom of God was coming, and he answered, "The kingdom of God is not coming with things that can be observed; nor will they say, 'Look, here it is!' or 'There it is!' For, in fact, the kingdom of God is among you."*

You can learn to be happy where you are in life and with what you have. If you are always wishing for something different or more of what you already have, you will never be truly content.

Because you are separated or divorced, you obviously did not get what you expected out of your marriage. You might be disappointed, heartbroken, angry or bitter. And all these feelings are perfectly normal, considering your current circumstances.

But it is possible for you to be content. Contentment is not truly dependent on life's external circumstances, but on your relationship with Christ. Rely on the promises of God and claim the power available to you. God can cure your discontent and help you to be fully content in him.

For example, if you're always wishing for more money, pray that God will remove this desire and teach you to be content with the resources that you have. And pray that you will learn to manage your money well. If you want your marriage to be restored, pray for God's will and trust him to handle your marital problems according to that divine will. If a larger house has always been on your wish list, you can ask God to help you to be happy that you have a house—no matter how small it might be. If you want your son to make straight A's on his report card, ask God to help you to be content with his combination A/B/C grades in this terribly stressful time of his life.

God can help you unlock the door to contentment with life.

*Philippians 4:11*

*Not that I am referring to being in need; for I have learned to be content with whatever I have.*

As marital separation continues, it becomes easy to get mired down in the daily problems that confront you. Lack of money, lack of help with the children from their father and lack of help around the house are sore spots that probably demand your constant attention. You are bombarded with life's many demands and feel overcrowded. Confusion may reign, and you probably often find yourself complaining and bemoaning the injustices of life.

However, instead of fussing and fuming, try to stay focused on the Lord. Love and revere him. Believe in him and trust in him. Honor and obey him. Worship God and God alone. Love and praise him. Keep his commandments. Let thoughts of Christ stay on your mind all the time. Be joyful in the Lord. Stay pure. Devote yourself to Christ. Grow in God's Word.

Know that God has a wonderful, fun and positive plan for your life. And if you stay on the path down which God is leading you, you will discover that marvelous blueprint. However, if you stray and let Satan lead you wrongly, it is possible that you will never discover God's supreme joy. The Lord's plan will be better than anything you had in your past life, better than your present and better than anything you can imagine for your future. Doesn't that sound wonderful? Only God knows the divine details, and he already has each bend in the road mapped out in an intricate way. Trust that he will reveal those plans to you in his good time.

Stay focused on the Lord.

*2 Corinthians 11:3*

*But I am afraid that as the serpent deceived Eve
by its cunning, your thoughts will be led astray
from a sincere and pure devotion to Christ.*

Do you have mood swings of incredible highs and incredible lows? Emotional peaks and valleys are the norm when a woman is separated or divorced, and you might feel as though you're riding on a roller coaster. One day you might be praying for your family to be reunited, and the next week you are thanking God that your husband is removed from your home.

This undulating pattern of joys and sorrows, hope and despair, could be fueled by your husband's offers of reconciliation. Predictable patterns might include declarations of changed behavior, professions of love for you and pleas to come home once he realizes that divorce is inevitable. The true test is waiting to see if your husband actually has God and family at the center of his life, and you may want to observe for a period of time in order to determine whether his words match his actions.

One friend, married for ten years, was separated due to her husband's Internet affairs. Ten months after he left their home, her husband called to admit his guilt while claiming to have just "lost his mind." He apologized and literally begged to come home in order to be a part of the family again, and she gladly consented. She was ecstatic! After a joyous reunion with the children, her husband was at home for just one week before his girlfriend called to inform him that their apartment was ready for them to move in. He quickly left his family for the second time within one hour of that particular phone call. Obviously, my friend was crushed and her emotions quickly plummeted due to extreme disappointment.

Tell God about your overwhelming emotional ups and downs during prayer time. He will help you to discern the truth as you steer through this emotionally laden time.

*Job 7:11*

*"Therefore I will not restrain my mouth; I will speak in the anguish of my spirit; I will complain in the bitterness of my soul."*

You may or may not be ready to accept the whole truth about the state of your marriage. Are you contemplating separation due to adultery? Do you have suspicions that his gambling addiction is out of control to the point of causing financial ruin and bankruptcy? Have you recently discovered that he has once again slipped back into his alcoholic drinking patterns, after having completed a treatment program? Has he relapsed and begun using street drugs again, followed by repeated domestic violence?

It is normal to proceed slowly when discovering the whole truth. You, your husband and your children may be denying the truth because it is too painful at this point in time. Just as you may not be ready to deal with the truth, your children may not be emotionally prepared to handle details of marital problems either.

Take your cues from your daughter's behavior. Tell her that you are available to talk whenever she needs to, but don't force her to hear about your marriage. It simply hurts too badly, and she may have no desire to know the complete truth about her parents. One friend informed her two adult children about every detail of their father's infidelity, and the children refused to speak to their father for an entire year. These revelations badly hurt everyone involved and served no helpful purpose at all. Remember the golden rule, and trust that your children will discover truths when they are emotionally equipped. Don't lie to your children; rather, answer questions honestly, but only inform them of what they must know at any given point in time. Reassure them of your love and God's love, and reinforce that Christ is the absolute truth.

*John 14:6*

*Jesus said to him, "I am the way, and the truth, and the life. No one comes to the Father except through me."*

You might have wondered if God has forgotten all about you in the middle of all this misery. Where is God? Has he abandoned you and left you alone?

God is right where he has always been. He is near and hoping that you will draw closer to him, even though you're in great pain. God has not deserted you and you are never alone if he is in your life. Imagine that he is standing in front of you with outstretched arms, ready to comfort and love you right now.

The Bible tells us in the book of James that we can become closer to the Almighty. Submission to God is critical, because we cannot both run from him and expect to draw near him at the same time. We want to be forgiven, and as Christian women, we want to honor God. We can confess any sin and remove this obstacle in our path toward our Heavenly Father. By resisting the devil, we will also turn toward God. If we are able to lead a pure sexual life, we will absolutely become closer to him as he shapes our lives.

Drawing closer to God and re-examining spiritual progress are positive outcomes that can be associated with separation and divorce. We cannot survive this hurt very well without the Lord having first place in our lives.

God is here.

*James 4:8*

*Draw near to God, and he will draw near to you. Cleanse your hands, you sinners, and purify your hearts, you double-minded.*

You may find yourself coveting your ex-husband's possessions. Coveting and envying his big new house, large-screen television, sports car or freedom without the responsibilities of daily child rearing can lead to unhappiness. You might resent his financial independence, since many men seem to fare better monetarily than women after separation. He might seem to be living the lucky life of a single man and loving every minute of it. Give yourself a minute or two to admit this envy, and recognize it for what it truly is. Then ask God to help you control it.

Remember that possessions and freedom from family obligations are not the keys to happiness, because true happiness is in the Lord. One woman became envious of her husband's country club membership after he left their family and she found herself coveting his luxurious lifestyle. He appeared to be happy-go-lucky and thrilled to be relieved of his wife. But she searched her heart and asked God to help her realize that true contentment was to be found in God, children, extended family and church family. She concluded that a country club life would bring her only temporary happiness, as contrasted with a deep inner peace she found while dwelling on Jesus Christ.

God can help you discover the underlying cause of envy and he can erase extreme resentment. Your Father in heaven will provide for your basic needs on a daily basis and show you what is truly important as you walk with him.

*Exodus 20:17*

*You shall not covet your neighbor's house; you shall not covet your neighbor's wife, or male or female slave, or ox, or donkey, or anything that belongs to your neighbor.*

Make a list of every material thing that you truly need—food, shelter, clothing, money for essentials such as the house payment and a dependable car to drive to work.

Now make a list of material things that you merely want—a larger house, a newer car, nicer clothes, an occasional night out at a great restaurant, a Caribbean cruise, a vacation to the beach and some mad money to spend just as you wish!

Next, make a list of intangibles that you actually need at this point in your life—God's love, the presence of your children, love from your family, endurance, courage, strength and joy.

What intangibles do you want? Do they include comfort, freedom from pain, hope, fun, greater relaxation and peace?

There is sometimes a vast difference between what you truly need and what you only want. God is aware of everything that you need in your life, both on a material and intangible level. And he will provide what you need. For example, his strength will be available to you during a particularly difficult moment of divorce. He and he alone can give you the courage to tolerate the penetrating hurt that accompanies separation and divorce.

Trusting in the Lord will give you discernment between your needs and your wants. God can slowly change your attitude from one of constantly wanting more and more to one of truly desiring him. As your shepherd, God is able to guide, provide and protect.

*Psalm 23:1*

*The Lord is my shepherd, I shall not want.*

You are probably fatigued from months or years of physical, mental and emotional challenges. It is important to recognize your fatigue level before you literally collapse due to sheer exhaustion.

Admit your weariness and give in to it. Allow yourself to take a 20 minute power nap the minute you come home from work. Just plop down on your sofa and listen to some soft Christian music as you close your eyes. Prayer works wonders when you're very, very tired. Give all of your mental and emotional trials to the Lord, because he is already at work on these problem areas before you even ask for help. Ask your children to help with household tasks and cook really simple meals.

You may have noticed that fatigue comes in waves. You might have the energy to cook a great dinner, dust the furniture and sweep the kitchen floor one day and then on the next morning you may not be able to drag yourself out of the bed, much less muster enough fortitude to read your daughter a story or wash the car.

Therefore, be aware of what your body is telling you. Rest when possible, take a multivitamin, pray and eat as well as you possibly can.

Recognize that surviving separation and divorce is a monumental task, and it sometimes takes immense amounts of physical and mental energy. Remember that God has a purpose for your life, and he is working in your behalf right now even as you are reading this page.

*Nehemiah 4:10*

*But Judah said, "The strength of the
burden bearers is failing."*

Father's Day might be difficult for you during separation or if you are recently divorced. If your husband has primary custody of the children, then you may feel alone and isolated as they spend this day together. Make plans to have lunch with a friend after worship service and Sunday School. Call your own father and remember him in a special way—you could even cook lunch for him if that is possible.

If you have primary custody of your children, pray that God will grant you the grace to arrange for your son to spend a good portion of the day with his father. Yes, it may be very difficult because your marital wounds are still fresh. But, in the long run, you are doing the best thing for your children if they are able to have a relationship with their father. Hold your head high and ask God for direction.

Perhaps you are in a situation in which your children's father is not stable enough to visit with them on Father's Day. In that case, pull the family picture album off the shelf and try to recall some better times. You could relate a particularly happy time of their childhood to them. Children of all ages, even in high school, enjoy hearing tales of their younger years. Just remember that some of those stories are best told only in your home, because they might be quite embarrassing to a teenager!

Make every attempt to have your children with their dad on this special day. You'll be glad, as you look back at some point in the future, that your actions matched your beliefs.

*Deuteronomy 5:16*

*Honor your father and your mother, as the Lord commanded you, so that your days may be long and that it may go well with you in the land that the Lord your God is giving you.*

It will take a tremendous amount of courage for you to stand up to sin and ask for marital separation. Sometimes you must adopt a stance of "tough love." Of course, it will be hard—phenomenally hard—to ask your husband to leave your home, but you may have no other choice. You simply cannot live with certain existing conditions, such as continuous physical abuse or adultery, in your marriage.

It also takes courage for you to simply survive separation and divorce. It hurts in every way, and it is very difficult! You will probably cry yourself to sleep many nights as you lie in your bed alone, while your husband might be with someone else. But take courage, because you can make it with God's help. Indeed, divine intervention is the only successful way to get through this time.

It will take additional courage for you to be willing to risk single parenthood. What an awesome, daunting responsibility this can be! This is a huge step that will test you to your very limits. But you can be a great mother, even if you have no choice but to raise your daughter alone. Often times, it just seems that the easiest road might be to simply beg your husband to return home. At the very least, you would have some help with the children and household chores again. But this may not be in your best interest or that of your children in the long run. God will show you what he expects of you.

The ultimate source of courage that you will need to endure the process of separation and divorce is God himself. He can give you courage that can renew and refresh—the courage to help you take each step on the journey down the path he is leading you.

*Psalm 27:14*

*Wait for the Lord; be strong, and let your
heart take courage; wait for the Lord!*

Remember that separation or divorce is a series of baby steps. So take a deep breath, proceed with caution and go slowly. Honestly, you cannot accomplish every task in one month or even one year.

It is impossible to completely heal your broken heart, adequately explain her father's absence to your teenage daughter, mend your son's shattered image of marriage and deal with child custody issues every day. Neither can you cope with your fluctuating emotions, grapple with dwindling financial resources, maintain your home and perform splendidly at work all at the same time. It's entirely too much to expect of yourself!

Therefore, attack one problem at a time. Then analyze your task at hand, whatever it might be, and ask God to assist you in taking a baby step toward your goal. For example, if you have decided to get your finances in order, you must begin with a careful assessment of your entire situation. What is your salary per month and how much alimony or child support money do you receive? Are there other sources of income? Next, make a complete list of monthly expenditures, such as your house or rent payment, utilities and church tithe. Remember to include saving some money for emergencies like car repairs for your teenager or yourself. Total your income and your expenses and pat yourself on the back if these two monetary figures are close in dollar amounts. If they are very far apart, seek some financial assistance from an expert who can help you manage with your new financial picture. Honestly face the facts and don't lie to yourself.

Approach each day and each challenge with small steps, and life won't seem so terribly overwhelming.

*Psalm 26:12*

*My foot stands on level ground; in the great congregation I will bless the Lord.*

Do you find yourself instinctively favoring one of your children over the other? Perhaps your older child is quiet, much more subdued and constantly doing things to make your life easier in this crazy thing called marital separation. Is her homework always completed on time and is she constantly volunteering for household chores?

On the other hand, your younger child might present a behavioral challenge on a daily basis. Maybe you've always disagreed and argued more with this child; indeed, he may pose a constant challenge during separation. Your son might try your patience every single night as he refuses to walk the dog and forgets to load his dishes in the dishwasher.

Make every possible effort to avoid showing favoritism between your children, even if you want to praise a particular child every minute for making your life simpler. Showing more love to one child over another can cause many hard feelings for years to come. Overt partiality from a parent to a child can carry over into the neglected child's adult years, as he or she struggles with feelings of inadequacy. Your child might continue to strive for approval even after becoming a parent. Even the favored child can develop emotional problems as a result of parental partiality. If your son knows that he is favored over her sister, it is possible that he will become a childhood brat and then go on to spend his entire life always trying to win others' approval.

Sometimes a mother will have a favorite child in her heart and maybe you have always been particularly close to one child. Such feelings may be natural to a small degree, and you cannot always control a thought entering your mind. But you can control your actions with God's help.

*Genesis 37:3*

*Now Israel loved Joseph more than any other of his children, because he was the son of his old age; and he made him a long robe with sleeves.*

Sometimes the smallest of things will start an avalanche of tears, unleash a new wave of anger toward your husband or cause you to spew coarse language from your mouth.

During the time of separation for one woman, both of her children went to summer camp. And once she began to fill out all the forms associated with her children spending a week away from home, the reality of separation began to set in one more time. She was hit squarely in the face with the fact that her husband was living in another town when she had to list his address on paper for the very first time. Then she had to list his phone number as being different from hers. Seeing that reality in black and white was startling, sobering and maddening.

The simple act of filling out forms for camp made her sad once again that her marriage had dissolved. She cried buckets of tears for the hundredth time and then became enraged. She stood in her kitchen, let out some blood-curdling screams before temporarily regaining some semblance of sanity and then proceeded to complete each required line for the camp forms.

You cannot avoid simple reminders that you are separated or divorced—such as those prompted by completion of forms. But be glad as a Christian woman that God is with you as you struggle.

You are not alone and he wants to help you, even as you tackle those applications.

*Philippians 2:13*

*For it is God who is at work in you, enabling you both to will and to work for his good pleasure.*

Reminders of the grim facts of your marital situation may confront you daily:

Completing a "next of kin" form when you have a mammogram.

Shopping for groceries and deciding whether to buy one pound of ground turkey for your previous family of four, or reducing the amount for a new family size.

Calling for a pizza delivery, and making a decision about whether to order a large or extra-large pepperoni pizza to feed your now-smaller family.

Changing the beneficiaries on your life insurance policy.

Taking up less room on your traditional family church pew.

Taking a family vacation to your usual beach location despite limited finances.

Running into an old high school classmate while shopping at the mall, who asks how your husband is doing.

Attending a PTA meeting at school alone.

Completing employment forms and checking a box for "separated" instead of "married."

Altering your will.

Filing a tax return as a single person.

Being alone at the end of the day.

Losing your prayer partner.

Remember that you always have a true partner in the Lord, as you offer prayers at all times for each situation that you encounter throughout your day.

*Ephesians 6:18*

*Pray in the Spirit at all times in every prayer and supplication. To that end keep alert and always persevere in supplication for all the saints.*

It may not seem fair that your husband appears to be thriving, while you struggle daily. You may feel deprived, while remembering a former financially-secure life as a married couple. It might look as though your husband is being rewarded and you may feel as though you're being punished. In fact you might feel socially, financially and physically challenged.

Are you struggling in your faith today? Maybe yesterday was emotionally stable, but the morning began poorly and the day has just gone downhill from there.

Commit your heart and life to God daily. Let the Lord rule your life through your loving commitment to him, despite the turmoil in life. Believe in God's promises and his divine provisions. It is often incredibly difficult to look down the road to the future when the present appears momentarily bleak. But believe that your future is in God's hands and that he is in total and complete control, as you remember that God loves you.

Believe in God's Word and his comforting assurances that a day will come when everyone will yield to him.

*Philippians 2:9–11*

*Therefore God also highly exalted him and gave him the name that is above every name, so that at the name of Jesus every knee should bend, in heaven and on earth and under the earth, and every tongue should confess that Jesus Christ is Lord, to the glory of God the Father.*

It is normal and expected that sadness will continue for many months—or even years—after separation. Separation is not a magic cure-all for the many problems that you have experienced on an every day basis. Instead, it may be just the beginning of a long healing process.

Admit your sadness and don't try to hide it. Allow yourself to sit and think, reflecting back to both better and worse times in marriage. You may not understand many of the behaviors that occurred in your marriage, and often they truly cannot be understood. Be still and let yourself think, because if you try to cover your sadness with constant activity, you will not properly heal. It is okay to cry, even a long time after divorce.

One woman had been divorced for four years, and her ex-husband had moved to another state. This woman is currently happily engaged to a Christian man who loves the Lord, while fiercely loving and protecting her. And even though she has been divorced for a while and is supremely content in her new relationship, she still becomes very distant and pensive in her sadness each time someone questions the circumstances of her divorce.

Sometimes you may feel that you can't be comforted at all. There will be days when even that dependable chocolate candy bar can't seem to lift your mood! All of this is normal.

Pray to God during these times. Just talk to him in a conversational manner. Tell your Heavenly Father of your heavy heart and pour out all your hurt to him. Trust that you will eventually be comforted in his way and in his time.

*Psalm 77:2*

*In the day of my trouble I seek the Lord; in the night my hand is stretched out without wearying; my soul refuses to be comforted.*

Do you feel as though you never have enough time? Is your to-do list growing in length instead of shrinking? Time is such a wonderful resource that we have at our disposal. We often wish that we had more. We have to make choices and you have important choices in how to spend your hours and occupy your days.

God will hold each of us accountable for how we spend our time, and we are responsible for using our days either for his glory or for wasting our time. Immediately after separation, it is normal for you to spend your hours crying and being consumed with thoughts of your marriage. You won't get very much accomplished. You just might be thrilled to simply exist from one day to the next.

However, God will eventually prompt you to get going with life once again. Spend time every day with God and that time will be multiplied elsewhere in your life. Children are wonderful reasons to continue with your daily routines. Make a conscious decision to stop neglecting precious moments. Love your son, laugh with your daughter and play with both of them.

One distant day you will even be able to focus on someone other than your own family. God will show you opportunities of service to him. An avenue may even present itself that allows you to witness to another separated or divorced woman who is in great pain. You could even share God's love as you work alongside her in the office.

Pray about the use of your time. Be purposeful in your management of your minutes and hours, and be wise with the time that God has given you.

*Ephesians 5:15–16*

*Be careful then how you live, not as unwise people but as wise, making the most of the time, because the days are evil.*

You may have been completely dependent on your former husband to meet your basic emotional needs. Did you depend on him for your sense of self-worth? Was there any balance in your relationship? Was your husband dependent on you to make him feel satisfied with life? In retrospect, you might be able to see that you were truly co-dependent.

You will be tempted, during contact with your husband, to slip into those old familiar behavior patterns. Marital recovery may include actually beginning to feel emotions and admitting past cycles of dependency. Only then you can start to grow and feel renewed as an individual and a child of God.

In the future, you can look forward to healthy and positive relationships with other people. Actually, you should seek growing relationships with others who are dependent primarily on the Lord. You can achieve balance in a romantic relationship that may blossom into marriage, if the Lord leads you in that direction.

Depending on God is not a sign of weakness, but it allows God's strength to show through you. God is the ultimate source of power and you can lean on him daily as you seek a new and different life without your husband constantly by your side. Rely on God's goodness as you move through separation and divorce.

*2 Corinthians 1:9*

*Indeed, we felt that we had received the sentence of death so that we would rely not on ourselves but on God who raises the dead.*

We all seek affirmation and want to feel worthy of being loved by others. God loves you and values you. He wants you to have a positive self-image.

During your marriage, you might have felt worthless due to comments from your husband about appearance, work habits, housekeeping, child rearing, sexual abilities or financial management. Such feelings have a way of permeating your entire being and leaving you feeling lifeless. And unfortunately, once you began to see yourself as inadequate, you may have begun to perpetuate this cycle with negative behaviors.

But you can be assured that God cares for you no matter what you look like, how much money you make, whether your house is clean or if you are a poor money manager. You can change your appearance in order to feel better about yourself and there is nothing wrong with that. You can also make more money and clean your house. But remember that faith in God and belief in his Son are critical steps toward feeling affirmed in life as a Christian.

Remember that you can also affirm your children with words and actions. You can let them know that they are loved by you, their extended family and their church family. You have amazing power to confirm their worth in life—through their faith in the Lord and through their love for family.

Affirm others, just as Christ affirms your worth.

*2 Thessalonians 1:3*

*We must always give thanks to God for you, brothers and sisters, as is right, because your faith is growing abundantly, and the love of everyone of you for one another is increasing.*

A very common explanation given by a man as a reason for change is that of a midlife crisis. It is indeed true that men do change at midlife! Exactly when the particular midpoint of life occurs will vary from man to man. One man may feel an intense urge to re-examine his life at the age of 40, whereas another may not experience any of these feelings until he hits 55 years of age.

Men's hormones, relationship to children, relationship to God, work environment and body all change at some point in midlife. Of course, these things all change for a woman as well and we call it menopause! Midlife—male menopause—is a critical time for a man to choose a path that may well determine the remainder of his days on earth.

A man may cope with a midlife crisis by experiencing a true clinical depression or he might buy a red convertible sports car. Another man will join a gym and work out six or seven days a week in hopes of looking 15 years younger. One man will change jobs, another might experiment with street drugs or alcohol and yet another will have an extramarital affair in order to seek a thrill. A man could also seek a closer relationship with his family and his Lord in order to make sense of midlife. One man actually moved to the desert to meditate for ten months when he hit his 50th birthday.

A man's response to midlife will depend on many factors such as his relationship with his own parents, marital happiness, his relationship with Christ and financial status. One man in my church got so exasperated with adulterous relationships being laughed off as a midlife crisis that he commented, "That is just their excuse to sin—a really poor one!"

God wants Christian men—and women—to respond to midlife with Christian actions.

*Leviticus 26:18*

*And if in spite of this you will not obey me, I will continue to punish you sevenfold for your sins.*

God calls us to be holy. Holy— not perfect.

God desires that we live according to his moral standards. As a Christian, you are set apart. All of your friends may be going to a bar where male strippers are present. You may be in a crowd that is going out to see a movie on Friday night and be surprised to find that it is X-rated. A separated acquaintance is dating other men, even though she is still legally married to her husband. You might even have a friend who is dating a married man. What will you do?

God might be leading you to avoid the bar, skip the illicit movie and postpone dating other men until you are legally divorced. Pray that the Lord will give you the power to avoid certain situations so that you can grow as a Christian and set a godly example to your children.

A friend's high-school-age daughter was going to the beach for a weekend with her boyfriend's family. My friend had discussed the entire weekend with the boyfriend's mom, and had been reassured that the sleeping arrangements were separate and that chaperones would be around the beach house on a continuous basis. Just as they were preparing to pull the loaded car out of the driveway, my friend discovered that the boyfriend's mother had a boyfriend herself who was going along. The mother openly shared that she was planning to sleep in the same bedroom with her boyfriend. My friend knew full well that this woman was not yet divorced from her husband, and she kindly voiced her disapproval and concern to her daughter. The other woman was genuinely shocked that anyone would object.

God wants you to be holy, and different, as his witness.

*1 Peter 1:16*

*For it is written, "You shall be holy, for I am holy."*

Are you too proud to admit that you have any faults? Perhaps you've made mistakes in marriage and mistakes in parenting. Pride can impede all relationships—with your husband, children, parents, friends and even the Lord. You may be blind to your own faults, while clearly seeing those of others.

Ask a trusted friend to honestly point out your areas of pride that you cannot see. What areas of your life need an assessment by someone on the outside of your situation? It may be that admission of your role in a problem area in marriage is standing in the way of reconciliation with your husband. If this is the case, ask God to help you in this area of pride as you attempt to repair your marriage.

Maybe your relationship with your daughter is severely damaged because of an error on your part, but pride is preventing you from admitting this to her. With the Lord's prodding, you will be able to humble yourself and have a heart-to-heart discussion with your child and clear the air.

Your former husband may also be puffed up with pride. Maybe he continues in behaviors because he is too proud to admit that he has been wrong. Remember that you can't force him to let down that prideful guard. Only God is in control of that.

As the Bible warns, pride is able to cause destruction both to oneself and others. Examine your life and ask God for assistance.

*Proverbs 16:18*

*Pride goes before destruction, and a
haughty spirit before a fall.*

Do you consider yourself to be a stubborn woman? You might be persisting time after time in trying to make your marriage work. If you have tried to reconcile and failed miserably, you might need to try something different. A new tactic or strategy might be in order. Quit doing the same old things over and over again, because stubbornness is not necessarily a desirable trait!

God has a better plan, so ask for his guidance. His plan may be for you to try a tough love approach and evaluate your marriage during a trial separation from your husband. Or he may show you a different loving angle from which to approach your husband.

Even though you may not believe in divorce and disposable relationships, God may show you that you just cannot control all situations. You expose yourself to spiritual, emotional and physical deterioration if you live under certain conditions. And in such unique circumstances, Christ pointed the way to divorce in the New Testament. Read the verses found in Matthew 19:1–12 and let God and God alone, fight this battle and point you away from your stubbornness.

The Lord's way is better than your way, so make the decision to yield to him. Submission to the Almighty can bring such incredible relief if you have been stubbornly trying to control a situation under your own power. God can use these experiences that you are undergoing now to teach lessons about submission, joy and future hope.

*Psalm 81:11–12*

*"But my people did not listen to my voice; Israel would not submit to me. So I gave them over to their stubborn hearts, to follow their own counsels."*

You will have ample opportunity to grow in your Christian faith during separation and divorce. You can learn to rely more on God and less on yourself and others. Acknowledge to your Father that you are aware that he will care for you and give you peace, no matter what your circumstances might be. Continue to talk with God and commit each day to him early in the morning. He can be your very best friend and also give you ultimate true comfort in the loneliness of divorce. He will supply your needs and some of your wants. Indeed, you will see daily miracles due to his power if you open your eyes.

There might be more time available to spend with God, because you don't have hours taken up each day with your husband's needs. You may not have been previously aware of your husband's demands on your life and time. Use any newly discovered moments wisely and give them to God. Establish a daily quiet time habit that can stay with you for the remainder of your life. You can take advantage of the time of separation to get to know Christ as your intimate Savior and Lord. Worship, trust, honor and obey him as you continue to grow.

It is possible to use problems and discouragement as opportunities for spiritual growth, because God loves you and is not going to give up on you. He urges and guides you every day—both in small and large decisions. Christ prompts you daily to grow more into his likeness in thought and action.

*Philippians 1:6*

*I am confident of this, that the one who began a good work among you will bring it to completion by the day of Jesus Christ.*

Be still and listen to God's voice. God can teach, comfort, guide and give direction with his words. He will give you a sense of peace and calm if you listen to his directives for your life as a woman in separation or divorce. You can also be assured that he will lead you confidently into the future, one that is full of joy and hope if you abide in his will.

However, if you're intentionally breaking one of God's laws and have veered off the desired path for your life, your Father will convey to you that he desires a change of behavior. If he corrects you, consider changing your actions or thoughts. But if you persist, keep praying, because God still loves you. He wants you to change for the better and not continuously yield to temptation, because he desires only your best.

One woman admitted her shame at being a separated Christian woman, even though she had no option because her husband was living with another woman. Still, she persisted in the shame and yearned for reconciliation. Wonderfully, she became aware that separation and divorce were absolutely not the worst things that could happen to her. Instead, she felt God reassuring her that an even-worse disaster would have been loss of faith in the Lord as a result of separation. That reassurance gave her wonderful peace and joy and enabled her to continue her future life with godly confidence.

Slow down and make a conscious decision today to listen to God's voice.

*Isaiah 30:21*

*And when you turn to the right or when you turn to the
left, your ears shall hear a word behind you,
saying, "This is the way; walk in it."*

You *can* endure the trials of separation and divorce with God's help!

It is normal to often feel frustrated and overwhelmed with all the daily challenges that confront you during this difficult time. But don't give up, because you have phenomenal power available to you. God can help you to keep going when you are weak—so weak that you are convinced that you cannot continue under your own strength.

One woman, very recently separated from her alcoholic husband who had physically abused her, began to fear for her safety once again when he began to stalk her outside her place of employment. He would sit in his car and wait for her to come out the front door after work. Then he would verbally threaten her and demand money to buy alcohol. She became panicky and worried that she would have to take him back into her home to prevent the loss of her job. Instead, she prayed and asked God for help to get through her trying ordeal. God supplied her with the necessary emotional strength to obtain a legal restraining order against her husband. Then a man from her church offered to change her door locks at her house free of charge so that she would feel safer. God most certainly gave her the resources to endure.

God has awesome power which he is willing to give you. He wants you to endure because he loves you. Your victory will honor the Lord and you can give him all the glory while continuing to endure one day at a time.

*Colossians 1:11*

*May you be made strong with all the strength that comes from his glorious power, and may you be prepared to endure everything with patience, while joyfully giving thanks to the Father, who has enabled you to share in the inheritance of the saints in the light.*

It is tempting during marital separation to simply replace your husband with a new man in your life. This solution might seem like it would solve some short-term problems and it certainly looks easy. A replacement male partner would definitely take away your loneliness.

Ask God to help you to resist this temptation. You need time to heal, detach, let go, pray, love your children, think and develop a stronger relationship with Christ. It may not be possible to accomplish these tasks of separation while focusing on a brand-new relationship with another man. You also cannot begin to analyze your portion of any marital problems by refusing to examine them or running away from them.

Instead, pray and ask God to replace your thoughts of your husband with thoughts of Him. No, it isn't easy. But it's certainly preferable to engaging in another romantic liaison at such a vulnerable and critical time in life. Plus, a new romance makes reconciliation with your husband almost impossible—and reuniting may be in God's will. How will you know this if you simply replace him with another man?

It is also very important to consider a biblical and moral example to your children. If you are still legally married to your husband, even though separated by distance or a piece of paper, you still have a binding commitment that you made both to him and God.

So think about God. His love, grace and mercy are sufficient to replace a relationship with your husband and to carry you through the darkest and loneliest days.

*Psalm 62:6*

*He alone is my rock and my salvation,*
*my fortress; I shall not be shaken.*

God is watching over you—even in the midst of stress, anguish, fear, anger and a broken heart. God loves you even more than your mother and father. That's amazing!

In fact, he has sent guardian angels to watch over you and other believers. There are many examples of guardian angels in the Bible and they are still present today. Angels will befriend you and protect both you and your children; they can be your personal bodyguards.

One friend reflected back to the particularly dark and hideous day when her husband left home after many years of marriage. She felt as if her head was disconnected from her body and that she was functioning in an auto-pilot mode. To this day, she still doesn't know how she made it home from the office while driving a car, as she has absolutely no recollection of operating that vehicle. However, God knew of her intense pain and pierced heart. He sent a neighbor to her house that afternoon to borrow an egg and that wonderful woman held my friend's hand and simply hugged her as she cried. The neighbor neglected her baking while she spent an hour comforting and helping my friend to stay rational in thought. The neighbor was God's angel on that day, and she has continued to operate in that capacity ever since.

Take a minute and ponder what angels God has sent to care for you during separation and divorce. Then thank God profusely for these people that he has placed in your life in such a divine fashion.

*Psalm 91:11*

*For he will command his angels concerning you to guard you in all your ways.*

Is jealousy ruining your life? You may be jealous of many things or people.

If your former husband is an alcoholic, you might be jealous of the attention and devotion he gives to his liquor bottle.

If street drugs are a problem for him, you probably are jealous of the power that they hold over the man you married.

If your husband has a girlfriend, you may be jealous of the money and time he gives her.

If he is a gambler, you are more than likely quite jealous of the time that he spends at the race track placing bets while ignoring your family.

If your husband is a workaholic, you might be jealous of the time that he spends at the office while forgetting your wedding anniversary.

If your husband is a free spirit who refuses to work and support his family, you may envy his low blood pressure and seemingly low stress level while you are spinning circles trying to monetarily support your family.

If your husband is thriving without you, you might be jealous of his material possessions and full bank account.

Jealousy can have terrible consequences. It can lead to fighting, gossip, hatred, violence or stealing. It can cause you to become hardened and bitter, instead of the woman that God desires you to be. Pray—and pray continually. Ask God to clean jealousy from your life and he will.

*Romans 13:13*

*Let us live honorably as in the day, not in reveling and drunkenness, not in debauchery and licentiousness, not in quarreling and jealousy.*

Is darkness closing in as you struggle in this awful thing called separation from your husband—the man you considered to be the absolute love of your life?

You will have dark hours, days and weeks. In fact, some darkness of mood is normal and expected. Face it—you feel wounded, bewildered and perplexed. Each Christian woman will approach her darkness in a different way.

One woman who was separated from her husband allowed herself to experience one hour of darkness every day. She specifically chose an hour at 9:00 p.m. after her young children were in the bed. Then she rocked in her special chair, thought, talked aloud, cried and let her anger out. She said that this daily dose of darkness at a specified time, for a specified duration, kept her from falling into an even darker hole. In order to put a more positive end to her day, she always closed her "dark hour" with praises to God and prayer.

Remember that God gave the Holy Spirit to us to help dispel darkness and gloom. We always have hope in the Lord, and he is our light. Pray passionately that Christ will enter your dark times and that they will be fewer as time marches on. If you find that your dark times are increasing and lengthening, consult both Christ and your medical doctor. Clinical depression can potentially overcome a separated woman who is struggling mightily with daily life.

You can have confidence in the Lord when attacked by the darkness of life.

*Psalm 43:3–4*

*O send out your light and your truth; let them lead me; let them bring me to your holy hill and to your dwelling. Then I will go to the altar of God, to God my exceeding joy; and I will praise you with the harp, O God, my God.*

In one sense, you are a different person now that you are separated or divorced. You're no longer one-half of a married couple and that may feel very strange to you. Just what is going on? Do you feel married, single, separated or divorced? You might be unsure of exactly who you are and that's okay.

Some things have not changed, and you can take comfort in those old familiar relationships. You're still a Christian, woman, mother, grandmother, daughter, friend, neighbor, cousin, aunt and niece. You also continue to be a teacher, cashier, accountant, doctor, nurse, secretary, lawyer, research scientist, homemaker or banker.

You may be more certain of those identities related to family and work, but your personal identity is probably in question just now. As a Christian woman, you became a new creation when the Holy Spirit transformed your heart. You were not the same person after deciding to live with Christ. Indeed, you began an entirely new life with the Lord as you discarded your old self.

You are now assuming a sort of new identity with your changed marital status. God will guide you, and you will be able to glorify him as you look around new corners at the appropriate time. Let Christ guide every area of your life. See what emerges.

*2 Corinthians 5:17*

*So if anyone is in Christ, there is a new creation: everything old has passed away; see, everything has become new!*

You might have a badly broken heart—one that is damaged, torn and shredded by hurtful actions. Is your pain indescribable? Maybe you are still crying yourself to sleep every night, or you may still replay in your mind the day of separation as you remember each sordid detail. You might even have imaginary conversations with your husband each morning while rolling out of bed alone—silent or mumbled conversations in which you "get even" with him. Are you still angry months after separation or years after divorce?

All of these emotions could be normal for a woman who tried for months or years to hold her marriage together. You, as a Christian woman, are aware that God does not smile on divorce, but you are also acutely aware that you cannot change another's behaviors. You are going through normal grief reactions, so allow yourself time to hurt and experience this pain.

One woman, who had given her husband a second chance after two extramarital affairs that were eight years apart, reported that her heart was "pierced." She said that she felt like someone had physically put a dagger into her chest and ripped the life out of her. She was hurting and was experiencing extreme anguish over her family's breakup.

Remember that you can still glorify God even with a broken heart. Hold your faith near to your heart, be a witness for Christ and let him shine through. The Lord can help you and other women with pierced hearts.

*Philippians 1:12–13*

*I want you to know, beloved, that what has happened to me has actually helped to spread the gospel, so that it has become known throughout the whole imperial guard and to everyone else that my imprisonment is for Christ.*

Some women who are separated from their husbands find great comfort in divorce recovery groups. If you think that this might help you to adjust to life without your husband, locate a group in your town and plan to attend the next meeting. You could even ask a friend to go with you so that you might feel more comfortable.

One woman attended a divorce support group and said that she found a new best friend who would let her call and cry at any hour of the day or night. She was thrilled that she wouldn't have to spend her Friday nights alone anymore, and she was happy to have a movie companion. She said that the group was especially helpful for her, because she had no children and felt all alone in the world. A supper club eventually emerged from her group, and the members began to eat monthly potluck dinners at each other's homes. It is sometimes comforting to know that you are not alone in your life situation.

Another friend, separated for two years, actually found her next husband at a support group meeting. Her future husband had simply come along for moral support for one of his separated male friends, who was quite intimidated at the prospect of attending a divorce support group meeting alone but was seeking some direction.

You might even be able to encourage someone else at a group meeting, if you are at such a point in your own recovery. Pray and seek God's leading about attending such a group.

However, be sure that any support group that you attend is Christian in nature. You may not benefit from a support meeting that has purely secular goals in mind; it is best to glorify God in all your actions.

*Galatians 6:2*

*Bear one another's burdens, and in*
*this way you will fulfill the law of Christ.*

Are you experiencing phantom pain?

Sometimes a patient in a hospital who has had a leg amputated reports that the pain still persists, even though the injured limb has been cut away. He is experiencing true discomfort—a phantom sort of pain.

That same phenomenon applies for a woman who is divorced from her husband. He has been legally cut out of her life, but the pain lingers. You may have these feelings—declaring that your pain is real and not imagined—similar to the amputee.

What are your options? What can you do to help yourself feel better and help the pain become less intense? Be faithful to God. Demonstrate your faith by continuing to read your Bible, praying and acting as a Christian mother. Attempt to keep gossip about your marriage to a minimum and focus on God. When you focus on your former husband and your pain, you take your eyes off God. And when you take your eyes off God, you will most certainly stumble.

You can also lessen your hurt by maintaining your relationships with family members and old friends. Reach out to other women who are separated or divorced, and you will make some new friends. After all, you have a lot in common. You will surely have an eternal reward, and your earthly tribulation will one day be over.

In the meantime, you can live joyously and victoriously through Christ. He can lessen your phantom pain now and remove much of it through the passage of time. Choose Christ's path for a life that is full of his promises.

*Revelation 7:17*

*"For the Lamb at the center of the throne will be their shepherd, and he will guide them to springs of the water of life, and God will wipe away every tear from their eyes."*

You feel betrayed by your husband. And now, unfortunately, you may find yourself also being betrayed by your friends.

Your friends may feel caught between you and your former husband. Some of your "couple" friends will more than likely come to the side of your husband, and some will gravitate to your side. This type of division commonly happens when a married couple divorces.

Try to cultivate your old friendships as much as possible, and verbally communicate your appreciation to friends who keep in touch with you. Old friends can be such a comfort when you sometimes feel as though you're the last person alive on the planet! They can offer a shoulder to cry on, pray with you, sit with you in church, dispense advice and even feed you supper.

However, there are some previous friendships that you will need to relinquish. You might find that some of your old friends support your husband's habits, and you may not be happy about these liaisons. You feel betrayed. In such situations, it might be best if you gently extricate yourself from regular contact with these folks. Ask God for guidance, and don't allow yourself to get mired down in an awkward controversy. It may be difficult to walk away from some old friends, but it may be necessary. Perhaps their current behaviors are causing you extreme pain, and you certainly don't need any additional pain added to your already heavy load.

Therefore, brace yourself for losing some old friends, but look forward to developing some fulfilling relationships with new friends that God has in mind for you.

*John 18:4–5*

*Then Jesus, knowing all that was to happen to him, came forward and asked them, "Whom are you looking for?" They answered, "Jesus of Nazareth." Jesus replied, "I am he." Judas, who betrayed him, was standing with them.*

Your role, as a Christian woman, does not have to be one of busyness for the Lord or for your church. You don't have to serve on six committees during the church year, teach a children's Sunday School class or hold the office of president in your own adult class. Neither are you required to volunteer for service on a couple of advisory boards in your community for social agencies whose aims are service to those in need.

Instead, your ultimate goal should be to know Christ.

Know him by communing through prayer, reading God's Word and listening to him. Other avenues include fellowshipping with Christ through worship, singing, searching his will for your life, attending church and listening to Christian music. Simply know Christ. He wants to be your intimate friend and constant companion.

Knowing Christ may mean that you have to sacrifice some things. You might need to omit an occasional recreational activity in order to have time each day to study the Bible or carve out moments for prayer. Any sacrifice is small, when you compare it to the sacrifice that Christ made for your salvation.

After you take time and begin to know Christ and pray for God's will in your life, he will guide you to service opportunities that fit you and his kingdom best. Remember to first ask for his guidance, and then follow the Spirit's urging.

Take a few minutes right now and begin to know your Savior on a personal level.

*Philippians 3:10*

*I want to know Christ and the power of his resurrection and the sharing of his sufferings by becoming like him in his death.*

Discipline yourself.

Self-discipline is hard work, but it can lead to greater joy. You probably have many areas of your life that need increased discipline, if you are like most women. Maybe you want to improve your habits of daily Bible study, exercise, correct eating, sexual self-control, taming your tongue, prayer, housecleaning or discretion.

Ask God which area of your life you should seek to discipline first. It is overwhelming to try to attempt to control all areas of weakness at one time! So be gentle with yourself, and be realistic in terms of what you are able to accomplish both as short-term and long-term goals.

It is particularly important that you discipline yourself now, since you are under increased stress relating to divorce or separation. Satan knows that you are especially susceptible to his attacks, so pray that God will give you more discipline in the specific problem areas of your life.

One woman said that her weak point of discipline was eating junk food during her afternoon break at work as a way to comfort herself. Each time that she prayed, God would specifically help her to resist eating a huge peanut butter cookie in the break room. But if she refused to pray and became stubborn, she would often find herself binging on the warm, freshly-baked goodies. And she knew that she could not afford to gain ten pounds from eating poorly, both from a health and financial viewpoint—she had no money to buy larger clothes!

Joyfully ask God for discipline help in your problem areas.

*1 Peter 5:8*

*Discipline yourselves, keep alert. Like a roaring lion your adversary the devil prowls around, looking for someone to devour.*

Are you anxious about the mere thought of separation from your husband? You may have been married for ten years—a large chunk of time out of your life. Perhaps you wonder if you can even summon the courage to tell him that you can't live with his domestic violence, alcoholism or adultery any longer. Maybe you are just simply scared of what the future holds for you and your children.

Are you anxious because you have recently separated from your husband? Your worry list may include finances, transportation of children to soccer practices, continued acceptance in your social groups and the ability to remain in your home to live. Many women are frightened of being alone during separation from their husband, and you may also share this very real concern.

Are you anxious due to being a divorced woman? More than likely, you feel a certain stigma associated with divorce. You don't want people to lump you in the category of being a "loose woman" because you are divorced, without a man by your side. Maybe the reality of divorce and all of its lifelong implications are just now hitting home with you.

In order for you to deal with all your anxiety, make a decision right now to totally trust God with your life. God loves and cares for you, and he is aware of all your needs in your particular stage of marriage. Don't let your circumstances weigh you down. Instead, allow God's strength to shine through in your weakness as you actively surrender your total life to him.

*1 Peter 5:7*

*Cast all your anxiety on him,*
*because he cares for you.*

Has your heart become hardened by everything that you have endured in the last few weeks, months or years? You may have placed a wall around your heart to avoid being hurt any longer. You are probably determined not to let anyone ever wound you again, and that reaction is perfectly normal in light of all the immense pain.

Unfortunately, a hard heart can rob you of joy in life and cause you to become a bitter woman. Hardheartedness can also rob you of happiness with your children and serve as a poor example to your son or daughter. Furthermore, an extremely hard heart can lead to social isolation and depression. But worst of all, a hard heart can remove you from God. Consider this possibility—you could become so removed from the Father that you will not allow him in your heart or be able to hear his voice. You could actually get to the place where you're unable to ask God for forgiveness. As a Christian woman, you surely want to avoid these terrible possibilities.

So take an honest inventory of yourself, and pray for God to soften your heart. Obedience is an excellent way to avoid a hard heart. Listen to God, read his Word and then follow his teachings. Ask God to help you avoid the bitterness and anger associated with a hardened heart of divorce. You can then rejoice in the Lord, and look forward to a brighter future.

*Hebrews 3:7–10*

*Therefore, as the Holy Spirit says, "Today, if you hear his voice, do not harden your hearts as in the rebellion, as on the day of testing in the wilderness, where your ancestors put me to the test, though they had seen my works for forty years. Therefore I was angry with that generation, and I said, 'They always go astray in their hearts, and they have not known my ways.'"*

Your Father wants you to ask him.

No request is too insignificant, because God knows all your needs. Avoid putting boundaries on God's power by thinking that you can't bother him with a need that you have. Your needs that you bring to prayer may be very small in the grand scheme of the world, but they're very important to you. Therefore, they are important to your Father.

Do you need help with your children? Perhaps they are trying your patience lately and you can't seem to give them the undivided attention that they need. Tell God about it and watch for his answers as they are revealed to you.

Do you need God's assistance with emotional outbursts or gossip? Openly confess this concern to your Father and ask for divine control.

Do you need a friend? Talk to God and discuss this heartfelt need.

Are you depressed over the end of your marriage? Discover a solution with God; don't decide upon a solution and then ask for a heavenly seal of approval.

Tell God about all your needs, large and small, and trust that he will answer your prayers. Some answers will be in the affirmative and others may be in the negative. Often you will receive the answer to wait. God's timing is perfect and in your best interests.

God loves you greatly and cares about your family. Don't ignore his power. Instead, faithfully ask and tell God your needs, bring your requests to him and watch what he will do.

*Matthew 7:8*

*"For everyone who asks receives, and everyone who searches finds, and for everyone who knocks, the door will be opened."*

There comes a point in separation and divorce when you simply have to move on. Move past all the hurt, anger, sorrow and pain in your marriage and look forward to the future. Decide right now to deliberately remove yourself from any ugliness in your marriage, and quit focusing on your husband if your marriage is irreconcilable. This needs to be a conscious decision on your part. Hopefully, after several months of separation and some Christian counseling, you are ready on some level to move beyond your past.

Yes, it may be hard to deal with your shame and guilt concerning divorce. But with Christ, it is possible to detach from your husband and your past. Some memories may be wonderfully good and others are probably quite bad. Maybe in some future time you will be able to retain some of the good memories, while discarding the horribly bad ones.

With Christ's help and strength, you can look forward to a future that is full and joyous. God will help you to become a woman who truly belongs to him. Press on toward Christ Jesus. Concentrate on your relationship with Christ, and not on your past marital relationship with your former husband. You can anticipate a full and fulfilling life, as you trust God to handle matters concerning your future.

Move past your former life filled with pain, as you look forward to what is to come. Press on.

*Philippians 3:13–14*

*Beloved, I do not consider that I have made it my own; but this one thing I do: forgetting what lies behind and straining forward to what lies ahead, I press on toward the goal for the prize of the heavenly call of God in Christ Jesus.*

Give yourself an attitude check-up.

Are you allowing God to control your life, resulting in a joyous disposition? Of course, every single moment of each day may not be happy; that is not a realistic goal. But overall, if you have the Lord in your heart, you will have an attitude of gratitude. You can be grateful for your health, children, home, work and play. You can learn to be content with what you have and enjoy peace in your heart. Your attitude of calm can serve as a positive witness for God. Your friends will notice your new demeanor, and you can verbally reveal the reasons for thriving during marital separation.

However, if you are bitter and sarcastic due to divorce, you will be a negative witness for the Lord. Unhappiness is contagious and cyclical in nature. You will make yourself—as well as friends and family—miserable. Negative attitudes tend to have a snowball effect, resulting in more misery and hostility for everyone around you. Your friends may actually begin to avoid being around you, which will make your entire situation even worse.

So examine yourself, and determine to be a positive witness for the Lord. Choose this path and dwell on Jesus Christ. Smile until you feel like smiling. Act pleasant until you actually feel pleasant. Force yourself to sing a worship song until you truly want to sing praise to God. Complain only in private to selected people but not to everyone you see on the street in your neighborhood.

Check your attitude every day.

*Proverbs 15:15*

*All the days of the poor are hard, but a*
*cheerful heart has a continual feast.*

It is entirely normal to continue to have regrets, doubts and dreams about your marriage—even after divorce. You may still occasionally wonder about the "what if's."

What if you had never married this particular man?

What if he had not had an extramarital affair?

What if you had loved him more fully?

What if you had turned a blind eye to his drinking?

What if you had refused to have children?

What if you had divorced earlier?

What if you had been able to reconcile?

What if you had been able to get pregnant?

What if you had been able to reach that goal of having a 25th wedding anniversary?

What if you had been able to actually change your behaviors, and those of your husband?

What if you had been able to lead him to Christ?

It is okay to allow yourself to occasionally have these thoughts. But try to remember that you cannot change another's behaviors and that you did your very best in the marriage. If a spouse is completely determined to leave a marriage, no action on the other partner's part can prevent this. Give all your doubts to God. Ask him in faith and be confident that the Lord will help to mesh your regrets, doubts and dreams about your marriage with his will for your life.

*James 1:6*

*But ask in faith, never doubting, for the one who doubts is like a wave of the sea, driven and tossed by the wind.*

Cling to the authority of God's Word. The Bible tells you that you are loved by God and that he cares about every minute detail of your life. Christ suffered—and to a much greater degree than you are suffering at the present moment. Jesus was fully human, and therefore, he sympathizes with your hurt and pain.

God's Word assures you that you will be honored for keeping his commandments and evildoers will not prosper. You are continuously told in the Bible that those who love the Lord will be rewarded with God's supreme peace, blessings and joy.

God's Word assures us of everlasting life, and it challenges us to obey. The Lord is able to look into our hearts and know if we are truly living for him or if we are living for ourselves only. We can live a full and complete life—one totally outside our bounds of comprehension—if we live according to God's Word.

God's Word is full of promise, hope, strength, faith and trust for your future. The Bible can shape your entire life. Therefore, look into the Word and live by it as you go through reconciliation, separation or divorce.

*Hebrews 4:12*

*Indeed, the word of God is living and active, sharper than any two-edged sword, piercing until it divides soul from spirit, joints from marrow; it is able to judge the thoughts and intentions of the heart.*

Does your soul thirst for God?

Are you hungry for his love and comfort? Do you want a relationship with Christ more than anything else? Do you want to be continually in his presence? Are you longing to abide with him? Do you truly need him for survival? Do you desire joy, peace and strength—the kind that only comes from above?

Do you want to understand more of his love for you? Is Christ your best friend? Do you find yourself actually carrying on a conversation with God during the day as you go about your everyday activities? Do you find yourself truly relying on him? Do you look forward to your daily quiet time when you dwell with him in his awesome presence? Do you want to know more of him?

You are thirsty for God if he occupies your waking moments.

Your very life depends on God. Pursue this relationship above all else, even when your marriage is disintegrating. Let God be your highest aim. Seek his face, reach for him and embrace your Father.

*Psalm 42:1–2*

*As a deer longs for flowing streams, so my soul longs for you, O God. My soul thirsts for God, for the living God. When shall I come and behold the face of God?*

You may find yourself spoiling your children. Are you buying toys for them that you never would have purchased before separation? Have you allowed them extra privileges, such as staying up well past their established bedtime hour? Did you increase their monthly monetary allowance the month after their father left home? Maybe you have ignored your teenager's curfew for the last month or two, allowing her to stay out past the appointed hour while saying nothing about her behavior.

Maybe you are feeling guilty that your children are deprived of an intact family.

It is tempting to spoil your children, especially when you see the hurt in their eyes. Perhaps you have justified your actions because of their pain or your feelings of guilt. Many women who find themselves in your circumstances admit to spoiling their children, so you are not alone if this path seems tempting. You probably feel like you are playing the parts of both mother and father now.

However, spoiling your children is not in their best long-term interests. Continued spoiling can cause them to become selfish and turn their eyes from the Lord. As a daughter becomes more and more self-absorbed, she may think that there is no right and wrong. If a son is allowed to constantly have his way, he will begin to push his limits to the extreme. And these behaviors can ultimately lead to disaster for your entire family.

Begin to examine your behaviors toward your children today. And then pray that God will help you to love your children while avoiding spoiling them.

*Proverbs 13:24*

*Those who spare the rod hate their children, but those who love them are diligent to discipline them.*

Having recognized the need to avoid spoiling your child, you can learn to discipline him or her instead. Just as discipline is important in a personal walk with Christ, it is important in your walk with your children.

God has given you a huge responsibility to raise, love and nurture children. If you love your children, you will set boundaries and begin to discipline them. You are displaying concern each time you help them sit down to complete daily homework assignments from school, each time you expect them to make their beds, each time you instruct them to take out the trash from the kitchen and each time that you reprimand them for breaking one of the household rules—such as failing to call for being out late with friends. Such behaviors on your part communicate that you love your children and care enough to set guidelines. After all, you are a parent and not your children's best buddy.

If you recognize that you have always been a parent who didn't know exactly how to discipline effectively, make this a matter of prayer. Check out a book from your church library about Christian child rearing and read the section that deals with discipline. Discipline is not synonymous with physical or emotional punishment. There are far more effective methods of discipline than delivering verbal abuse for mischief and you should not use a child's behavior as a reason to batter. God does not approve of domestic violence in any form.

Instead, lovingly discipline your child. Begin this process early in his life, and it will continue through the teen years when rebellion can be very common. Remember that your acts of discipline can point your children toward God or away from him for the remainder of their lives.

*Proverbs 13:1*

*A wise child loves discipline, but a*
*scoffer does not listen to rebuke.*

After a long marriage which ended in separation from her husband, one woman wanted to protect her children from suffering. She wanted to shield them from as much pain as was humanly possible. Therefore, she tried doing fun activities with them, such as a hike and picnic in the nearby mountains. They spent time playing board games together, cooking and singing around the piano. And she prayed daily that God would protect them from hurt and pain, so that their childhoods could be as normal as possible with divorced parents.

They all enjoyed the special planned activities—healthy fun ways of playing together as a new family. They all laughed and began the slow, laborious process of healing.

However, it soon became apparent to her that she would be unable to prevent her children from feeling the hurt and pain associated with the separation. So, instead of protecting them from suffering, she chose to suffer along with them, knowing that we sometimes need to feel the pain in order to recover. She allowed her children to see her cry and let them know that she was hurting just as they were. They occasionally talked about the reasons behind the separation when the children asked, but the mother tried to avoid poisoning them with venomous words about their father. She let them judge his behavior for themselves, and they were able to come to conclusions about right and wrong. The children had a sure foundation that held firm as they learned that actions have consequences.

Suffer with your children instead of hiding your feelings. They can then know that Christ also suffered and that the Holy Spirit is able to comfort you and them.

*1 Peter 2:21*

*For to this you have been called, because Christ also suffered for you, leaving you an example, so that you should follow in his steps.*

Did you consider your husband to have been your best friend in the whole world?

He probably was the one person you could tell about the mundane and ordinary happenings of your day, such as going to the grocery store or shopping for clothes. You could cry with him if you were upset over the way a meal turned out after you tried a special recipe for his boss, and you could laugh with him over a "hot meal" of a hot dog and fries. Did you ever call him at work and take him out for a surprise lunch? Maybe you felt like you could tell him anything and he would still love you just for being you.

Was he able to rub your shoulders in a special way if you were tense after a particularly difficult work day? Did you have a special way that you held hands? Perhaps you liked to swing dance with him because he was an excellent dancer. Or did you watch old movies together?

You could kid with him about something silly, or you could scream about some huge disaster in your family. Did you ever get stressed out about having his parents over for a birthday supper and complain to him? You knew he would understand your frustration, because he was your best friend.

It's natural for you to feel a void, because the person who listened to you and shared your joys is now gone. He was your husband, lover and very best friend. You understood each other for many years, but now life has changed. Perhaps he decided that he wanted something different for the remainder of his life.

Let yourself grieve over this monumental loss of your best friend.

*Song of Solomon 5:16*

*His speech is most sweet, and he is altogether desirable.*
*This is my beloved and this is my friend,*
*O daughters of Jerusalem.*

Pray for clarity, totally clear thinking about your marriage and family. God can grant this request, and such a clear vision can enable you to steer through separation toward your ultimate destination. Only God knows where that final destination will be, and you can learn to trust him in this regard. But for the interim, you need clear thought in order to properly function as a Christian woman and mother. The Holy Spirit can help you clear your mind and find answers.

As your marriage was nearing its end, you may have been desperate to keep your husband at home. Just the mere thought of living without him might have thrown you into a panic mode! You may have been completely dependent on your husband instead of the Lord. Was your heart filled with marital turmoil and anxiety instead of the Holy Spirit? One woman who was separating from her husband admitted that she was extremely confused and couldn't even remember the month of the year at times. You might also have been totally irrational in thought as you struggled toward family unity; many women in troubled marriages suffer from extremely muddled thinking and a gross lack of concentration.

In order to avoid irrational thought, ask God to bless you with clarity. Trust that he will clear your mind of thoughts of your husband and whatever he may be doing on a daily basis and will instead fill your mind with divine thoughts only. Clarity will help you to analyze your marriage from a godly viewpoint, as opposed to one that is truly secular.

God knows your heart and your desires. He also knows what you need in order to live for him, and he will show you his will for your life when your mind is clear from distractions.

*Romans 8:26*

*Likewise, the Spirit helps us in our weakness; for we do not know how to pray as we ought, but that very Spirit intercedes with sighs too deep for words.*

Ask God to bless you with clarity of speech. Tell others in your life what you want, need and expect from them. Talk without embarrassment or shame.

Speak directly, without mixed messages or double meanings. For example, tell your children exactly what you mean when you assign them household chores. Avoid telling them that they have the responsibility of cleaning their rooms without checking to follow up on your request. If you have told your son that he is free to talk to his father on the telephone every evening, don't monopolize the phone and make this impossible for him.

Take a deep breath and clearly ask your husband for that child support check that is four weeks overdue. If he is obligated to pay you the required amount on the first day of the month, don't simply allow him to establish a habit of bringing it whenever it suits his individual budget. You shouldn't be belligerent, but it is your right to ask for the money in order to provide for your children.

Say exactly what you mean at work as well. Quit letting words to your boss be wishy-washy. Speak up and state your position slowly, firmly and clearly— without ambiguity or hesitation. Be brief, not long-winded and boring.

Your speech reflects your heart. As a Christian woman, you have acknowledged that the Lord is your guide and is leading you to be his witness even in your speech. Be clear and truthful in your words, in order that all people will know exactly what you mean when you speak.

Glorify God in all things, even clarity of speech.

*Luke 6:45*

*The good person out of the good treasure of the heart produces good, and the evil person out of evil treasure produces evil; for it is out of the abundance of the heart that the mouth speaks.*

Dear Father, I love you. I worship you as the Creator of everything in the entire universe. I know that you are Lord of all and the Source of all blessings. You are the One who has taken care of me in the past, and you are in charge of my future. I give you praise, glory and honor.

Please forgive me for my many sins—unresolved anger, jealousy, bitterness and gossip. Also, please forgive me of my worldly concerns when I take my eyes off you.

I'm so glad that you are in control of my life and that of my child. Thank you for all you've done for me in my life up to this point! Thank you for my friends, family and work. Thank you for my marriage because I loved my husband with all my heart, and we had a wonderful child together. Thank you for your love, goodness, strength, joy, peace and hope. Thank you for getting me through each day, even though sometimes I feel that I can't go on.

You know that separation from my husband is unbelievably painful to me, and I know that you're aware of the pain that my child is enduring. Please, God, comfort us as we try to please you every day. Help me to live for you and to be the best mother possible. I ask for your strength every single day and for joy to be your witness. Help me to trust that you know what is best for my life, and to wait on you to reveal yourself to me. I will survive with your help and I will thrive as a Christian woman.

I'm so glad that you are in my life! I can look forward to the future because you gave us your Son and you are faithful. In Christ's very strong name, I pray. Amen.

*Psalm 4:3*

*But know that the Lord has set apart the faithful for himself; the Lord hears when I call to him.*

You will experience many "firsts" as a separated or divorced Christian woman who is alone.

It is possible to live through the first time you sit in church without your husband, your baby's first step, your first school open house when you go alone with your children to prepare for the new school year, the very first Christmas holiday and your daughter's first date. You can survive the Sunday your child is baptized, your first vacation with just you and the children, the first time you hear "your song" on the radio without your husband to dance with you, your first child support check and the first wedding that you attend alone.

Other events that will present themselves are your son's first prom date, the first time your daughter wears make-up, your child's visit to a college campus as he tries to decide where he will attend and your child's wedding when your husband brings his second wife.

Others include selling a car alone, the first major appliance that you purchase independently and the first home improvement that you undertake all by yourself.

These "firsts" can be overwhelming, and you might be tempted to beg your husband to return home so that you can share the joys or problems together. Remember that God will triumph as you endure trials and hardships, because the Lord feels all your hurt and pain. God promises to prevail if you trust and obey.

*Revelation 14:12*

*Here is a call for the endurance of the saints, those who keep the commandments of God and hold fast to the faith of Jesus.*

You have a natural right to all of your feelings.

Joy, sorrow, elation, devastation, hurt, anger, jealousy, pain, revenge, hope, despair, relief, retaliation, apathy and distress are some of the emotions that are quite normal for a woman who is separated or divorced.

One woman became so exasperated when her friends constantly told her, "You shouldn't feel that way about him. After all, he is the father of your children." She was relieved when her Christian counselor told her that she shouldn't be afraid to express her feelings, because that was one avenue for healing. However, she was reminded that having certain feelings did not necessarily give her permission to act upon them!

Likewise, God made you complete with all your emotions and feelings. They are a normal part of you that shouldn't be ignored. If you continue to suppress certain feelings, you can become physically and emotionally sick. Don't hide your feelings of grief over the loss of your marriage, because these emotions simply show that you loved your family unity. Admit your feelings of being heartbroken to yourself along with your counselor and friends, and let yourself go through all the steps of grief.

Recognize your feelings, and thank God for the ability to actually feel something after coming out of the numbness and shock of separation. Then thank him for the outlets that he has provided for you to talk with friends and family.

*Job 1:20*

*Then Job arose, tore his robe, shaved his head,*
*and fell on the ground and worshiped.*

Have you recently been mad at God, blaming him for your impending divorce? After all, you may reason, isn't God in charge of everything and everyone? Couldn't he have prevented your husband's abandonment?

Separation or divorce is not God's fault. Yes, God is sovereign, omnipotent and in ultimate control of your family. But he loves us enough to allow us to make our own choices—choices of our own free will. Both you and your husband have free will to make choices.

God does not force us to comply with what may be his ideal plan for our lives and he does not treat us like puppets. We can willingly submit to God and give him control of our lives, instead of trying to take total charge ourselves. Alone, we may steer a course that may not be in our best interests. Sadly, as human beings, we often let our natural emotions and selfish desires overcome our rational side and we may turn our backs on God. And when that happens, pain will inevitably follow.

This may have been what happened in your marriage. But it's crucial to your spiritual health that you learn not to blame God for desertion, emotional abuse, battering or adultery. Neither should you blame God if any of these were your own past behavior patterns.

God did not cause this marital heartbreak and disappointment, but he is present to love and care for you in the middle of all of it.

*Job 1:22*

*In all this Job did not sin or charge God with wrongdoing.*

You might be patting yourself on the back, thinking that you are blameless in the marital separation. Are you telling yourself that you are better than your husband because you are not guilty of adultery or abandonment?

Humility is a rare virtue today. However, this is what God desires. It is inappropriate for us to elevate ourselves for any reason at all—because of our actions, lack of certain behaviors, having a higher educational degree, a large income, a position in a firm, a big house or a new car. It is also wrong for you to consider yourself superior to your husband because of problems that he may be currently having. Remember that God loves him too. "Hate the sin, but love the sinner" is an old saying that is particularly fitting in circumstances where you are tempted to think more highly of yourself than you ought. Christ died to absolve everyone of sin.

God can use you best when you are humble, when you don't put yourself above others. Allow God to have his way in your life, and avoid bragging about your accomplishments, your actions or your avoidance of certain other actions. Steer clear of playing the role of martyr.

God knows what you are doing for him and that's what truly matters. If it's appropriate, God will exalt you if and when his timing dictates it.

*1 Peter 5:6*

*Humble yourselves therefore under the mighty hand of God, so that he may exalt you in due time.*

Do you continue to be under your husband's influence?

Does your heart still race when you talk to him on the phone, discussing the children or separation agreement? Do you automatically defer to his judgment in these matters? Maybe you're still weak in the knees when you remember past tender moments or special celebrations of marriage. Naturally, if you had a long marriage, you forged a strong bond that may continue even now. It may be possible for you to occasionally forget his current behaviors and dream about the past as you pretend that he is still the man you married many years ago. If you're like most separated women, you are still financially dependent on your husband to help support your children. You are probably hesitant to ask for money for extras for the children, like summer camp or a sweet sixteen birthday party for your daughter.

Are you still under his control to some degree?

Be strong and ask God to help you as you boldly approach your husband about financial, household or custody issues. As time goes on, your husband's influence over you will greatly lessen. You will find this to be particularly true if you depend more and more on the Holy Spirit to strengthen you in your spiritual walk.

*Psalm 60:11–12*

*O grant us help against the foe, for human help is worthless. With God we shall do valiantly; it is he who will tread down our foes.*

Was your marriage filled with deception? Your husband might appear to the world to be quite a charming man and the perfect husband and you may also seem to be the perfect spouse. In fact, your friends and acquaintances may constantly question the reasons behind this separation in your "ideal marriage."

However, you know the story of your marriage in a way that no one else can. Only you know the intimate details of any emotional or physical infidelity that occurred. No one else is aware of the alcohol use from 8:00 p.m. until 12 midnight every single night of the week. Likewise, the battering may be completely unknown in your community since your marriage seems to be made in heaven.

God is not deceived, and he knows our true hearts. Your Father knows each ugly detail of any marital abuses that continued for months or years, and he is aware of each disturbing incident in your marriage that led to separation.

As a Christian woman, you are very precious to God. He loves you fully and wants only the best for you. If you continue to live as a witness for Christ and cultivate a godly path for your life, even in the midst of great emotional trauma, you will be rewarded. On the other hand, if you persist in certain deceptive behaviors, even while knowing them to be contrary to God's laws, the consequence may not be a full life in the Lord.

God will reward each of us with the type of fruit that we plant in our orchards.

*Galatians 6:7–8*

*Do not be deceived; God is not mocked, for you reap whatever you sow. If you sow to your own flesh, you will reap corruption from the flesh; but if you sow to the Spirit, you will reap eternal life from the Spirit.*

God made each of us and, therefore, loves all of us.

God loves you, your children, parents, brothers, sisters, in-laws, grandparents, aunts, uncles, cousins, friends, neighbors, work colleagues and fellow church members.

God also loves your former husband, his girlfriend, children that they might have together, people at work who have mistreated you, neighbors who gossip about you and friends who have abandoned you since the divorce.

It is often hard to accept that God still loves people that have hurt you and your children. After one husband's extramarital affair became public knowledge, a woman in their church sat down with the wife to have an honest talk. "You know that God still loves your husband, don't you?" was one of the first questions. The wife, who had felt so betrayed and injured, admitted that she almost felt like God shouldn't love her husband because he had been so awfully wicked to her. But she said that she was humbled to realize that God's love did indeed extend to him and that God was in control of reconciliation possibilities.

Remembering that God loves all people is an important part of healing from the trauma of separation and divorce. This realization can be quite sobering. Read the Lord's Prayer from the book of Matthew and notice the wording. It does not contain the word *my* father, but instead uses the word *our* father.

God's love is broad enough to encompass all of humanity, and his desire is that we all will accept his love before the end of our earthly lives.

*Matthew 6:9*

*"Pray then in this way: Our Father in heaven, hallowed be your name."*

Have you seen a bracelet, license plate, hair clasp, bookmark or other reminder of the phrase, "What Would Jesus Do?" These are visual prompts and challenges to each of us to act in a Christ like manner, regardless of the situation in which we find ourselves.

What would Jesus do if he found himself in your circumstances of life?

Would Christ choose to smile, even though wounded? Would Jesus tell your children every sickening detail about their parents' arguments? Would Christ continue to shine for God, his Father, despite ill treatment by others? Would Jesus gossip endlessly about your husband to everybody within earshot? Would the Lord continue to minister to your children's physical, emotional, spiritual and social needs on a daily basis? Would Jesus hate your husband? Would Christ thank your friends for their continued friendship?

Your Father yearns for you to seek his will for behavior. Pray diligently and ask God to show you how to act when challenges come your way. Search your heart and strive to act in a manner in which our Lord would.

If you're in doubt about how to act in a particular moment, pause and ask yourself, "What precisely would Jesus do right now?"

*Matthew 6:17–18*

*"But when you fast, put oil on your head and wash your face, so that your fasting may be seen not by others but by your Father who is in secret; and your Father who sees in secret will reward you."*

Are you still waiting on your husband to take care of you?

In life as a married couple, you probably relied on him for many things. You may have depended on him to fill the gas tank of your car with gas each Saturday morning. Or maybe one of his standard chores was taking the children to the park one evening a week so that you could catch your breath for a minute or two. Of course you relied on him to meet your physical romantic needs of hugs, kisses and sex! How about all the times he helped the kids with their math homework? You absolutely expected him to care for you and your family from a financial viewpoint. Maybe he kept the yard looking well-manicured because he considered himself to be an expert in that certain area.

Quit depending on your former husband to take care of you and ask God for strength to learn to take care of yourself—maybe for the first time in your life. Your Father in heaven will provide resources to solve those daily problems. If you've never filled your car with gas, drive to the gas station and simply follow the directions on the pump. Call a friend and take your children to the park together, while planning to go down the slide or swing with them. Patiently sit down with your son and try to help as he wrestles with that stubborn pre-algebra problem. Establish a budget; then tackle your bills and financial concerns the best that you possibly can. And ask for help from your neighbor, as you figure out how to crank the lawn mower so that you can mow your grass.

Trust that God cares for you, in a far better way than any person on earth is able.

*1 Peter 5:7*

*He cares for you.*

Admit it. You have been hurt by some of the behaviors in your marriage—confused, torn and devastated beyond belief at times. Your children's lives have been forever changed. You've seen them cry and you've held them as they questioned you about their father's absence from home.

You have tried to understand exactly what has happened, but you continue to shake your head in bewilderment. Many times you have sat and pondered while analyzing your marriage. And, more than likely, you may have concluded that it just doesn't make any sense at all.

One woman had married later in her life, around the age of 34. She and her husband immediately began to try to start a family, and she quickly got pregnant. They had a beautiful blond-haired little girl who was the joy of their lives. Two years later she once again gave birth, this time to a healthy baby boy. A wonderful happy family, she thought. One Sunday evening after attending church together and putting their two toddlers to bed, her husband announced that he no longer wanted to be a husband and father. He immediately packed his suitcases and left their house, never to return. What a shock! Like many Christian women who are separated or divorced, she sought pastoral counseling and began to try to cope with her losses. And she eventually forced herself to choose to "shake it off."

This is a conscious effort and it doesn't come easily! It takes effort, strength from the Holy Spirit, practice, discipline and a tremendous amount of prayer. However, you must walk away from certain events and not let them control you. Walk away from wrong choices and shake them off.

*Matthew 10:14*

*If anyone will not welcome you or listen to your words, shake off the dust from your feet as you leave that house or town.*

A special occasion can present very difficult challenges for a separated or divorced woman who may be struggling to reconcile her grim marital situation with her family dreams.

One separated woman, a professional trumpet player, was scheduled to play at a wedding for the first time since her husband left their family. She was glad for the opportunity to play, because the $250 fee that she charged would pay for new school clothes for her three children. She had braced herself for being at the wedding ceremony, knowing how emotional it would be for her as she would inevitably recall her own marital vows made 20 years prior. All of the pieces of music had been rehearsed many times so that she would be well prepared and in control of the situation.

On the morning of the wedding, she felt very calm and in charge of her ragged nerves. These feelings of peace continued through the ceremony until the pastor began to speak of the importance of a lifelong commitment when the bride and groom began to exchange rings. "I just came unglued at the point," she recalled. She had taken the precaution of having a glass of water nearby just in case such an emergency arose, and she began to slowly sip water so that she wouldn't cry. Luckily, a box of tissues was nearby in the choir loft and she dabbed at her wet eyes. She was able to continue playing for the service only through divine intervention, but cried for hours that night at her home as she reflected on her own wedding day.

Sometimes you will be able to prepare for such events as this, and sometimes they will just present themselves. Know that God will sustain you as you continue to live for him.

*Psalm 18:31–32*

*For who is God except the Lord? And who is a rock besides our God? —the God who girded me with strength, and made my way safe.*

God is perfection and only his way is perfect.

How often we try to control our lives under our own power, and fail miserably. As humans, we sometimes feel that we know the right way to handle every area of our lives—marriage, parenthood, separation or divorce. We develop a haughty attitude and may even turn our backs on God when our lives are smooth and peaceful. Sooner or later—and usually sooner rather than later—some sort of disaster strikes. And at this moment, we generally acknowledge God as ruler of our lives and ask for his help.

How much better our lives would be if we lived each day giving God control of our lives in his perfect way! He can protect and strengthen and sustain us through good and bad times, and he has a master plan that will exceed anything that we have in mind. We can rest in God, as he provides and guides us toward the greater good every day.

Trust God in his most wonderful and perfect ways.

*Psalm 18:30*

*This God—his way is perfect; the promise of the Lord proves true; he is a shield for all who take refuge in him.*

Are you broken down, weighed down, under all your daily responsibilities and duties? Has this feeling caused you to be generally apathetic and to lose your zest for life?

One woman, separated from her husband of 18 years, said that she was just sick and tired of life. She cried often and thought that things pretty much seemed hopeless from a marital point of view. Her husband helped very little with their four children, she was constantly short of money, and she felt overwhelmed with managing daily life. Her spirit was completely broken. After seeing her medical doctor, who assured her that all her feelings were normal in light of her current life circumstances, she agreed to begin taking a mild anti-depressant medication for a short period of time.

She also began praying on a daily basis, and she earnestly sought God in her Bible reading. She asked her Father to guide her on an hourly basis as she was striving to be a good mother to her children, even in her own hurt of separation. Because she was trying to sort out her own feelings and contend with her raw pain, she had been feeling guilty about sometimes neglecting her children. Her emotional state slowly began to improve as she noticed both physical improvement from her medication and spiritual improvement from her godly medicine. After she came through this dark and emotionally flat period of her life, she was better able to appreciate God's goodness and see how he had built her up.

If you find yourself emotionally apathetic and these feelings get worse instead of better, seek spiritual and physical medicine. Do not ignore this apathy, because it could get worse without help.

*Ecclesiastes 3:3*

*A time to break down, and a time to build up.*

Have you heard the phrase, "everybody's doing it," given as an excuse for divorce?

A separated woman was attending an open house—at the beginning of the school year—for her daughter, who was beginning kindergarten. She was still very teary about her separation and was somewhat ashamed about her whole situation, because her husband had been an abusive alcoholic for years. Even though this woman had endured years of misery and battering, she continued to hold some small shred of hope that she could make her marriage work.

She entered the school building and was hesitant to approach her child's teacher because she knew that she would be questioned about her husband's absence. He was a well-respected businessman in town, and their marital separation had shocked all their friends. Just as she was about to speak with the teacher, a friend of her daughter walked up along with her mother. This woman kindly put her own hand on the newly separated woman's shoulder and casually remarked, "Oh, don't worry about your separation. A lot of the kids in this school have parents who are divorced. You know, everybody's doing it."

This tired, old cliché angered this particular separated woman. She tried to smile at the other woman but was speechless. Somehow she managed to make it through the remainder of the evening without either uttering words that she would later regret or collapsing in tears.

The increasing divorce rates and the frequency of failed marriages should not always be seen as reasons to give up on a marriage. Using the behavior of others does not justify our actions. Instead, God wants us to follow his laws. As we seek God, he will reveal his will for our marriages, and he will show us how to live within that will.

*Ephesians 5:10*

*Try to find out what is pleasing to the Lord.*

You have wonderful protection in God, your Father!

He promises that he will protect you if you abide in his will. God will not prevent all hurt and danger from befalling you, but he will shelter you even in the very midst of it. He is God, not a god, and he has power and strength that you cannot imagine. With his shield, nothing that your former husband says or does will be able to totally destroy you. Sure, his actions may temporarily sideline you from active duty, but he cannot separate you from God's love.

God will keep you, love you, strengthen you and guard you. He will save you, help you, heal you and shield you. He is Almighty and can do wondrous things.

Visualize your heavenly Father protecting you from Satan and his schemes. What an immense comfort this can be in times of emotional distress, hurt and pain.

Ask God for His glorious protection. He will safeguard you as you endure separation, reconciliation or divorce.

*Psalm 91:3–4*

*For he will deliver you from the snare of the fowler and from the deadly pestilence; he will cover you with his pinions, and under his wings you will find refuge; his faithfulness is a shield and buckler.*

Companions are a blessing from God, and they can provide wonderful comfort. A true companion can sit silently and say nothing for hours or be willing to talk with you as you scream about your marriage. Just the mere physical presence of a special friend is balm for the wound in your heart. A friend is someone to offer advice, help you solve problems and help you see problems from an entirely new perspective. Friends can help you as you work and learn to play. Burdens are lighter if shared with another person, and laughter is sometimes richer when it is shared with a best friend.

A spiritual companion can pray with you and pray for you. It is a true joy to know that someone is thinking of you in prayer! It makes me feel valued to know that another person mentions my name before God. As I look back over some particularly dark moments of separation and divorce, I could truly sense the power of prayer from my Christian friends and family members. I know that I would not have survived this specific trauma without the power of friends lifting me up.

We are not to be an island unto ourselves, but we are meant to lean on each other. Once you are on the road to recovery and have begun to heal from your divorce, you can then begin to help others who are in the same situation.

Identify all your present companions individually by name, thank God for each of them, pray for them and then thank them for their continued friendship during this particularly difficult passage of life.

*Ecclesiastes 4:9–10*

*Two are better than one, because they have a good reward for their toil. For if they fall, one will lift up the other; but woe to one who is alone and falls and does not have another to help.*

Do you have a bad habit of putting things off until tomorrow? Is your calendar for today full of items that you had planned to do yesterday? Do you always plan to clean your house or pay your bills or call a friend on another day? Do you need to call your daughter's elementary school teacher, shop for tennis shoes for your son and cook a dessert for a church potluck? Have you put off establishing a daily prayer time?

If you frequently find that your to-do list is too long for each day and you need to quit procrastinating and get busy, start with one project. This single accomplishment can give you a sense of satisfaction and strength. Clean your toilets, because letting them sit for one more day will only add to the slime that is growing in the toilet bowl. Vacuum the carpets, since they are now visibly dirty with chunks of dirt cluttering the den floor. Hug your kids today. Combine your shopping trip to buy tennis shoes with a quick stop at the grocery to purchase eggs for that dessert that you need to fix. And admit that it's certainly okay to use a brownie mix. Find a few minutes today to pray with God and get to know him better.

The key to solving a procrastination habit lies in two little words: *do it.* You will probably feel tired for a while as you try to catch up from multiple chores left undone, but you will eventually climb out of the debris. And you will feel so productive and glad about what you've accomplished.

You want to do your best in handling life's challenges, and God wants your best.

*Joshua 18:3*

*So Joshua said to the Israelites, "How long will you be
slack about going in and taking possession
of the land that the Lord, the God of your
ancestors, has given you?"*

You need to giggle!

You have plenty of worries and negative thoughts running through your head, if you're similar to most women who are separated or divorced. So let yourself giggle out loud.

Giggle at a silly joke that your grade school child tells at the supper table. Giggle even if the joke is very, very bad. Let yourself giggle at the worm that your toddler pulls out of his pants pocket as he tries to scare you. Laugh loudly at your dog that is running around in circles and trying to catch his tail. Giggle at the comic page. Go ahead and laugh at that horrible mess that you made of a new recipe for a broccoli casserole. How about that terribly horrible outfit that your preschooler put on this morning as he greeted the world? Giggle away the tensions in your life.

Help your children laugh, as you lightly tickle them. Sing a perfectly silly song in the car together and laugh about the lyrics. Show them that joy still exists in the world.

Find something in your life, no matter how trivial, to giggle about. Laughing is so beneficial—it reduces stress, helps you relax, lowers your blood pressure and it's contagious! If your children see you laughing, they will be much more likely to laugh themselves. Giggling can help you see a brighter side of life, when you are convinced that the whole world is dark and gray.

God wants you to be joyful in his goodness, and in salvation through Jesus Christ.

*Isaiah 12:3*

*With joy you will draw water from the wells of salvation.*

You are God's witness. Good, bad, indifferent, hot, cold or lukewarm—you are always God's witness everywhere you go.

Reflect on some times in your life when you were a positive witness for God. Your words matched your actions, and you were confidently living with your Heavenly Father in your life. You knew that the Lord was present in your life, and your friends could see it as well. You were full of God's power, joy, strength, hope and love. During these particular times, you were a powerful witness to the Creator's power at home and at work.

In addition, allow yourself to remember some moments when you may have been a negative witness for the Lord. Maybe your language was foul or your actions did not match those of a Christian. Have you recently been short-tempered with your children due to financial worries? You may not be proud of your Christian witness as you recall those times. You know that God forgives you when you ask forgiveness for wrongs committed, but he then hopes that you will change your behavior and turn from negative acts.

You are always witnessing for God in one form or another. Just the smile on your face could cause someone to ask about the reason for your joy. On the other hand, rude behavior toward another might cause a bystander to turn from God if he knows of your Christianity.

Pray that God will mold you and that you will be bold with the power of the Holy Spirit. You can be a strong and confident witness if you allow your Father to use you for his glory.

*Acts 1:8*

*"But you will receive power when the Holy Spirit has come upon you; and you will be my witnesses in Jerusalem, and in all Judea and Samaria, and to the ends of the earth."*

A very difficult challenge that many separated and divorced Christian women face is that of remaining sexually pure. You are naturally lonely during this painful time of life, and it might be tempting to seek some physical affection from a man who is not your husband. Are you aching for someone to simply hold you in bed?

Pray to God and ask the Holy Spirit to comfort you as you resist this temptation. Satan will attempt many methods of trying to trick you into believing that it is acceptable to follow any natural impulse you may have. But God wants you to follow his laws for you.

If you are separated, remember that you are still morally and legally obligated to your husband. To be sexually intimate with another man at this time could be considered the equivalent of adultery. If you are already divorced, God desires for you to follow his teaching against sex outside of marriage. God wants to be involved in every single area of your life, not just your Sunday morning hours.

Talking with other women, prayer, physical exercise, laughter and relaxation are great alternatives to pursuing a sexual relationship with a man outside of marriage. Of course it doesn't help if your former husband has another partner, but God doesn't intend for you to focus on his behavior. Instead, focus on yourself and your relationship with the Lord. Daily commit this sexual area of your life to your powerful and all-knowing Father.

*1 Thessalonians 5:23*

*May the God of peace himself sanctify you entirely; and may your spirit and soul and body be kept sound and blameless at the coming of our Lord Jesus Christ.*

I once had a very moving experience in a Sunday School class that focused on the nails of Jesus' cross.

There were about 35 or 40 adults in our class on that particular morning, and we were in the middle of a lively discussion about biblical responses to our emotions. The teacher then distributed a dull blunted wrought iron nail to each class member and asked us to examine it. I rubbed the nail in my hands and noticed the peculiar smell it left on my palms. Then, as she read aloud the story of the crucifixion, our leader told us to push the nail tip against our wrist—an act that caused us only minor discomfort for about three or four minutes.

Before that morning, I had never considered what true physical pain Jesus Christ endured as he was crucified on the cross. And that lesson led me to ponder how truly human the Lord was in his earthly existence.

Christ is able to identify with all the hurt, pain, suffering, agony and humiliation of your separation and divorce because he experienced some of those very same feelings. He was God, but fully human on earth. Because your heavenly Father lived on earth through the Son, he is now able to supremely comfort you in all your sorrow and anguish associated with marital unrest.

God is intimately aware of all your life circumstances, and he loves you deeply.

*John 20:25*

*So the other disciples told him, "We have seen the Lord."*
*But he said to them, "Unless I see the mark of the nails in*
*his hands, and put my finger in the mark of the nails*
*and my hand in his side, I will not believe."*

What has your response been to the pain inflicted during your marriage? Are you still struggling to control the very human emotions of anger, rage and blame?

It is important to first acknowledge your emotions. Don't deny your hurt and don't stifle your disappointment, because these responses are natural when you are separated or divorced. Denial of feelings can lead to spiritual, mental and physical sickness if it is left unchecked. Next, slow down and think about why you have the emotional responses that you have had. Allow yourself to reflect on your marriage and the true reasons for separation and on the behaviors of both you and your husband since the date you parted. And then thank God that you are not alone, because he is with you as you move your life in a new direction.

But now look at the response that the Bible has outlined for you—loving your husband in some fashion through the Holy Spirit and praying for him as he struggles through parenthood as a single dad. It is hard to love the man who may have verbally abused you for years, but God will help you move toward that goal since hatred will make you a bitter woman.

And, of course, you might want to retaliate. However, the Holy Spirit can help you to steer clear of vindictive behaviors. And only the Comforter can help you pray for your husband to come to know the Lord. You want to be a strong Christian, but not a doormat, in responses to hurt and pain.

You want to glorify God in all of your actions.

*Luke 6:27–28*

*"But I say to you that listen, Love your enemies, do good to those who hate you, bless those who curse you, pray for those who abuse you."*

Are you feeling pretty badly about yourself? Have you convinced yourself that you're a failure as a wife? Are you letting yourself remember only the negative things that your husband told you for years? It is easy to feel overwhelmed and have a pity party for yourself.

Naturally, you may be doing a great deal of complaining about your challenges as a single mother—constant cooking, housecleaning, work at your job, laundry, packing school lunches, yard work, bills, money shortage and loneliness. You might reason that this was not your plan for your life and that you just have to vent your frustrations.

Or maybe you're blaming yourself entirely for marital failure. It is often easy to forget that there were two people involved in a marriage. You might be wondering, just now, how you are going to face your future alone. After all, you had planned to retire with your husband to that dream log cabin in the mountains.

Perhaps you have such a hard heart that you cannot forgive your husband for his actions under any circumstances. You might be noticing that you just don't smile anymore because you are still so incredibly mad!

If you are filled with despair at the prospect of a bleak future and an uninviting present, your entire outlook on life might be negative. Even though these feelings are temporarily normal due to separation or divorce, God does not want you to adopt a negative attitude for the long-term. Instead, he wants you to live a life that is full of his promises.

*Numbers 14:2*

*And all the Israelites complained against Moses and Aaron; the whole congregation said to them, "Would that we had died in the land of Egypt! Or would that we had died in this wilderness!"*

Try being a positive woman—just for today. This can eventually turn into a daily habit if you practice it often enough. Think of your survival during separation, because you are making it through a horribly difficult time. Some days might not be pretty, but you are making it!

Reflect on a positive minute you shared with your daughter. Maybe you snuggled with her at bedtime last night as you read her favorite book together.

Or how about that home-cooked dinner you prepared this past weekend? It might not have been chicken cordon bleu, but that spaghetti was probably delicious when you and your children gobbled it with that garlic bread and a salad.

Did you set a boundary with your husband? Maybe you would not let him change his visitation schedule for your son, merely for his convenience, because you had already made plans to go to a singles dinner at your church.

Perhaps you were a good listener when your friend called yesterday in tears to complain about a family problem.

Did your entire family make it to church on time yesterday? This is sometimes a minor miracle, as everyone runs from room to room looking for a particular black patent leather shoe that somehow manages to walk away from the closet on Sunday mornings.

Instead of dwelling on the bleak future of a fragmented family and all of the problems that it entails, choose to look at the positive things that are indeed happening in your everyday life.

*Psalm 73:26*

*My flesh and my heart may fail, but God is the strength of my heart and my portion forever.*

Praise God always—in every way and in everything.

God made you, loves you, cares for you and protects you. He is your refuge from the deluge of life's storms.

Praise God when you get out of bed in the morning. Literally roll out of bed on your knees and give thanks for another day. Verbally praise him and give him the glory for a night's rest.

Praise God as you pour that milk over your cereal and utter a blessing over your food.

Continue to praise him as you pack your child's lunch for school and as you walk her to the bus stop. You can praise God through your actions, words, songs, thanksgiving and prayers.

Keep on praising him as you drive to work. Be glad that you have the ability to earn an income and help support your family.

Praise God for small things during your day, such as a green traffic light as you hurry to work in the morning. Also praise him for large events, such as attending an outdoor play with your daughter and her Girl Scout troop.

Don't save up your praises and thanks until you get to church on Sunday. Instead, praise God regularly and habitually. Then you will be better able to keep a positive outlook through life's storms, and you will be able to see your many blessings more clearly.

Praise the Lord!

*1 Chronicles 16:4*

*He appointed certain of the Levites as ministers before the ark of the Lord, to invoke, to thank, and to praise the Lord, the God of Israel.*

Your life may be very difficult right at this exact point in time. You might be at a low point where you are even questioning God's control of the horrible conditions in your life and whether he really cares about every detail of your divorce.

Perhaps your children are hurting and behaving poorly in school in order to get someone's attention. They want someone to take notice of them since they feel their father's absence so acutely.

You may still be angry at separation and not even ready to talk to your husband about a legal agreement.

Maybe you've never worked outside of the home and have very limited education. You might be wondering how in the world you can financially care for yourself, especially if you were married to your husband for 35 years and were a homemaker for your entire married life. Your future, therefore, is uncertain.

You are scared of the future with all its unknowns. Your children are crying every night, and you're crying yourself to sleep most nights as well.

Life is hard at times, but God is good and powerful. He will care for you. Put yourself in his hands each and every day. Think about every good thing that your Father has done for you in the past and think about how much more he will do for you in the future.

*Jonah 2:2*

*"I called to the Lord out of my distress,*
*and he answered me; out of the belly of Sheol*
*I cried, and you heard my voice."*

Stop whatever you're doing at the moment, close your eyes and empty your mind. Visualize the glorious, beautiful, majestic mountains that God has made.

In your mind, you can see great tall peaks and low valleys. Look at the gently rolling hills, and the mass of trees covering the mountainside. Feel the cool, gentle breeze blowing on your cheeks as you stand on the side of a grassy bank. Continue on this hike and smile broadly at this awesome show of God's creation.

Enjoy the warm sunshine that God has provided as it shines down on the earth. Take a deep breath, exhale and let your shoulders relax as you blow away all of the stressors in your life.

Do you somehow feel a bit closer to God in the mountains, while you walk along a trail and see the many intricacies of nature? Watch as a hawk soars over the glorious hills. Simply marvel at all the magnificent scenery that is right before your eyes.

Reflect on the quiet serenity of the valleys below, while enjoying God's glory and the beauty made for you to enjoy. In this place of solitude, give your Father many thanks for his creation and the calm that you have found in this particular spot.

Remember this peaceful time in the mountains, and close your eyes often so that you can come back for a quick mental visit when the tensions mount in your life.

*Psalm 121:1–2*

*I lift up my eyes to the hills—from where will my help come? My help comes from the Lord, who made heaven and earth.*

Just get up and go to work on a regular basis. Sticking to a routine is comforting for both you and your children during separation and divorce and assures all of you that life goes on.

Your formal work may be in the role of a secretary, nurse, doctor, teacher, lawyer, clerk, social worker, homemaker, writer, sales associate or researcher. Thank God that you have this function in life, and remember that your Father has given you work for many purposes. You can be a positive witness for Christ in your workplace, and you can influence many people for good.

One divorced woman discovered a support group of fellow teachers at her school; many of the women there were also from marriages that had dissolved. They helped one another through the many crises of separation and divorce, and this woman openly shared her Christian faith with non-believers.

Consider your work at home as you minister to your children on a daily basis. The role of motherhood can never be over-emphasized! It is crucial that children grow up in a godly home if they are to grow in their own faith from childhood on into their adult years. They will be able to see your strength, courage, dignity and grace as you endure heartbreak. What a powerful witness you can be to God's power. And you can share your reason for optimism despite divorce—your faith in the Lord.

Be assured that God is with you in all your work and that your work is not in vain.

*Haggai 2:4*

*Yet now take courage, O Zerubbabel, says the Lord; take courage, O Joshua, son of Jehozadak, the high priest; take courage, all you people of the land, says the Lord; work, for I am with you, says the Lord of hosts.*

Recovering from divorce is a long process. It does not happen overnight, and that is okay. It is better that this be a slow process, in order for you to learn to depend totally—not partially—on God. Complete trust and total surrender to your Higher Power is a vital part of recovery from a dissolving marriage.

You need time to rest, think, remember, pray, reflect, hope, grieve, heal, ponder and be alone. Also, you need to be with family and friends. And you need time to laugh, cry, scream, play, work, have fun and smile again. All of these experiences are necessary for true recovery.

A work colleague was made aware of this process of recovery during separation from her husband at around the one-year anniversary date of their parting. Although she thought that she had made a complete psychological break from her husband of 15 years and the father of her three children, she was assaulted by a flood of memories at this point—memories both good and bad. She became enraged once again at many marital behaviors and then experienced many emotions that she had thought were far behind her. She began to cry each morning and actually wanted reconciliation despite her husband's continuing to live with another woman. After three tear-filled miserable weeks, she acknowledged that she was just beginning to recover from marital wounds. Once again, she realized that she definitely had more work to do and called her counselor for yet another appointment. Then she got on her knees, and began to pray anew.

Trust that God will bring you to the right place at the right time in your recovery process.

*Mark 6:31*

*He said to them, "Come away to a deserted place all by yourselves and rest for a while."*

Your character is being shaped by the events surrounding your separation and divorce. Who exactly are you and what are your beliefs?

The fibers of your spiritual, moral, mental and ethical being are being strengthened by each event in this very difficult time. Really take time to think and decide what you want your reputation to reflect about you as a human being. Ultimately, your testimony for Christ is determined in large part by your character. Your actions will speak loudly to others about your true values and priorities.

God desires for your character to be one that is filled with the fruit of the Holy Spirit and one of honesty and integrity. Therefore, it becomes important for you to critically examine each choice that you're making. For example, be honest with your children about your feelings concerning separation, but don't slander their father. Neither do you want to lie to your children about the true reasons for separation if they are old enough to ask you.

You need to admit first to yourself and then openly to God what is in your heart. Do you need to rid yourself of some dishonesty and deceit? Then confess these sins and give them to the Lord so that he can give you a fresh start and develop your character as a godly woman.

The Holy Spirit can work in your life much more effectively if you are consciously trying to live a full and joyful life in Christ, one full of his truth.

*Acts 5:3–4*

*"Ananias," Peter asked, "why has Satan filled your heart to lie to the Holy Spirit and to keep back part of the proceeds of the land? While it remained unsold, did it not remain your own? And after it was sold, were not the proceeds at your disposal? How is it that you have contrived this deed in your heart? You did not lie to us but to God!"*

You can be assured that God loves you and is with you constantly. He will not abandon you in the middle of your trials. Instead, he is there to guide you and draw you even closer to him.

He is present when your children cry and blames you because their daddy is living somewhere else. Your heavenly Father is aware of your continued love for your husband, in spite of his alcoholism which led to your family's disintegration. And he knows how much you are still hurt by your husband's actions. He feels your pain as you sit alone with tears in your eyes in the church pew that your family has occupied for years. God hears your daughter telling you that she doesn't love you anymore because you are getting a divorce. He knows that you cry as the result of seeing tears in your son's eyes because his parents are living apart.

God's love is vast and it certainly is bigger than the problems associated with your divorce. His love can change lives. God's love is great and consistent, and it does not change with the different seasons of your life. Your Father upholds you in the intense heat of summer decisions, the changing colors and moods of autumn, the emotional bleakness of winter and the new growth of spring.

God is here. What a wonderful assurance!

*Romans 8:38–39*

*For I am convinced that neither death, nor life, nor angels, nor rulers, nor things present, nor things to come, nor powers, nor height, nor depth, nor anything else in all creation, will be able to separate us from the love of God in Christ Jesus our Lord.*

Thank the Lord for your dirty laundry! And for suppers to cook, dishes to wash, toilets to scrub, grass to mow, beds to make, preschool carpools to drive, dirty sinks to clean, carpet to vacuum, dust to wipe, bathtubs to clean, school lunches to pack and children to bathe.

You might be rebelling at this long list and refuse to thank God for all these chores. After all, housework is definitely not a glorious carefree idea of a fun way to spend Saturday morning! But try to see all these daily tasks as the normal, everyday events of life. These events can give you a temporary focus, keep you going and give you a routine. They let you know that life can continue on in spite of separation and divorce.

If you have no children, then these household chores alone will kick you in gear because it's hard to lie in bed and cry all day if your grass is six inches high in the front yard. If your children are toddlers, be glad for the opportunity to give them their wet and messy nightly baths. If your children are teenagers, they are grateful for all that you do for them. They may not always verbalize their thanks, but they do notice that you are continuing to provide a home for them.

So give God thanks for that dirty laundry and all that it represents. And for his strength that enables you to wash the third load of laundry on this particular Saturday morning.

*Ephesians 5:20*

*Giving thanks to God the Father at all times and for everything in the name of our Lord Jesus Christ.*

Examine your past marital life and be honest with God. Are you at fault? Did your actions lead to divorce from your husband? Maybe you have become a Christian since you separated from your husband and deeply regret your former behaviors. Your heart may be heavy with guilt, while God has shown you that you need to take steps toward reconciliation.

If you are guilty of adultery, abandonment of your husband and children, gross sinful behaviors, drug or alcohol abuse in your past life, then you need to confess those sins immediately. You cannot enjoy fellowship with Christ if you have unconfessed sins in your life—sins that are weighing you down and separating you from the Lord. God loves you and wants to forgive you for any past wrongs that you committed that may have ended your marriage.

Ask God right now for forgiveness, and he will extend it. Of course, remorse and repentance are a vital part of forgiveness. Your spiritual growth is not enhanced by mere verbal regret, and actions must accompany words. God can help you change, and he will be in control once you truly turn your life over to him. And you don't have to confess the same sin over and over. God will forgive and help you to move forward and move past your sin. Talk with your pastor. He can give you valuable assistance with life changes.

Next, you must take steps to reconcile with your family members. Admit to your former husband that you are aware that your adultery, abandonment or addiction hurt him and your marriage. Be honest with him, apologize and ask for forgiveness. If you have unspoken issues with your children, bring them out into the open. Let them know of your genuine sorrow for any actions, and then you can show them your changed heart. Your altered life can be a powerful witness to God's power.

*James 5:9*
*Beloved, do not grumble against one another, so that you may not be judged. See, the Judge is standing at the doors!*

Friday and Saturday nights can be lonely for a separated woman. Your partner for going to see a movie on a regular basis is gone. He might even be dating a new girlfriend tonight. Who are you going to ask to go out and eat with you at the new Italian restaurant in town? You don't have your standard partner to sit with you at the football games at your daughter's high school where she is a cheerleader. Maybe you and your husband had a habit of always renting a videotape to watch on Saturday nights after you had given your children their baths and put them in bed.

Friday and Saturday nights are hard! You might be able to make it through the week pretty well, because you have a set routine at home and work for the next day. But weekends can be difficult to maneuver around in your newly single state.

So get moving and find some activities to take up those lonely hours. After you have survived several weekends of crying, you might be ready to join a dinner club in your neighborhood or at church. During one woman's separation, her church began a dinner club as a means of fellowship and outreach. They always had dinner on the second Saturday night of each month. She was thrilled, because she had something to do on a regular basis! Along with many other single women in her church, she made that dinner club a top priority.

Don't hesitate to call another woman to go with you to see the latest movie release. And still rent an occasional movie to watch on Saturday nights. You just might want to avoid the steamy romantic ones—unless you *really* need a good cry.

*1 John 1:3*

*We declare to you what we have seen and heard so that you also may have fellowship with us; and truly our fellowship is with the Father and with his Son Jesus Christ.*

God is alive and thinking about you. He is caring for you and your children, and he wants first place in your life.

If you are struggling in any way, acknowledge this battle to the Lord. Lay it out plainly in your prayer time and admit your sorrow to him. For example, if you literally cannot afford to buy groceries due to a financial emergency, cry to God about this. Let him know that you're very concerned. One friend who was recently separated had no money for her week's food bill and placed this expense on her credit card. Then God provided her with a bonus check from work the following week! God will provide a solution; our part in these battles is to trust and obey with our eyes on God.

If you are struggling with your children who are depressed over their father's absence, admit this to God. Continue to love your children and lead them to Christ and his truths. Seek an appropriate Christian counselor for them, because they may not feel comfortable discussing marital separation with you. If you cannot afford a counselor for your children, consult your pastor. He may provide the counseling himself free of charge or direct you to emergency church funds to pay for outside counseling. Endure and focus on God. Remain steadfast.

If you are struggling with continued anger even a couple of years after your divorce, tell God about it. Ask for removal of these remnants that are damaging your emotional well-being.

If you are struggling in any way and are at a low point, be assured that God is aware of it, and he wants to reward your faithfulness. Your increase is coming! Keep your eyes on God and watch his plan unfold.

*Psalm 115:14*

*May the Lord give you increase,*
*both you and your children.*

What will you choose? Good or evil—life or death?

Some choices may sound simple, but in reality, they may not necessarily be simple or easy. Consider many of the life-changing choices that you have confronted in the past. Did you choose to believe that Christ was your Savior many years ago? Did you choose to marry your husband? Did you choose to have children? Perhaps you chose to remain childless. Maybe you chose to attend college. Did you choose to accept the job in which your currently work? Did you choose to buy your house? As you now reflect back, these may have been easy decisions that you made. And, hopefully, they were good choices that were filled with the promise of an abundant and full life.

Now consider the dilemmas you face each and every day. Are you going to go on a date with another man while still legally married? Are you planning to get up a half-hour earlier tomorrow morning to talk to God in the fresh hours of morning? Maybe you are planning to move to another city for a job opening that you've dreamed about for years. Are you choosing to become engaged to your boyfriend while still married to your husband? Are you re-committing your life to Christ? You can do that even though you are still angry about your marital mess. Are you choosing the good or evil, life or death?

Each day, in each situation, we have the opportunity to choose good or evil. God does not force his will on us, but he wants us to choose life in him so that we may receive his blessings.

*Deuteronomy 30:19*

*I call heaven and earth to witness against you today that I have set before you life and death, blessings and curses. Choose life so that you and your descendants may live.*

You do not have to constantly talk abut your problems and marital upheaval. Listen instead.

Listen to God. Let him have time each day to talk to you. Structure several minutes for listening to the Almighty. Rest in your bed in the morning and let him speak to you. What does he want you to do this day? What is his long-range plan for your life? If you're so busy talking to everybody else about your marriage, you won't be able to hear the Lord talking to you about the wonderful things he has planned just for you. And just for your children.

Listen to your children. Your son may have a new piece of art work that he's just bursting to tell you about—ready for your refrigerator door. Or your daughter may be ready to finally talk with you about separation and divorce. Simply be still and listen.

Listen to your parents. They have your best interests at heart and may have some valuable advice to offer with a different perspective than yours. You may not heed each piece of direction that they give for your marriage, but try to listen and be respectful.

Listen to your trusted and valuable Christian friends that God has supplied for you during this turbulent time of your life. They can sometimes help you see a situation in your life that is foggy to you because you are in the thick of the dilemma.

Listen to your pastor as he prays with you about your marriage and family.

And then listen to the Lord some more, because he will always have some encouragement for you.

*Proverbs 13:3*

*Those who guard their mouths preserve their lives; those who open wide their lips come to ruin.*

Who is your family? Of course, your parents and siblings constitute your family—as well as your children, aunts, uncles, cousins, in-laws and grandparents.

But your family is much bigger.

Christ asks us to broaden our definition as we consider our family to be all believers who follow God's will. This concept of a spiritual family can be very comforting as you muddle through marital separation and divorce. You will need lots of comfort, prayers, shoulders to cry on and laughter.

Openly accept forms of assistance from your church and spiritual family. Isn't it glorious that God has provided such a huge resource for you during this time of need? During one woman's early weeks of separation when she wasn't thinking clearly and felt very alone, she literally received dozens of cards from church members. This mail encouraged her tremendously! She was very surprised at such an outpouring of love and support at a time when she needed it greatly; she even received a letter from a man—a true shock. He exhorted her to "hang in there." She still has all of these cards in a folder and will occasionally pull one out if she's having a rough day as a single mother.

Another divorced woman received two dinner invitations from a church family during a summer week while both of her children were at camp and she was feeling alone. She said that these invitations boosted her spirits when they were sagging.

Tap into your family of believers and thank God for such a wonderful family.

*Matthew 12:49–50*

*And pointing to his disciples, he said, "Here are my mother and my brothers! For whoever does the will of my Father in heaven is my brother and sister and mother."*

Are you filled with shame because of being divorced? Perhaps your children are also ashamed. This is somewhat normal, and you can be assured that you're not alone. Just hearing that specific term "a failed marriage" used in conversation can certainly lead a woman to feel like a failure as a wife.

You may be ashamed of your former husband's addictions that are well-known within your community. Continually repeat to yourself that you cannot control his actions, because they are his behaviors and not your fault. On an intellectual level, you know that you shouldn't be ashamed of another's deliberate, toxic repetitions, but you may continue to feel that it reflects on you in some way. You can be comforted in knowing that many women feel some degree of shame in separation and divorce and this shame may be related to regret. Are you also ashamed of your own choices during the marriage and what you are hiding?

Recognize your shame for what it is, and ask God to help you as you struggle through this emotion. Give your shame to God and he will work in your life. God will give each of us many opportunities to make better choices in the future.

*Deuteronomy 30:15,17–18*

*See, I have set before you today*
*life and prosperity, death and adversity.*
*But if your heart turns away and you do not hear, but are led*
*astray to bow down to other gods and serve them, I declare*
*to you today that you shall perish; you shall not live long in*
*the land that you are crossing the Jordan*
*to enter and possess.*

Pour out your soul before God. Don't just give him a laundry list of your concerns each day during your quiet time. Instead, feel free to continually pour out your heart to him. As your heavenly Father, he wants to know what is on your heart. God loves you and cares for you.

Are you still in love with your husband even after your divorce? Tell God and ask for his guidance. His answers will come. Do you still fantasize about family togetherness? God knows your innermost desires. Are you aching for the love and affection of another man? The Lord is aware and welcomes your sharing this with him. Are you wanting to follow Christ's teachings concerning sexual purity but feeling vulnerable in this area? Confess this to your Father. Have you harbored angry and bitter feelings toward your husband or others? Give them to God. Are you still struggling with depression over a very recent separation? God wants to help. Have you just seen your divorce papers today, finalizing the end of your marriage? Let him begin to heal you. Do you still hurt in a visceral way for your children's pain over losing their intact family? God wants you to tell him about it.

Your Father in heaven cares about all these needs and will intervene on your behalf as you mature and are capable of handling future developments. He will act in good time. Tell him everything that is both a joy and a burden for you.

God cares about our big problems and also our small worries. He wants us to get on our knees, talk to him and pour out our souls.

*1 Samuel 1:15*

*But Hannah answered, "No, my lord, I am a woman deeply troubled; I have drunk neither wine nor strong drink, but I have been pouring out my soul before the Lord."*

Are you finally able to focus on someone other than yourself? Or do you find that you can't quit thinking about your own multitude of problems?

Service to others is a wonderful remedy for self-centeredness. Look for opportunities to serve God. As a newly-separated woman and mother of two, I was often alone on Sunday evenings as my children attended youth fellowship in our church. One Monday morning, our youth minister called and asked if I would volunteer to work with the junior high school group as a member of the youth leadership team. I prayed about this opportunity, joined this wonderful group of people and then found extreme fulfillment by reaching out to others in the middle of my pain and confusion.

Other divorced women have found short-term mission work to be a fantastic way of service to God and mankind. How about volunteering as a tutor in your local school system? Maybe you can offer to babysit for a new mom while she does her grocery shopping. Another possibility is serving meals at your local homeless shelter; almost anyone can dip soup!

Even though you're incredibly busy and stretched thin, you will find that using your gifts to serve God through serving others is very satisfying. Your horizons will be broadened, and you will be able to see beyond yourself and your marital woes. This will also serve as an excellent example to your children when they see you growing stronger.

If you feel like you have no gifts to offer, pray and ask your Father to reveal them to you. Everyone has gifts. Your talents may simply be hidden momentarily as God seeks to uncover them.

*1 Peter 4:10*

*Like good stewards of the manifold grace of God, serve one another with whatever gift each of you has received.*

Actions have consequences. As my pastor once very appropriately quoted, "You can't unscramble an egg."

You may have learned this as a very young child when your mother warned you about playing near a hot stove. Did you ever just lightly touch the hot burner to see if she was right? If so, then you remember that terribly painful burning sensation!

Perhaps you have given your husband so many chances to reform his abusive behaviors that he began to think that you would always forgive and "take him back." And maybe you have only now decided that you can no longer live with his choices. Both your emotional and physical health may be suffering due to years of mistreatment.

Any action that results in sin will have consequences. You certainly do not have to tolerate specific actions on the part of your husband even if commonplace and frequently cited as a cause of divorce. Neither do you have to continue to suffer abuses toward you or your children, because they can destroy your self-esteem and emotional well-being.

Your own actions also have consequences, so be careful. An old adage about publicity certainly applies here. If you're trying to decide about whether to participate in an activity, simply ask yourself—*Do I want my actions known to others?* or *Could I tell my pastor about this?*

Seek guidance from God, your pastor and the Bible before acting. Be sure to follow the Lord's leading as you choose paths of actions during your separation and divorce.

*Ephesians 5:11–13*

*Take no part in the unfruitful works of darkness, but instead expose them. For it is shameful even to mention what such people do secretly; but everything exposed by the light becomes visible.*

Is it time to finally tell your children that you are indeed getting a divorce?

At this point, they have known for months about their parents' separation. You have probably seen their grief displayed in some form of anger, sadness, depression or even bargaining behaviors. Divorce is incredibly hard for children, even if they are trying to cover up their fears and concerns by telling you that everything is "all right." They may be hurting all the time they are smiling as they go visit their father.

Perhaps you're now satisfied that you have given your marriage every possible attempt at reconciliation, and you and your husband have decided to divorce. There are several important considerations for both of you to ponder. First, consider not telling the children early, because it may spare them grief for several months before divorce becomes final. Next, remember that you and your husband should jointly tell the children about the coming divorce. Both of you were in the marriage, and the responsibility of informing the children should not fall to only one parent. Then ask God for his guidance as you prepare to carefully tell the children about the divorce.

Make your announcement short and factual, because your children do not need a long speech at this point. Neither do they need a fight from their parents about fault issues. Reinforce to your children that the divorce is not their fault and remind them that they are not to blame. Verbally acknowledge their pain as they struggle with the full reality of their parents' divorce and remind them that you are available to talk. Reassure them of your deep and abiding love, and tell them that you want them to continue to have a relationship with their father and their heavenly Father. Then you should hug your children and, as always, pray for them.

*Psalm 15:3*
*Who do not slander with their tongue,*
*and do no evil to their friends.*

A time of intense national tragedy can either draw people closer to God or cause them to blame God for their pain and sorrow. In times of heartbreak, most people don't believe that God stands up in the heavens like a dictator and decides who will die and who will live. I believe these moments of immense sorrow also cause pain to our heavenly Father.

If you are a woman who is separated or divorced, emotional pain and feelings are likely to be greatly magnified whenever any national tragedy strikes. You are emotionally vulnerable, and in times like these, you may fear for your own safety. You're probably also concerned for your children's welfare in the event that something should happen to you. Likewise, your children might also wonder if they will be safe during a time of terror or violence. They are fearful about what will personally happen to them, and they worry about what will become of them if you were suddenly taken from them due to terrorism.

It is your duty to be well-informed, and make rational decisions both for yourself and your children in times of national crisis. Turn to God, as he knows what has happened and what the future holds. Instead of blaming the Lord for a tragedy that has struck, grow closer to your Father. Pray to God for guidance, read his Word and wait. His direction may come in a variety of ways. Comfort your children and pray with them.

You can turn a time of national tragedy into a time of growth in God.

*2 Corinthians 12:10*

*Therefore I am content with weaknesses, insults, hardships, persecutions, and calamities for the sake of Christ; for whenever I am weak, then I am strong.*

Should you separate from your husband? Is it time to file for divorce? Should you sell your house? Are you trying to decide whether to accept a new job that would require twice the number of hours, but yield much more money? Should you continue with separation as you pray for reconciliation? How long should you wait after your divorce before you begin to date again? Should you ever date again?

If you are unsure what course of action to pursue as you consider life-changing decisions, stop and pray. Hesitate and wait as God reveals his plan. If you are tuned in to God and his will for your life, you know that he wants only the best for you.

Don't rush into a plan of action without God's input. In matters of marriage and divorce, haste can most certainly make waste. Give God plenty of time to reveal a master plan to you, because his ways are perfect and methods infallible.

One friend of mine was determined to avoid being alone. She began to date other men just one month after separation from her husband. Sadly, her children began to feel neglected as she pursued her romantic interests. The kids' grades at school began to deteriorate, and they began to misbehave at home. To further complicate the picture, this friend rushed into a second marriage the week after divorce from her husband, and then was completely miserable with her new husband. She realized that she should have waited much longer to become involved with another man, and her hurry to move forward without consulting her Father made her problems worse.

If you are in doubt or uncertain—wait. Hesitate, think, pray and look for God's will.

*Acts 1:4*

*While staying with them, he ordered them not to leave Jerusalem, but to wait there for the promise of the Father.*

Have you fallen victim to the crazies? You know—done something stupid that you vowed you would never do. Many separated and divorced women do some wild and crazy things!

A woman warned her friends in this situation that they would do some things that they had never before considered. "You might just go crazy," she predicted. She explained that separation was a time during which she had forgotten about some biblical and moral principles that had always previously guided her life.

"I felt so hurt because the love of my life had rejected me for a young redhead girlfriend, that I went to a bar and picked up a man and had a one-night stand," she confessed. She wanted to show her husband that she was still desirable and that someone would want her. This wonderful Christian woman went on to explain that she never saw the man again and that she felt immense waves of guilt over her actions. She actually experienced some depression related to her uncontrolled drinking at the bar and the casual sex, something that she declared that she would never have done at any other time in her life. Her emotional panic had very definitely led her toward some crazy behaviors. But, she went further and told me that she asked God for forgiveness for her bizarre actions and then tried to obey her Father's directives for her life as she abided in him.

She met a great Christian man a couple of years later and married him. He has been an absolutely terrific father to her small son. And now my friend is actually a seminary student, joyfully serving God on a daily basis in thousands of ways!

God can forgive even "the crazies." He loves you and wants you back in his fold.

*1 Corinthians 6:11*

*And this is what some of you used to be. But you were washed, you were sanctified, you were justified in the name of the Lord Jesus Christ and in the Spirit of our God.*

In contrast to actively choosing to participate in "the crazies" on a regular basis, strive to stay sane and pure. Peace, joy, calm, strength and hope are yours in the Lord.

If you know that your weakness is sexual temptation, remove yourself from sexually ripe situations. Don't go to bars or other places where the focus may be on finding a casual sexual partner. Leave those breeding grounds totally alone. Just steer clear of them!

Maybe your point of temptation is abusing your body through overeating. Enlist a friend or family member to assist you as you attempt to uncover the root of your gluttony. Pray passionately. And don't visit all-you-can buffet bars for a lunch or evening meal. It can be hard to control yourself in this environment where you want to get every bite for the money that you paid.

Perhaps you know that your trigger point in avoiding crazy behavior is alcohol abuse. Do you notice that you have a drinking problem that has manifested itself after separation? Are you drinking every night to dull your pain? You can actively engage in counseling, along with a recognized program for alcohol treatment. Consult your pastor and develop an action plan.

Have you been known to be verbally abusive toward your former spouse? Don't put yourself in situations where you are likely to yell at him. Try to turn around and literally walk away if you are alone with him and ready to blow off steam in unhealthy ways.

Pursue purity and Christ-like behaviors. Talk with Christian friends who are experiencing separation or divorce. They will help you as you try to stay sane. While struggling through these hard times, it is possible to come to terms with separation and thereby grow closer to God.

*2 Timothy 2:22*

*Shun youthful passions and pursue righteousness, faith, love, and peace, along with those who call on the Lord from a pure heart.*

How long has it been since your last physical examination by a doctor, nurse midwife, nurse practitioner or physician assistant? Like many women in separation and divorce, you may have been neglecting your health during marital ups and downs.

Make an appointment to get your Pap smear. Let's face it—very few women actually look forward to a gynecological exam with wild anticipation, but this is something that should be done. You need to take care of yourself so that you can have the healthiest life possible. Plus, you're setting an example for your daughter. Maybe it has been three years since your last Pap smear. Tell yourself to get up right now, look up your doctor's telephone number in the directory, make the call and find a time to go for your appointment. Do it today!

Likewise, you might not be able to even remember when you had your last mammogram. Was it two years ago, maybe three? Time can certainly slip away from you during very stressful periods. If you are over forty or have risk factors, ask your doctor if you need a mammogram. And if you have never practiced monthly breast self-exam, now is the time to start. As women, we are at risk for breast cancer. You might be like my 35-year-old friend who had refused to check her breasts because she was afraid of finding a lump. Remember that most lumps are not cancerous and that any cancer is usually more curable the earlier you discover it. Ask a nurse or doctor for help.

Do you have a chronic medical condition, such as high blood pressure, that requires annual blood work? Make it a top priority to regularly visit your doctor and monitor your health.

God wants us to take the best possible care of ourselves, and we honor him by doing so.

*1 Corinthians 6:15*

*Do you not know that your*
*bodies are members of Christ?*

Have you ever felt as though you were wearing a big sign on your back that reads "I am separated" or "I am a divorced woman?"

Many women who are in marital changes feel a certain stigma attached to separated or divorced. Some degree of shame or embarrassment can be normal as you relinquish your marriage.

One divorced woman confided that she was so ashamed that she didn't want to leave the house for days at a time. "I felt like I was branded as a divorcée and I thought that people would consider me to be one of those loose women." Furthermore, she became a bit paranoid and thought that everyone was looking at her when she was out in public. "I felt disgraced," she confessed.

If you share some of these feelings, remember that you have a right to each of your emotions and they are acceptable. It's okay if you associate some discredit with being divorced. After all, divorce was not the ultimate goal for your marriage. However, Christ died to cover your shame and embarrassment. You are a child of God, a woman of God, and as such you do not need to let that shame persist. Place it at the foot of the cross, thank God for covering it and walk with God every day.

Christ will remove your stigma if you turn it over to him in prayer and trust him to take care of it.

*Luke 3:6*

*"'And all flesh shall see the salvation of God.'"*

If you have a problem area in your life that needs intensive work, find a partner and tackle this difficulty together. Joint effort sometimes produces increased results! Having a partner increases your likelihood of success and can force you to be accountable to another person.

Do you need to start an exercise program? Then find a partner. The two of you might be able to attend an aerobics class together at your church or a yoga class in the gym during your work lunch hour. Perhaps you can walk together in your neighborhood if your joints can't handle a formal exercise program.

Are you having a hard time staying pure as a divorced woman while dating the most handsome man you have ever seen? Locate another woman in your same situation and share your concerns. One woman read a book about surviving dating as a newly single person, asked her friend to also read it and then they made a covenant to be accountable to each other. They both wanted to save themselves physically for their next marriages. "It was so much easier," she admitted, "if we could talk out our sexual frustrations over coffee every Tuesday night, and we knew that we couldn't ask God to bless us if we intentionally planned to engage in sexually immoral behaviors."

Is your problem area that of being short-tempered with your toddler? You are not alone! Talk to another mother who is also struggling with this self-control issue and make regular contact with her as you devise some sort of treatment plan for your tempers.

Your best partner in life is the Lord. He is always present and wants to help you in times of trouble. When Christ comes into a life, hope and new possibilities always exist.

*Proverbs 18:24*

*Some friends play at friendship but a true friend
sticks closer than one's nearest kin.*

Are you still angry over your marriage coming to an end?

Anger is a very potent emotion and God wants you to be careful to avoid true rage. However, there is surely such a thing as righteous anger; it is sometimes quite appropriate to express this particular emotion. Try to overlook minor problems and reserve your righteous anger for sin. God doesn't want you to smile at abuse, addictions, abandonment or adultery. Instead, he wants you to label these actions for what they are and steer clear of such behavior. He also wants us to clean existing sin from our lives, because God is not pleased when we continually disobey.

One woman who had been separated from her husband for only one week discovered that he had bought a new house and moved his young girlfriend in with him. Of course she was hurt and angry! After all, she is human and was incredibly wounded by such painful behaviors.

Another woman's husband quit work after their divorce, in order to avoid paying any child support monies for their daughters. Naturally, she was angry.

Indeed, even Christ was angry as he drove the merchants out of the temple; his anger was righteous because of the injustice and sin occurring in a place of worship.

*John 2:15–16*

*Making a whip of cords, he drove all of them
out of the temple, both the sheep and the cattle.
He also poured out the coins of the money changers
and overturned their tables. He told those who were
selling the doves, "Take these things out of here!
Stop making my Father's house a marketplace!"*

Like many separated and divorced women, you may be tense because of all the complex bits of your life.

One woman said that she felt like a jigsaw puzzle and that she could never quite fit all the pieces together in the correct way. She said that she was constantly making lists—then lists of lists—in order to stay organized. To get through each day, she had developed an amazing method of organization in her household. She always served supper at a certain time, helped the children with their homework, ushered them to the bathtub and finally put them in bed at precisely the same time every night.

She had become so rigid, out of perceived necessity, that she was truly miserable. All her happiness was gone while she was attempting to get everything done. When one of her toddlers asked her why she never smiled anymore, she knew that she had a big problem on her hands.

In her prayer time, she told God that she was unhappy and asked for help. She asked God for his promise of true joy and for a way out of her situation. Then this woman decided to cook more modest meals, give the children baths every other night and play with them right before bed. They rediscovered joy and fun in their lives as they laughed together. She let her house get somewhat cluttered—and no one noticed or even cared.

Flexibility and being willing to bend enriched both her life and those of her children.

*John 16:20*

*"Very truly, I tell you, you will weep and mourn, but the world will rejoice; you will have pain, but your pain will turn into joy."*

Are you satisfied with what you have in life?

Many of us are always wishing that we could have more—more money, newer clothes, more vacations with the children, greater inner strength or more prestige at work. We may want more new furniture, increased happiness, greater amounts of leisure time or a bigger house like our neighbor's. We just might constantly be wanting something newer, bigger or better.

We can have something newer, bigger and better if we put God first place in our lives. New and improved is definitely available!

You can have more strength, joy, hope, and peace with your Father by your side. Try to focus on what you do have—instead of on what you don't have—as you see your neighbor's new sports car. Thank God for all that he has provided for you from a material standpoint—food, shelter and clothing. Then thank him for all your spiritual blessings—salvation, protection and comfort. Acknowledge his guidance for helping you to survive marital separation and divorce.

You can have a sense of satisfaction, knowing that you have obeyed God and tried in every way possible to salvage your marriage. You can be satisfied with the knowledge that you have continued to strive to set a Christian example for your children.

Be satisfied with who you are as a woman of God. You can experience true satisfaction by abiding in God's will and walking with him every day.

*Acts 20:33*

*"I coveted no one's silver or gold or clothing."*

Christ, the Good Shepherd, loves you and knows your name—your very own name. Think about that and ponder what it means for your Lord to know you individually. You belong to him and you are quite special in his sight.

He protects you from harm and wants only good for you. He leads you in the right directions in life, not down some dark and scary path. Jesus modeled behaviors for you to imitate.

Just as sheep belong to their shepherd, you belong to the Lord. He truly wants you to be in his flock every day as he shows you the best food available through him.

You simply have to be willing to follow where he leads you. Just like a sheep with its shepherd, you must follow your Shepherd each day in order to receive daily nourishment. And if you follow Jesus, you will have an incredibly full and abundant life as his special child!

Christ Jesus knows your name and calls for you. Listen.

*John 10:3*

*"The gatekeeper opens the gate for him, and the sheep
hear his voice. He calls his own sheep
by name and leads them out."*

Are you in need of a good gripe session?

Then feel free to talk, blow off steam, scream and get it all out. Call your best girlfriend and invite her over for dessert. And as you eat a brownie topped with vanilla ice cream, you can complain for a couple of hours about anything that is on your heart and mind. Are you still angry at your husband? Did your car insurance bill just double since your son obtained his driver's license? Has your teenager disobeyed her curfew hour once again? Or has your toddler started to wet his pants since his father left home? Did your divorce notice arrive in the mail today? Is your job stressful and hectic this month? Maybe you are just tired—exhausted from maintaining a rigorous schedule of activities. Are you upset because you have been divorced for a year and no one has even asked you out for a date? Perhaps you're tired of being alone . . . or feeling like you're missing out on life in general.

You don't have to feel guilty about griping on an occasional basis. Remember not to abuse this privilege, because no one wants to hear you talk about your divorce every single day! A weekly or monthly gripe session with a trusted friend can actually be very therapeutic and can be a sure step in the healing process following divorce. These sessions can also lower your blood pressure and help you feel less depressed.

And don't expect your need for talking to a loyal companion to go away just because you might have recently gotten divorced. This need will continue to re-surface, because it may take you a couple of years to feel as though you have talked it all out. So keep talking to God and your Christian friends when you need to gripe!

*Habakkuk 1:2*

*O Lord, how long shall I cry for help,*
*and you will not listen?*

Approach God with confidence and continually seek his will for your life. Acknowledge that God is God of the entire universe. He is in charge of everything— your past, present and future. He knows all things and is in control. Just stop to really consider God's power; he is indeed majestic and awesome!

God is real to those who believe in him and can speak to you through the Bible. Be reverent as you read the Word and pray. Keep your silence and listen to him. God wants to communicate with you and wants to guide your daily life.

Do not make the mistake of assuming that God is only in heaven, far removed from your joys and sorrows on a daily basis. Nothing could be further from the truth. Even though he most certainly is all-knowing and all-powerful, he still cares about your individual marriage, separation, reconciliation and divorce. His power, joy, hope and peace are available to you now.

Call on God, keep silence, listen and wait.

*Habakkuk 2:20*

*But the Lord is in his holy temple;*
*let all the earth keep silence before him!*

A friend of mine from church, divorced from her first husband and currently remarried to a great guy, is always ready to listen to any woman undergoing separation. Women with marital troubles feel as though she truly understands all their feelings of anguish because she has experienced them firsthand.

This friend's present husband has a very dependable habit of giving hugs to all the women who are either separated or divorced whenever they are all together, such as at a church dinner. In fact, he is well known for greeting each individual woman in that particular setting with a huge bear hug.

My friend readily acknowledged that the terrible span of time during separation and divorce was "a lonely walk" for her. She reassures women that they are never truly alone and that they always have God and their Christian family by their sides. This encouragement speaks volumes to all these struggling women.

She once explained that she had instructed her husband that one of the ways in which he could actually demonstrate his love for her was to reach out to all of her separated and divorced friends. She had told him how lonely she felt during her past marital trials, and she asked him to freely hug all women of our church who are in similar straits.

"Do you need a hug today?" was her kind husband's greeting every Sunday morning at church where he was an usher. Our lonely walks were certainly a bit less lonely because of this Christian couple's loving actions.

*John 16:4*

*"I did not say these things to you from the beginning, because I was with you."*

Do you have or are you striving for the mind of Christ?

Christ was humble and ready to be used by God for divine purposes, while yielding to his Father's plans. Any Christian woman can desire the mind of Christ in this fashion. Admittedly, it would be easy to be self-absorbed and focus only on your desires during this trying time of separation, but you need to ask yourself if this is in line with God's ideals for your life.

Have you begun to work longer and longer hours at the office, trying to save money for the new car you want, while asking all your friends to care for your children? Are your children asking you to come home earlier in order to attend a school function with them?

Are you stubbornly refusing to attend counseling sessions and work toward the possibility of marital reconciliation? Is your husband truly trying to change his behaviors, while you have closed your heart and mind?

Ask God to help you give up insisting on your own way. Your heavenly Father can guide, mold, lead and steer you in the right paths of life. He can alter both your attitude and your actions in a way that will serve him and give you his unending joy. God can and will use you for his glory during this awful thing called divorce. No, it won't be easy. And, yes, you might be alone temporarily while you grow closer to God and begin to know yourself again. But aligning yourself with the Lord and having his mind will give you a far better reward of peace in the end.

Pray that God will empty you and fill you with his purposes and a desire for obedience.

*Philippians 2:5*

*Let the same mind be in you that was in Christ Jesus.*

As women, we have all heard messages to take care of ourselves. "Take care of number one because if you don't, nobody else will." It is a popular selfish refrain of society today.

It is very true that you should care for your physical, emotional, social and spiritual needs. You are in a unique position during separation and divorce. You must handle your needs by yourself and you have responsibilities to many other people as well. However, strive to find a balance when caring for yourself and others at the same time.

If you are a mother, you must provide for your children in a way that you never have before. They are probably confused and frightened over the prospect of their father living elsewhere. Your son and daughter have so many needs right now that you might be spinning in circles just trying to wash laundry, dry tears and help with homework. It can certainly be overwhelming if you are in the position of having very little help from their father.

You might be the primary caretaker for aging parents. This is a very common situation for middle aged women whether single, married, separated or divorced. And if you have been in this role for the past several years, the expectation is probably that you continue in this capacity even if you are struggling with your marriage.

Naturally, your job still requires that you give of your time and energies.

Pray to God that he will direct you each day in your ministry to others, as you ponder where to place your time and talents. You can show God's love, learn time management skills, gain personal satisfaction and serve God while you selflessly serve others.

*Philippians 2:4*

*Let each of you look not to your own interests,*
*but to the interests of others.*

Do you continue to doubt God?

Can your marriage be reconciled? Will he provide the money to finance your son's college education? Is it possible to ever recover from such a severely broken heart? Will you be financially able to afford to stay in your family home? Can your children remain emotionally and spiritually stable through separation and divorce? Is there any possible way that you can ever forgive your husband for his actions? Can you forgive yourself for specific marital behaviors? Will your parents be able to remain in the same room with your former husband during your daughter's upcoming wedding?

Some doubt is quite normal and natural. Therefore, don't feel badly because you occasionally doubt God—and perhaps question your own sanity as you survive divorce proceedings.

Try to develop a battle plan for doubt—for those times when you temporarily don't have enough faith in God. Pray, and ask God to draw you closer to him. You belong to God. Spend time with God himself, not simply reading books about him. And remember to listen for his answers.

Ask your friends to have faith *for* you, even if you waver periodically. I called a wonderful Christian friend many times during my separation and divorce when I needed a shoulder to cry on. And, more often than not, she would assure me that she had prayed for me that very morning. What comfort! She exhorted me to remain strong in my faith, even if I was having a rough day.

Rest assured that your moments of doubt can and will resolve themselves if you remain in God's Word and in Christian fellowship.

*Matthew 28:17*

*When they saw him, they worshiped him;*
*but some doubted.*

No woman is immune from trouble, even if she is a Christian. Faith in God does not serve as a barrier to ward off turbulence in our world, and neither does it defend you from all hurt and pain. Your faith is not a layer of insulation to keep you away from the trauma of separation or divorce.

One woman was divorced from her husband of many years, and their two daughters were living with her in the family home. She was facing a lengthy list of worries—long work hours in an unpleasant workplace, the failing of a high school calculus course by one child, college choices for another and receiving no child support monies from her unemployed former husband. Due to the overwhelming nature of her concerns, she felt as though she had no place to turn and was becoming depressed. A friend listened to her as she cried and began to pray with her. At her friend's suggestion, she approached her pastor for counseling sessions, which were provided free of charge. She told the minister about all her misery, and they jointly worked toward some solutions.

God will not shield you from problems and trials. You are human, after all, and difficulties will come your way. But the Lord is most surely present—in the middle of all the mayhem and upheaval—to comfort you and enable you to persevere.

Therefore, place one foot in front of the other and move forward with God's help. Look upward.

*Philippians 4:19*

*And my God will fully satisfy every need of yours according to his riches in glory in Christ Jesus.*

Get in the healthy habit of drinking water every day for the rest of your life.

Drinking water has many potential benefits. It keeps your skin clearer, helps you stay more mentally focused, reduces swelling of your feet in the hot summer months, cools you off and assists in maintaining your weight—or even losing a few pounds. Once you're accustomed to drinking water on a regular basis, no other fluid will truly quench your thirst. Apple juice or lemonade may help for a moment in the summertime heat, but only water has the ability to fully help satisfy your body's need for fluid.

Likewise, partaking of the Living Water has many benefits. Giving yourself to God and your life to Christ can produce true joy and peace. You can avail yourself of God's power to endure your current trials, and you can experience strength to withstand life's temptations if you have the Living Water. This water can refresh you when you are emotionally drained, can fill you even in separation and divorce and can invigorate you for another day as a single mother. Gulping the true water of the Lord will renew your body, spirit and soul.

Just as drinking water is essential for your physical body, only the water of Jesus Christ can completely satisfy your spiritual needs and thirst.

*John 4:10*

*Jesus answered her, "If you knew the gift of God, and who it is that is saying to you, 'Give me a drink,' you would have asked him, and he would have given you living water."*

Your marital difficulties, separation and impending divorce are God's battle. Let him fight for you. You may feel frightened and exhausted as you struggle through the misery of indecision, fear, anger and loneliness. Do you ever feel like just giving up? Then by all means, go ahead and give up. Give it all up—to God.

God will triumph as you battle temptation, financial difficulty, children's tears and heartbreak. He is bigger than we are. In fact, we cannot even fathom his greatness. We are limited as humans, but God is limitless. You may feel weak, but God is very strong. Perhaps you feel fearful, but God is able to conquer fears. You might be unable to solve your current problems alone because you've been trying for several months now, but God is quite able.

So quit trying to fight all your daily battles alone. God has a battle plan, and it is filled with his wonderful strategies. Wave that white flag in front of God and surrender to him. Verbally give him your marital woes as you recognize your weaknesses and then get on your knees. Pray and ask God to direct your life and joyfully let him do his work.

What a privilege and comfort to be able to give God all our problems and rest in the knowledge that he will take charge.

*2 Chronicles 20:15*

*He said, "Listen, all Judah and inhabitants of Jerusalem, and King Jehoshaphat: Thus says the Lord to you: 'Do not fear or be dismayed at this great multitude; for the battle is not yours but God's.'"*

The beatitudes can give you, a woman in separation or divorce, a blueprint for living in relationship to God and your fellow man. These scriptural guidelines describe how to be a joyful follower of Christ, and they are particularly applicable in this uncertain time of your life. However, to some degree, they might be contrary to what you've heard all your life. Maybe you've been told to "just give people what they deserve." In contrast, the beatitudes offer a more Christ-like life.

What does it mean to be poor in spirit and have the kingdom of heaven? You just might feel poor in spirit right now. But remember that only when you are empty can you be filled with Christ, who emptied himself to be crucified. God can beautifully mold you into one of his own if you're destitute from a spiritual viewpoint. God wants you to completely depend on him, and not totally on yourself or others. What a paradox – only when you are poor in spirit do you have the wonderful opportunity to become spiritually rich and filled.

My pastor once preached a sermon about the kingdom of God, and declared that it starts small and then can grow large. He went on further to say that each time God's will is done, there is a little bit of the kingdom of God added in that action. Therefore, God's kingdom can get stronger with each small step you take, even though badly wounded by marital turmoil and pain. The kingdom of God is not a church or a specific location but instead begins when you, a woman quite poor in spirit, choose God's will in the face of hurt and a broken heart.

Poverty can lead to true riches. Being poor of spirit and then choosing to follow God and live in his kingdom will lead to happiness and your Father's blessing.

*Matthew 5:3*

*"Blessed are the poor in spirit,*
*for theirs is the kingdom of heaven."*

Any woman who is enduring the agony of watching her marriage dissolve is certainly in mourning. You may mourn for your own lost romantic dreams or for the lack of seeing your children each day. This thing called alternating weekend custody may be causing you untold anguish. Your sadness may, despite the passage of time, still result in tears and a wet pillow as you try to get to sleep. Do you still have arguments with your former husband months after the divorce is final, causing you to grieve for the man he used to be?

Perhaps you're also mourning for your children, as they plod to their father's house through their own tears. Maybe your six-year-old daughter doesn't want to spend the night with her father and his new bride, because she misses her own bed and the comforts of home. Or perhaps your son continues to be angry and mumbles curse words about your separation.

Go ahead and let some more tears flow as you are mourning this terrible loss. Continue to visit your pastor or Christian counselor on a regular basis and vent your feelings in a safe environment. *Your feelings are completely normal, and you're entitled to each one of them.*

Be assured that God will comfort you as you stay close to him. Pray that your Father will help you avoid alcohol, food, drugs, other addictions, and extramarital sex as ways for comfort. Instead, God will send the Great Comforter in the Holy Spirit to give you some balm for your wounds. He can most assuredly soothe your soul. Your Creator will wrap his arms around you and give comfort that is true, real and lasting.

*Matthew 5:4*

*"Blessed are those who mourn,
for they will be comforted."*

A meek Christian woman has the opportunity to reflect Christ in her life. Meekness is not to be equated with weakness, but rather with humility. Christ was humble and sacrificed himself on the cross.

God wants you to be strong in his power alone and not a weakling in the world. You're able to be strong in the Lord precisely because of your meekness, but you shouldn't falsely elevate yourself because of your Christian faith or any worldly attribute. If you let Christ have first place and put yourself second, you will be tremendously blessed in life. You can inherit the earth and all the good things that God has planned for you if you live in him, because he does indeed have marvelous plans for your future.

A physician, separated from her husband due to extreme physical abuse, was relying on her own strength and power in order to cope with her horror. Sadly, she was continuing to "take him back" and the cycle of battering was becoming more intense with each reconciliation attempt. Finally, her pastor was able to guide her in a different direction – one of admitting that she needed God's help to separate from her abusive husband until he was able to seek help and demonstrate true change. This doctor totally humbled herself, asked for God's incredible strength, yielded to him, and then inherited a much better plan for her life here on earth.

This concept illustrates another paradox in the beatitudes—be meek and, as a result, be powerful in God. Claim this power, persevere, and inherit the good on earth planned for you.

*Matthew 5:5*

*"Blessed are the meek, for they will inherit the earth."*

Have you ever been extremely hungry? Maybe you have tried to lose five pounds in two weeks in order to try to fit into a new dress to wear to a Christmas party. Or your doctor may have told you to drop 15 pounds in the span of three months in order to avoid being placed on medication for high blood pressure. Remember those hunger pangs as you denied yourself a piece of chocolate cake or a scoop of your favorite strawberry ice cream? Perhaps you actually salivated as you saw some warm oatmeal raisin cookies in your neighbor's kitchen. You certainly might have thought you were starving at that precise moment!

Right now, imagine being that hungry for God's Word and his righteousness—spiritual starvation. Maybe you're at the point of being so ravenous for God in your life that you want nothing else. In the past you sought God's direction as you considered marital separation, reconciliation or divorce. Don't stop seeking now. Instead, continue to search every day.

What is the cure for spiritual starvation? An open heart for the Lord, for his ways, and for obedience. God is waiting to show you his wonderfully good plan for your life.

All too often, the advice that a separated or divorced woman receives from well-meaning friends is just to "have a little fun." This path may be tempting, especially if you feel emotionally neglected and hungry. But instead, make the conscious decision to fill your hunger with the Lord in order to be truly well-filled.

Even in the presence of hurt and sorrow, your cup can be filled to overflowing as you turn your eyes toward your heavenly Father.

*Matthew 5:6*

*"Blessed are those who hunger and thirst for righteousness, for they will be filled."*

What exactly is mercy? A pastor once used the following story to illustrate this concept: A father was very angry at his son for disobeying and stealing some money from his mother's wallet. In the heat of the moment, the father began to repeatedly spank the boy until he began to cry out and scream. He begged his father to have mercy, to stop punishing him. And luckily for this young boy, his dad stopped hitting him at that very moment—showing mercy instead of justice.

God displays mercy toward us each day. Even though our actions will often bring consequences, he doesn't punish us for any sins, although he does correct us as a loving Father. Instead, God allows us to ask for mercy and grace through the cross. As imperfect women, we know that mercy from God is definitely close to the top of our wish lists!

But you may be asking yourself what mercy has to do with separation or divorce. It's important for you to show mercy toward others if you are to receive mercy. For example, be merciful if your former husband is an hour late to pick up your daughter to take her out for Saturday lunch or when he plans an outing with his girlfriend instead of attending your son's soccer game. Certainly tell him that you hope for improvement in the future, but don't berate him because you can't control those actions. And getting terribly upset simply raises your own blood pressure. Instead, enjoy those few extra minutes with your children, and they will see your dignity and grace.

We are promised to be recipients of heavenly mercies, if we can find it in ourselves to accept the challenge of asking for the Holy Spirit's help and dispensing some mercy of our own.

*Matthew 5:7*

*"Blessed are the merciful, for they will receive mercy."*

The beatitudes promise that the pure in heart will see God—actually see God. Doesn't that sound wonderful? To actually see your heavenly Father would be awesome.

How can you get to that point? By having a heart for the Lord, one that is pure in purpose—unblemished and totally clean. Then you can know God here on earth and in heaven.

Admittedly, you have probably been in the middle of countless impure behaviors and actions over the past few months or even years. You might have been involved in a marriage filled with patterns of domestic violence, substance abuse, pornography addiction, verbal abuse, adultery or abandonment. Now you may be so entrenched in the daily grind of getting up and going to work in order to afford a house payment that you don't exactly feel pure of heart in a heavenly sense. Or you may still be crying in the bed for six hours a day and suffering from depression over a surprise separation from your husband of 14 years. Are you still so angry that you continue to have wicked thoughts about harming him every day? You might feel that you don't have a pure bone in your body right this very minute, and you can be assured that some of these thoughts are perfectly natural.

But you need to ask yourself if you want to continue to have this focus forever. Work, crying and hatred shouldn't be your life's goals. Instead, try asking God to take control, yield to his leading, and make a decision for purity of heart. Let him be your aim. In this way you will definitely be able to see God at work in your life every single day, and others will be able to see your faith as well.

*Matthew 5:8*

*"Blessed are the pure in heart, for they will see God."*

It is often very hard to be a peacemaker as a woman in separation or divorce!

One friend shared the following story: Her former husband called her on the phone, accusing her of ruining the Thanksgiving holiday for his new bride. This friend and her three toddlers had been asked to go to her grandmother's house to eat turkey and dressing at 3:00 p.m., and her former husband was quite angry. He had planned to take the children out to a restaurant for a Thanksgiving Day buffet meal at the exact same time but had not bothered to share this information with anyone. "You're just trying to mess up the holiday for everybody," he yelled into the telephone receiver. "You could have told me before now," she yelled back. Just before slamming the phone down in her ear, her ex-husband informed her that she was disturbed and unreasonable. Definitely not a peaceful exchange of words, and she did not feel like a peacemaker! God urged this woman to be calm and peaceful with her own words, and to avoid screaming in return. Unfortunately, this heated exchange caused everyone involved to be in tears before the issues could be resolved.

God does desire peace for you, and living within his will leads to peace. Make a conscious choice to respond with words of peace, because God doesn't want you to retaliate with ugly words and actions if they are hurled your way. Your children will also learn God's ways of peace from your example.

Ask the Holy Spirit for help, practice peace, and live as a child of God.

*Matthew 5:9*

*"Blessed are the peacemakers,*
*for they will be called children of God."*

Take a moment to recall a time during the past year during which you felt persecuted.

When you scheduled an appointment for joint marital counseling.

When you separated from your husband in order to protect your children from further physical violence at their father's hand.

When you refused to allow your children to visit their father for the weekend when he came to pick them up in an obvious state of alcohol intoxication.

When you went to divorce court.

Perhaps you endured verbal abuse and taunting from people during such times. If you're like most women in these situations, you have been told repeatedly that all the marital problems were your fault, and you were probably told this "fact" during a rather heated shouting match. Indeed, you may have been persecuted because you insisted on living according to God's righteous laws.

Christ assures us that the kingdom of heaven belongs to those who suffer persecution for the sake of righteousness. Continue to be steadfast in God's assurances that the Word directs you in paths that are good and true. Cling to Christ's examples of right and wrong, and watch your faith mushroom in its growth.

*Matthew 5:10*

*"Blessed are those who are persecuted for righteousness' sake, for theirs is the kingdom of heaven."*

A dear Christian friend was separated from her husband of 15 years due to his infidelity. He was in the middle of a hideous affair with his secretary when my friend discovered this truth. When he was confronted and refused to cease the affair, she asked him to move out of their home while she remained there with their three-year-old daughter.

This wonderful woman gathered herself, continued to teach her child Christian patterns of living, and struggled with everyday life as best as she could. Sadly, her husband was furious that she had asked him to leave. He called her a false Christian and laughed as she took their child to church. She ignored his verbal insults and demeaning threats, and muddled through each day alone.

Her husband got more and more angry at her refusal to let him have his way and began to circulate rumors about her in their town. He told his work colleagues that his affair was simply a way to get back at his wife for her own affair, and he attempted to elicit sympathy for his plight. On the phone with her mother-in-law one day, she discovered that her husband had even told his own family these same lies about her committing adultery.

This friend denied the rumors when asked about them, held her head high, and persevered through the very tough times. She served as an example to her child and set her eyes on God's earthly and heavenly rewards that she knew were coming.

The beatitudes from the book of Matthew offer insight for all women who are separated and divorced. They can help us to grow in our faith and live more peaceful and joyful lives.

*Matthew 5:11–12*

*"Blessed are you when people revile you and persecute you and utter all kinds of evil against you falsely on my account. Rejoice and be glad, for your reward is great in heaven, for in the same way they persecuted the prophets who were before you."*

Go ahead and smile. Think about your best female friends and let a huge grin spread over your face. Women understand other women in ways that no one else possibly could. We're able to laugh, cry, talk, cook, work, play, giggle, plot, and scream together. We can spend hours talking and forget all about cooking that spaghetti that we had planned for supper. We will also encourage a friend who is also separated or divorced to call us at 3:00 a.m. if she needs an ear—it's just what we do. Most women are nurturing, supportive and caring.

Treasure these friendships as you go about your journey of separation, divorce or reconciliation because they are true gifts from God above.

A group of single and divorced women from my church gathers every few weeks for food and fellowship. Every person brings a dish to share, so the meal is not a financial burden for anyone. One fall Saturday night we had gathered at one woman's house at 6:15 p.m. for appetizers, and began talking. We discussed every topic imaginable – money, lack of money, weight, dates, lack of dates, children and work. During the main course we proceeded to discuss our pastor's inspirational sermons, house decorating, house cleaning, lack of cleaning, husbands, former husbands, attorneys, Sunday School, parents and the upcoming holidays. Then we ate dessert and began to talk about getting older as we drank our coffee. Absolutely no subject was off limits. Next we began to play a popular board game, laughed like crazy, and finally broke the party up at about 12:30 in the morning. After all, we had to go to church in a few short hours!

Female friends can be great when they love the Lord and each other.

*Proverbs 31:30*

*Charm is deceitful, and beauty is vain,*
*but a woman who fears the Lord is to be praised.*

In your new existence as a woman in separation or divorce, you must choose. Will you be more like Martha or Mary?

We are told in the New Testament that Martha opened her home to Jesus. She made all the very necessary preparations of cooking, cleaning and serving others. Martha, the older sister in the family, took charge and wanted everything to be right for the Lord. She was a hard worker and loved Jesus very much. These preparations were vital, because someone had to perform all the necessary functions associated with having people in a home to eat a meal.

On the other hand, Mary sat at the feet of Christ. She loved the Lord, valued her time with him, and consciously chose to remain by his side. Mary allowed Martha to continue in her service without offering to help, because she wanted to spend these precious moments with Jesus.

This biblical account holds many lessons for women in times of transition. It is so incredibly easy to focus on your everyday necessary chores that you neglect time with God and family. Of course, you must physically care for your children and your home. Cooking, cleaning, laundry, homework and grocery shopping are necessary parts of everyday life. And Christ would not be honored if we neglected these duties. But remember to spend time with your children and get to know them, instead of always doing tasks for them. Balance is the key.

Likewise, service to God in a church is quite important, but it is not a substitute for a personal relationship with Christ. Don't allow service to get in the way of worship and intimacy.

*Luke 10:41–42*

*But the Lord answered her, "Martha, Martha, you are worried and distracted by many things; there is need of only one thing. Mary has chosen the better part, which will not be taken away from her."*

Beware of the big wave.

You might feel as though you have life under control. Work is going smoothly, and your income is almost enough to make financial ends meet on the home front. Things are on an even keel right now as you are attending joint marital counseling sessions with your husband, in the hope of becoming a family together again. The children appear to be adjusting to rotating between two homes. And you're caught up with the necessary housework, as you just finished cleaning the children's rooms that had gotten completely out of control. You can let yourself exhale with a big sigh, and allow your shoulders to relax for a minute or two. Wonderful!

Then along comes a big wave that knocks you completely over—and under.

Maybe your husband started using drugs again and quit attending his recovery program. Or he is still calling his girlfriend on the phone, after denying any further contact with her during a counseling session. On a whim, have you gone on a shopping binge to cope? Perhaps your son just told you that he wants to leave your home and live with his father on a full-time basis. You might have just learned that you're in danger of losing your job because of a possible layoff.

A Christian counselor once said that these occurrences are like big waves. These emotional waves, just like those at the ocean, can take your breath away. You may not see clearly for a while, as you try to get the water out of your eyes and stand in the middle of a huge wave. This new revelation may startle you so badly that you literally lose your balance.

Just as a wave suddenly knocks you over, it will recede. Regain your footing, and look forward in order to anticipate the next immediate wave. God is there. He will not leave you.

*Psalm 34:19*

*Many are the afflictions of the righteous,*
*but the Lord rescues them from them all.*

Do you always seem to be remembering some terrible event from your marriage? You might have just recovered from one of those gigantic waves, only to be assaulted by a memory that makes you ache.

Recollections such as these are entirely normal.

One friend thought that she was going crazy, because even after 18 months of separation she couldn't clear all of these events from her brain. She tried. She truly tried to completely erase them all. On one particularly rough day, she began to cry while paying yet another $100 to her attorney. Her husband had abandoned the family after she had weathered very serious health problems, but insisted that he didn't want a divorce. He informed her that he would just continue to live a single life and remain married to her as long as it was convenient for him. All of his ugly comments periodically came flooding back, as her erasure attempts had failed.

She related these concerns to her counselor the next time she went to see him. She felt frustrated and asked for his magic "cure." He assured her that women are different than men, and that the female sex is more emotional by God's design. Naturally, we will remember verbal taunts and emotional wrongs long after men wipe them from their memory bank. But the counselor comforted her, saying that time would diminish the sting of recall. He went on to say that every month that passed would help her take each time of remembrance in greater stride, and recover more quickly than the previous month.

His comments were wonderfully comforting and provided her with some reassurance of sanity, and they have proven to be true over a period of time.

*Ecclesiastes 3:4*

*A time to weep, and a time to laugh;*
*a time to mourn, and a time to dance.*

Who is God? Describe who God is.

Holy. Glorious. Good. Wonderful. Almighty. Worthy. Great. Total. Giving. Awesome. All. Deliverer. Merciful. Right. Majestic. Perfection. Faithful. Provider. Forgiving. Righteous. Wisdom. Compassionate. Foundation. Healer. Renewal. Enduring. Conqueror. King. High. Exalted. Refuge. Forever. Grace. Protector. Justice. Generous. Steadfast. Covering. Powerful. Always. Helper. Excellent. Fortress. Truth. Unfailing. Lord. Answer. Sovereign. Available. Open. Knowing. Close. Breath. Ruler. Continuing. Near. Rich. Triune. Strong. Mercy. Redeemer. Friend. Full. Loving.

God created the earth, everyone in it, and everything on it. Praise him as you talk with your children today; give him credit and glory for his goodness to your family. Sing a song of praise to God, both today and always. He is your Refuge. Remember all that he has done for you in the past and imagine all that he can and will do for you in the future!

It is impossible to adequately describe our heavenly Father, as we are only human. But we can bask in his love and tell others of everything he has done for us, how he is carrying us through our hurt and pain.

*Jude 1:25*

*To the only God our Savior, through Jesus Christ our Lord, be glory, majesty, power, and authority, before all time and now and forever. Amen.*

What are your excuses for not following God right now, for not spending time with your Father, or for not maintaining fellowship with other Christians?

Sunday morning is a great time for some sleep. After all, the weekdays are incredibly tiring.

You must clean your house—your bathtub even has some orange scum in it.

Work is very demanding, and you have to pay for your car insurance all by yourself now.

You're even looking for a second part-time job, in order to pay for your son's college tuition.

Exercise class three times a week is very important to you as you deal with your stress.

You're going on a date for the first time since your divorce, and you're shopping for new clothes.

Carpool for your daughter's soccer practice two times a week keeps you on your toes.

You must attend a PTA meeting at your son's elementary school tonight.

The neighborhood block party is coming up, and you're cooking a new recipe to serve.

There is nothing inherently wrong with the items on this list, or on your personal to-do list. Prayerfully consider your priorities and analyze any reason for either a lack of time to foster a relationship with Christ or lack of obedience.

Consider Abram. He was 75 years old when he left all his worldly possessions and the comforts of home to obey God. He dropped everything and did as God directed. Abram made no excuses and, as a result, was blessed beyond measure in God's kingdom. What a wonderful example for us as women in separation or divorce.

*Genesis 12:4*

*So Abram went, as the Lord had told him; and Lot went with him. Abram was seventy-five years old when he departed from Haran.*

Do you have some good memories from your marriage? Then allow yourself to think about them. Don't allow anyone to convince you that your entire marriage was totally bad.

A college friend who is separated from her husband was talking and crying about their courtship years. She remembered how sweet her husband had been during those days and spoke about a special necklace that he had given her. After going to her jewelry box and fishing through the bottom drawer, she pulled out a beautiful gold heart locket with their pictures in it. He had given it to her one beautiful summer day on the anniversary of their having dated for one year. They had been on a picnic in a park that they had considered their special place. She wondered aloud what had happened to him to have changed so much through the years. My friend recalled her husband's many extra-marital girlfriends, but insisted that he had once been so wonderful to her.

Another woman fondly remembered her husband during the years that he coached their daughter's softball team. He had regularly taken their daughter to practice, thrown the ball with her in the back yard to help her improve catching ability, and gone to countless games at the ball field. And now, her husband wanted nothing to do with his daughter. "It's like he is an entirely different man. But I won't let my husband take away the good memories that I have of all our years together," she insisted.

It is wise not to let another person rob you of good memories. Instead, treasure those times, because both you and your children may need them to help you endure some painful days.

*Luke 2:51*

*Then he went down with them and came to Nazareth, and was obedient to them. His mother treasured all these things in her heart.*

God is molding you into something beautiful.

Have you ever seen a potter at work? My daughter once took a pottery class, and I was amazed to see this art form in action. She started out with a brown lump of something wet, cold, and a bit yucky. Then she proceeded to rotate this glob of clay on a wheel with her own little hands, changing it into a beautiful shape that grew to be completely unrecognizable from its humble original beginnings. The bowls that emerged at the end of the process were quite pretty, and they still decorate our home.

Likewise, women are often yucky lumps of clay on the day of separation from their husbands. A total mess! They may be weak, not truly themselves, and controlled by an earthly man instead of by their heavenly Father. Separated women frequently feel that they are worthless and unable to survive an existence without their husbands. But over time, God is able to transform women in separation or divorce, by the power of the Holy Spirit, into women who love him more than ever before, into Christian women who are not perfect, but who yearn to be more like Christ.

God is the master potter; we can be clay in his hands and allow him to shape us. He can indeed work miracles!

*Isaiah 64:8*

*Yet, O Lord, you are our Father; we are the clay, and you are our potter; we are all the work of your hand.*

Ask God to completely protect you.

God can protect you from evil thoughts, from dwelling on past negative events that almost robbed you of your sanity, from hatred, and from depression. He can also protect your children. God is mighty, vast and limitless in power.

One woman in my community who had been separated for six months was struggling with the issue of whether to allow her children to spend time with her husband and his girlfriend. She thought that the moral influence would not be positive for her young girls who were nine and ten years old. But her husband stated flatly that he wouldn't spend any time at all with his daughters unless his girlfriend was there. They were touting themselves as a new family already. The girls cried to see their father, and the woman relented. She prayed, and prayed often.

Then she asked God to protect the girls when they were with their father and his girlfriend. She did not agree to let them sleep over at his house while the girlfriend was there, but gave them her blessing to go to eat with them, shop, or see a movie. In this way, they were still able to see their father.

This woman said that this decision was gut-wrenching, but she left it in God's protective hands. Then one day her daughters came home and surprised her by confirming that their parents were still married, and wondering why their father had a girlfriend who was living with him.

God had protected her daughters in many ways.

*Psalm 16:1*

*Protect me, O God, for in you I take refuge.*

What path do you want for your life? What dreams do you have, and what have you always wanted to do?

Go to college? Return to college to complete a degree that you started many years ago, before you had your first child? Be a more patient mother? Serve as a church deacon? Take a flower-arranging course at a local community college? Take dance classes, so that you could learn to waltz? Lose weight? Travel to London? Sleep all night long? Become healthier? Have red hair? Exercise regularly? Go on a church mission trip? Learn to play bagpipes? Bake homemade bread? Get a wild hairdo? Go to France to attend a week of cooking school? Serve as a volunteer at a homeless shelter? Hike the Appalachian Trail? Get a really great job? Clean your house thoroughly? Sing in the church choir, even though your voice is not star quality?

With God, all things are possible. God loves you immensely, and he cares about all of your hopes and dreams—even the wild and crazy ones. After all, he is the one who gave you a mind for dreaming. The future is truly limitless with God.

Choose God's path, and you are promised fullness of joy. You might not be able to book that flight to France tomorrow for cooking school, but you will have a full life of happiness in the Lord if you follow his directions for you. After all, his plans for you are infinitely better than what you can even imagine!

*Psalm 16:11*

*You show me the path of life. In your presence there is fullness of joy; in your right hand are pleasures forevermore.*

Have you ever wondered how long you might live?

My paternal grandmother died when she was 95 years old, after having a stroke that left her quite sick for two weeks prior to her death. I have many wonderful memories of my grandmother taking me shopping, putting my hair up in a fancy twist, saying prayers at the kitchen table, and wearing pink clothes. Ninety-five years is a long time to be on the earth—a very long time to be a wife, mother, and grandmother. Yet, she died.

One of my great-grandmothers lived to be over 75 years old and left a legacy of farming and hard work. I can still recall her favorite hymns. I also remember her wearing a brimmed bonnet to plant strawberries, which we picked each spring to make homemade ice cream and pies.

Another grandparent died while I was in college, but I still remember his quiet strength. My grandfather displayed family values and complete intolerance of certain actions, such as illegal business transactions. He made his mark in the community as a fair businessman and was well-respected.

Will your legacy be one of witness for the Lord? You will live for the number of days on earth that God decides and then you will surely die. You don't know when you will die and that's for the best. It is normal to occasionally wonder how long you might live, but don't allow yourself to dwell on this. Instead, decide to leave a Christian legacy of trust and obedience.

You can be true to him, even in the midst of your many trials. You have a tremendous opportunity to cast a long shadow that can exert a godly influence long after your earthly life.

*1 Chronicles 29:15*

*For we are aliens and transients before you, as were all our ancestors; our days on the earth are like a shadow, and there is no hope.*

Have you been feeling a tug lately?

Perhaps you're unsure of certain actions to take regarding reconciliation with your spouse, separation, or impending divorce. On Monday you might be mad enough to march down to the courthouse and demand an immediate divorce if such a thing were possible. But Tuesday morning, after calming down, you're more rational and prayerful. Maybe you really don't want a divorce after all, and you feel an inner voice telling you to wait.

This tugging may be the Holy Spirit guiding, leading, showing, and telling you which path to choose. The Holy Spirit can help you pray, transform your mental status, and point you directly to God. You cannot control the Holy Spirit, and at times, you may not be able to understand his working. That's normal, and it is part of God's plan. We are not meant to understand every spiritual concept while here on earth. Instead, thank God for the gift of this Comforter.

A pastor once said that if you feel the tug, you know the Holy Spirit is present and active in your life.

*John 3:8*

*"The wind blows where it chooses, and you hear the sound of it, but you do not know where it comes from or where it goes. So it is with everyone who is born of the Spirit."*

A Christian woman who is separated or divorced might try to fill her life with many different things.

New clothes, different bedroom furniture, borrowed dishes, or a new house might sound wonderful! At first glance, this new stuff promises to make you happy. After all, you'd look great in a new purple dress to wear to work. And you wouldn't have to look at the bed that you once slept in with your husband. Different dishes for breakfast each morning might remind you less of your former life. Certainly a totally different place to live would shed a changed perspective on your marital breakup.

But all of this stuff is momentary—it is not enough.

The only things that last and make a core difference are things of God. Belief in God the Father, Jesus Christ the Son and the Holy Spirit are eternal. This belief and acceptance can make your life abundantly full and meaningful, because earthly things can be empty and will fade away. The new dress might get torn, the different bedroom furniture could burn in a fire, borrowed dishes can shatter if dropped on the kitchen floor, and a new house could be lost in a financial battle with the bank.

But God is everlasting!

Most certainly, stuff is not enough.

*Matthew 10:39*

*Those who find their life will lose it, and those who lose their life for my sake will find it.*

Can you remember the last time you went to the dentist to have your teeth cleaned?

One friend was so muddled during the first year of separation from her husband that she totally forgot to go to the dentist for her regular check-up. The thought of any preventive care had gone completely out of her mind because she was so scattered. However, after she developed a throbbing toothache, she gave her dentist a call and went in to have the problem corrected. Sadly, she wound up having the tooth pulled because of a raging infection that was out of control by that point. She became quite sick, and was out of work for a week.

Remember to take care of yourself, as you care for others. Naturally, you're consumed by your own emotional pain and that of your children. Plus, you're busy arranging visitation schedules with your former husband, or you may have an older parent who needs your physical assistance due to a chronic illness. Maybe your neighbor's dog might have just bitten your toddler as she played out in the back yard. Your plate is full to the point of overflowing!

But you can't care for others if you're sick. If your dental appointment is overdue, call your dentist today and schedule a time to go. God made your body, and you need to keep it in good working condition in order to serve him and others.

God cares for both your spiritual and physical body.

*Romans 12:1*

*I appeal to you therefore, brothers and sisters, by the mercies of God, to present your bodies as a living sacrifice, holy and acceptable to God, which is your spiritual worship.*

It is normal to cry during marital difficulties, separation, divorce, and even after divorce. Grief takes many forms and might last for months or years, because your life has been irreversibly changed. Even though your marriage didn't last forever, your divorce probably will indeed last forever. More than likely, you won't be married to your former husband again. Allow yourself to cry and express sadness over the many losses you're enduring.

A woman who had been divorced for three months went shopping one Saturday morning in order to complete all the errands that she didn't have time for during the week. She left her young children at home in the care of a babysitter so that she could quickly polish off her chores. As she was walking by her favorite restaurant, she looked in to find her former husband and his new bride sitting there eating lunch together—in her favorite eatery! The one at which she could no longer afford to eat due to their high prices and her pinched financial status.

All of the unfairness of her separation and divorce slapped her in the face once more when she was out there on that sidewalk peering into that wonderful restaurant. She was working hard to care for their two children, and tears quickly sprang to her eyes when she saw her ex-husband.

She immediately ran to her car, drove home, hugged her children, and then went into her bedroom for a well-deserved cry. Tears bubbled over as she cried to the Lord. After a half-hour she was able to emerge from her room and tackle life again. Her tears had actually refreshed her and served as a much-needed emotional outlet.

*Psalm 3:4*

*I cry aloud to the Lord,*
*and he answers me from his holy hill.*

Christ can help you overcome any difficulty associated with marriage, separation, or divorce. Christianity does not guarantee you an immediate deliverance from all troubles, but you can be assured that God is present in the middle of your brokenness and imperfection.

Difficulty can strengthen you and help you to grow closer to God. Don't fight whatever difficulties you may be facing, but accept them as he gives you strength. Your heavenly Father is indeed strength itself! Some good can come out of your misery, because you can grow infinitely closer to your Lord as he uplifts you and carries you every day.

Let God be the first place you turn when you encounter difficulties during reconciliation, separation, or divorce. Always ask for his strength and guidance.

You will surely face more struggles and difficulties than you can imagine during this time of trial and grief, but you are not alone. The Lord will not abandon you—he is certain, sure, true. And in this knowledge, you can move forward.

*Judges 4:3*

*Then the Israelites cried out to the Lord for help.*

Take measures to keep you and your home safe if you are enduring an emotionally explosive separation or divorce. Tempers can flare, threats are sometimes issued, and your personal safety may become an issue.

If you receive hang-up phone calls at 3:00 a.m. or hear strange noises in the middle of the night, be sure to protect yourself. You might find it necessary to change the locks to the doors at your house. Some women are hesitant to take such a drastic measure, because they view it as the end of any trust that they may have in their husbands. They may fear that their husbands will immediately file for divorce if he can't gain entry into the marital residence, but that is not necessarily the case. After all, you are a woman all alone in a house and you may have small children in your charge. You might realize that you are not the only person with a key to your front door, resulting in a need for some semblance of control. Therefore, the safety of your family becomes an absolute priority.

Call a locksmith and make an appointment for him to come to your home. Changing the locks is not usually an extremely costly venture. One woman chose to have the locks changed to her outside doors during separation, and the locksmith gave her a very reasonable rate once she explained the circumstances. He even offered to let this woman pay him over the span of three months, if necessary.

Pray about your safety, and ask God to show you what you should do in order to be as physically safe as possible. Listen to him, and he will guide you.

*Psalm 18:3*

*I call upon the Lord, who is worthy to be praised,*
*so I shall be saved from my enemies.*

Sadly enough, ugliness often rears its head during marital strife and separation.

A work colleague, who had been married for 28 years, came into the office one Monday morning with bloodshot eyes and a tear-streaked face. She began to sob as she closed the door to her office. This woman had been completely devoted to her husband, and had seen him through graduate school and then the start of a glowing academic career. Their three sons were adults by this point and were parents themselves.

Her husband had told her the previous night that he was leaving home. He had a girlfriend who was 25 years younger and their affair had been going on for over a year. My friend was shocked. She had been totally clueless. She had no idea at all of what had been happening behind her back.

The really devastating turn of events happened next as she called her adult children to inform them of their impending separation. She was quite surprised to learn that her husband had already told the children of the marital demise and had warned them that their mother was emotionally unstable. He had actually called their mother schizophrenic and had told the children that she would lie about him and falsely accuse him of adultery. Her husband had completely turned the children against her, told them that the impending divorce was through no fault of his own, and called their mother a crazed woman who was hallucinating.

Naturally, this loving woman was devastated, but she felt totally unable to defend herself. Therefore, she felt that she had no choice but to hold her head high and continue to live a godly life. She prayed and trusted that the full truth would be revealed in God's time. Such ugly behaviors are not part of God's plan.

*Proverbs 11:20*

*Crooked minds are an abomination to the Lord, but those of blameless ways are his delight.*

Blessings come in many shapes and sizes.

A friend's budget was incredibly tight when she separated from her husband. She clipped every grocery coupon that she could find, bought new clothes only if they were on sale, made only the necessary house repairs, and was still unable to make financial sense of her budget.

One day her department secretary came in to work with a bag of clothes for her. Unfortunately, the secretary's cousin had gained about 25 pounds and could no longer fit into her great-looking clothes. Lucky for my friend! She was thrilled to accept these hand-me-downs, as she was very tired of wearing her one pair of black pants to work two or three days a week.

Then on another day she received a phone call from a neighbor whose mother had died and left a closet full of beautiful clothes, many brand-new with store price tags still attached. She wondered if my friend would like them, because it was common knowledge that her finances were limited. She literally jumped up and down, squealing with delight in her kitchen after getting this call.

God cares about every part of our lives—emotions, finances, spiritual wellness, physical health, and even clothing. And he is able to provide unexpected solutions when we have problems that confront us.

Pray about every obstacle that presents itself. It is truly wonderful to know that God is in charge.

*Matthew 10:31*

*"So do not be afraid; you are of
more value than many sparrows."*

God is everywhere, all-knowing and all-powerful. He made the universe and everything in it, and he is an awesome God!

He loves you, and wants you to have a relationship with him through Christ the Son. God is both vast and personal. He has sent his Holy Spirit to minister to you and comfort you during trying times.

God does not want to be ignored or rejected, and he commands reverence. Your heavenly Father wants you to have a healthy fear and respect for him in all stages of life. He demands your attention as his child and will lavish unfathomable blessings on you as you walk with him each day in trusting obedience.

Bow before God on your knees today in the quiet of your bedroom—early in the morning, midday, or at nighttime. Acknowledge him to be your Maker, the Source of all life and then thank him for all the goodness in your life.

Revere him.

*1 Peter 1:17*

*If you invoke as Father the one who judges all people impartially according to their deeds, live in reverent fear during the time of your exile.*

Do you long for spiritual milk?

A newborn baby longs for its mother's milk many times a day, and cries when there is none available. In fact, a baby will root around and try to find the source of the milk when she is hungry. This child absolutely will not stop until she is satisfied, and her stomach is filled.

Likewise, a new Christian longs for spiritual milk in order to mature and grow as a believer. A new believer reads the Bible, prays often, talks with other Christians, and seeks regular fellowship at a church in order to satisfy her appetite for things of God. This person is usually excited and preoccupied with learning and stretching the limits of her faith. Such a base is necessary to serve as a foundation of spirituality.

Even if you're a more mature believer, you can also continue to grow. Read God's Word, and seek out an organized Bible study group. This type of interaction can encourage a Christian at any time, but might be particularly important as you struggle with issues of separation or divorce. Always remember to pray. And make church attendance a good regular habit at this time, because you need to fellowship with others who will pray for you and your family.

This scripture passage urges us to long for pure, spiritual milk. Be certain that you seek only those pure godly beliefs. Yearn for the Word and its full truths.

Like a newborn baby, seek until you are receiving pure spiritual sustenance and then drink liberally. In this way, you can grow closer to God and maintain your Christian walk.

*1 Peter 2:2*

*Like newborn infants, long for the pure, spiritual milk,*
*so that by it you may grow into salvation.*

God is calling you.

Young or old. Christian or non-believer. Single, married, separated or divorced. Mother or childless. Beautiful or plain. Short or tall. Well-dressed or naked. Thin or full-figured. White, Black, Hispanic, Asian or mixed race. Rich or poor. Well-educated or not. Black-haired, red-haired, brunette, blonde or gray. Sick or well. Wrinkled or flawless. Working or unemployed.

God is calling and he has a plan for your life, a good and perfect plan. We need an open heart in order to hear God's call. Then we must be ready to listen, wait, and respond to our Father.

How can you commune with God? Through reading of the Word and through prayer. This wonderful privilege is always an open door for you.

Be ready to answer "Here I am" when God speaks in mysterious ways, leads you, and reveals his plans to you.

*1 Samuel 3:4*

*Then the Lord called, "Samuel! Samuel!"*
*and he said, "Here I am!"*

An acquaintance from church called recently, because she was having a really bad day and needed to talk with someone.

"I have that awful hollow feeling that comes when the children go to their father's house to spend a few days. It's just like an appendage has been cut off," she said. She went on to explain that the divorce had left her with a sense of brokenness and emptiness. But she admitted that she was even more broken and empty when her three wonderful daughters weren't with her, as they had been constantly during the marriage.

You will have some hollow feelings during your separation and divorce, too. They come with the territory, and they are almost unavoidable. And it is normal for you to feel this way—after all, you have experienced many losses! At times, your life might be emptier than it was last year. So go ahead and let yourself feel some of the pain, but try not to let it wholly consume you.

You can take measures to fill up that hollow space. Call a friend and talk, go to lunch, read, take a bubble bath, pray, play the piano, clean your kitchen, or just sit and think. A little bit of "down time" can recharge your batteries.

Those hollow moments will get better with time, and you will learn to enjoy your own company. Such times can help you to heal from your marriage and its disappointments, so you won't be constantly mired down in the past.

Remember that you are never truly alone. God has sent the Holy Spirit to comfort you.

*Numbers 6:24*

*The Lord bless you and keep you.*

Keep your life turned toward God, and the Holy Spirit will work to transform you. You can see God through Christ's life in the Bible. Indeed, you will want your life to parallel that of Christ as you grow to be more like him. The more Christ-like thoughts and behaviors you have, the more you will want to have as you walk further into the wonderful circle of being in God's care. You have daily opportunities to apply Christ's teaching in your life, no matter what terribly horrible events might be happening within your marriage.

Others can then see God through you, as you model after your glorious heavenly Father in word and deed. In this way, you will serve as a mirror to reflect God's love to your friends, neighbors, family members and work colleagues. Many opportunities will present themselves for you to be a witness to other people.

No one becomes a perfect Christian, since Christ himself was the only perfect individual. However, it is possible to slowly and steadily grow into his likeness through study, prayer, trust and obedience.

Never allow any crisis in your life to separate you from a relationship with Christ. Guard this treasured and intimate journey.

*2 Corinthians 3:18*

*And all of us, with unveiled faces, seeing the glory of the Lord as though reflected in a mirror, are being transformed into the same image from one degree of glory to another; for this comes from the Lord, the Spirit.*

You might feel as though you've been attacked on many fronts. On the home front, your husband may have abandoned your family. People at work might be gossiping about you. Your family might be blaming you for separation, because you are a convenient scapegoat. In fact, your husband might even be blaming you for his misery as well.

Blaming others for upheaval or leveling criticism at your husband will not help your situation. Indeed, he may be at fault for some problems, and you might feel that you're responsible for others. But your duty is to step away from all the condemnation and hard-heartedness that you see around you. Step away from these negative behaviors, and pray. Seek God's will.

You shouldn't berate yourself, or feed an inferiority complex about past behaviors and sins. You can't change the past; you can simply move on from the here and now. Focus on the present, and go forward with the confidence of the Lord. As of today, don't allow doubt, fear and guilt to conquer you. In fact, Christ has conquered that doubt, fear and guilt for you on the cross!

God has a plan, a good plan, for your life. He has stayed with you to this point, and you can trust that he most certainly will not abandon you now.

You can find solutions to your problems, as God strengthens you in the here and now.

*1 Samuel 30:6*

*David was in great danger; for the people spoke of stoning him, because all the people were bitter in spirit for their sons and daughters. But David strengthened himself in the Lord his God.*

Are you sad, brokenhearted or frustrated? Do you feel unable to continue with life as it currently exists? Have you recently viewed your life as a complete wreck?

Then take heart because all is well if we completely trust and abide in God.

Think for a minute, and let yourself remember days during childhood when you played the game of hide-and-seek. I loved this game as a young girl. It was fun to run and find a secret hiding place, one where no one could find me—one that I could claim for my very own. If I discovered a really wonderful hiding place inside or outside, it was my secret. I can recall one spring day as I went outside and sat down beside the chimney while waiting for someone to find me. But no one ever did. I knew right then that this was a perfect place, completely surrounded on all sides with either brick of the house or very thick forsythia shrubs. For several days to come, I went outside and read my favorite book all alone in my hiding place. Or I could just go outside to my favorite spot and look up at the clouds. But it was my special hiding place, and mine alone.

Do you have a current hiding place? It might be a well-worn and shabby chair in your den or a rocking chair out on your back deck. It could be your own bed where you feel comfortable and secure.

God is the best hiding place. He is supreme, true and everlasting. He will comfort, protect and reassure you that all is well as you abide in him.

*Psalm 119:114*

*You are my hiding place and my shield;*
*I hope in your word.*

Holidays can be especially difficult when you are separated or divorced. You could be flooded with memories of holiday gatherings from your courtship and marriage. Maybe you're remembering your first Thanksgiving as a mother, or that one very early Christmas morning when your toddlers woke you and your husband at 4:30 a.m. And now, your life is very different from how it ever has been as this holiday season approaches.

Get an early start, and begin to make plans now—a few weeks before the holidays actually arrive. Pray, talk with your children and your husband, and try to make arrangements that will be as fair as possible. Remember to keep the children's concerns and interest in the forefront, because this isn't easy for them, either. Make every possible effort to avoid bickering about the holidays in front of your children.

Your Thanksgiving and Christmas Days will be different, but they don't have to be disastrous. You can spend time with friends, neighbors, or family members. Or you could do something entirely different, such as serving lunch at a homeless shelter. You do have choices!

Thanksgiving Day and Christmas Day are just two days in one year, and you can survive them. These days belong to God, and he can deliver you from immense grief. Acknowledge the difference from years past, make some plans, and determine to have as good days as possible.

*Esther 9:22*

*As the days on which the Jews gained relief from their enemies, and as the month that had been turned for them from sorrow into gladness and from mourning into a holiday; that they should make them days of feasting and gladness, days for sending gifts of food to one another and presents to the poor.*

Every single thing going on inside you is important to God. All of your thoughts, attitudes, needs, wants, dreams, emotions, desires and motives are known by him—and all this determines who you really are.

Of course, your outer self is also important. You do get up at 6:00 a.m., after all, in order to get a quick shower and wash your hair every weekday morning before work. You might even try to exercise a couple of times a week. Maybe your doctor has prescribed a medication to help control your high blood pressure and you are complying with this regimen. That laundry that you wash is important, and you might even occasionally get the iron out of the laundry closet to get rid of some of those wrinkles in your favorite green cotton shirt. You're acutely aware that your external appearance plays a part in your life, but you also know that it is not the primary statement about who you are as a person and a Christian woman.

God looks on your spirit, and in your heart. He knows that you love him, and is aware of your desire to be obedient. Your heavenly Father knows that your inner self is what matters most. God is much more pleased by your offering of a sweet spirit and a pure heart, instead of trying to perfect your outer appearance.

If you are not pleased with your inner being just now, surrender to the guidance of the Holy Spirit. You can be molded by this Spirit to align your own spirit with that of God.

*1 Peter 3:4*

*Rather, let your adornment be the inner self with the lasting beauty of a gentle and quiet spirit, which is very precious in God's sight.*

God made this day—this very day—and he wants you to be joyful in it.

Some days are definitely not ones of joy for women who are separated or divorced. If your mood is unpleasant or you are overwhelmed with grief, you may be extremely sorrowful. Joy might be the last thing on your mind! Are you always looking toward the distant future when things will improve in your personal life? You might not even want to think about today, because things are so wretched.

One friend, divorced from her husband of 10 years due to his relationship with another man, was experiencing a period of depression. She was understandably confused, and her children were as well. Their entire lives were turned upside down, and this woman felt that she was unable to function as a stable mother to her children. She sought help from many sources—her medical doctor prescribed a mild antidepressant medication for her to use for a short period of time, her pastor met with her weekly for a counseling session, and she confided in a few select friends.

Her life slowly began to improve, and her prayer life also increased. Her pastor let her know that God already knew about her agony and pain, but urged her to pray anyway and pour out her heart to the Almighty. The simple act of telling her Father about her grief made her feel better, and God then revealed to her some reasons for joy. Over time, her prayer life naturally became one of praise and adoration, and she was able to experience joy in her life once again. As she acknowledged all the blessings of her life, she was able to rejoice in her days.

It is difficult to continually be sad and disgruntled when you are praising God.

*Psalm 118:24*

*This is the day that the Lord has made;*
*let us rejoice and be glad in it.*

Decide to commit your life to the Lord. Your whole life —marriage, children, faith, extended family, friends, work, material possessions, money and health. Your heavenly Father is trustworthy; you can depend on him to care for you always. Mostly certainly, he will not let you down. In truth, God can care for you far better than you are able to care for yourself. He is the Source of all life and all good in this world, and he loves you deeply.

One divorced woman was continuously taunted by her former husband with regard to child custody of their two toddlers. Whenever her ex-husband got angry about events with his new wife turning sour, he began to threaten to take the children away from his former wife, a Christian woman. She was in a state of constant turmoil, because her ex-husband was not a happy man. In fact, he was miserable because of his current circumstances and choices, but was determined to force his children to accept his new wife.

This woman accepted her ex-husband's verbal mistreatment for a few months, then grew weary of the threats, and chose to commit this issue to God. She had known all along that her Creator was in charge of everything, including concerns like child custody, but she'd been hesitant to yield all of her marital fallout to the Lord. Instead, she had tried to manage her divorce all alone. She finally surrendered her entire life to God, trusted in him, and watched as he acted in her behalf and that of the children. The child custody problems were eventually resolved to her satisfaction, and with a minimum of verbal abuse from her former husband.

Commit, trust and wait—knowing that God will care for you.

*Psalm 37:5*

*Commit your way to the Lord;*
*trust in him, and he will act.*

You are probably curious about a multitude of events right now.

What is your husband doing every night since your separation two months ago?

What are the subjects of conversations between your former husband and your children during their visits?

Does your husband have his pornography addiction under control?

Do your children really like your ex-husband's new wife?

How many times a day does your husband think about you?

Has your husband really quit drinking?

Curiosity such as this can seemingly drive you crazy, and it is natural to some degree. Any woman who is separated from her husband will normally wonder about what he's doing. But you shouldn't let this curiosity consume you, because it serves no useful purpose at all. When your husband brings your children back from a visit, simply give them a hug and ask if they had a good time. Avoid asking about all of the details of the visit, because you can't control them anyway.

Dwelling on your former husband and his actions could become an obsession, lead to confusion, and prevent the Holy Spirit from helping you to think positively. Pray that God will control your curious thoughts, and focus on Him instead of your former husband.

*2 Corinthians 10:5*

*And every proud obstacle raised up against the knowledge of God, and we take every thought captive to obey Christ.*

Nothing is too hard for God. He can repair your marriage, guide you through an unwanted separation, or help you maintain your sanity during a hotly-contested divorce.

God can minister to your children, keep them close under his wings, and help them to discern right from wrong. He can assist your sons or daughters to find their way in the dark pit of their parents' divorce.

Your Father can heal your depression, then take your broken spirit and mold it into something whole and productive. The Creator of the universe can help you to smile again, even after years of crying because of a terribly unhappy marriage. He can help you to become financially responsible once again, after a marital lifetime of being in tremendous debt.

God can indeed work miracles. He can bring you from a weak, lonely woman into the fullness of a strong Christian fellowship within a church family. God can do anything and everything, because he is God himself. He is everywhere, all-powerful and all-knowing.

Put your life, along with all of its associated problems, in God's hands and then watch as his wonderful plan unfolds for your life.

*Jeremiah 32:27*

*See, I am the Lord, the God of all flesh;*
*is anything too hard for me?*

Slow down and take time, lots of time, when considering the prospect of remarriage after divorce. There truly is no hurry, and you shouldn't rush into a second marriage soon after your first one has ended.

Many women feel totally desperate to quickly find a man after divorce, and they reason that they can't be alone. But you can be alone with the Lord. In fact, you need to be alone with him. You need time to pray, study, heal, think, grow and decide what is really best for you. Plus, you don't want to drag unresolved issues from your first marriage into any other relationship.

One Christian woman chose to separate from her husband due to his chronic alcoholism. His alcohol abuse reached the point where she was afraid to ride in the car with him, for fear of his hurting someone while under the influence. This woman wanted her husband to quit drinking in order that their marriage might be restored. Sadly, this didn't happen—even though they had sought counseling, both before and after separation. After the divorce, she read God's Word for guidance about remarriage. She felt that God was directing her to stay single and, therefore, made the difficult decision not to even date another man, since dating could potentially lead to marriage.

Many women respected and admired her because of this decision. She demonstrated how vital it is during this time to seek the counsel of a pastor, read the Bible, and pray before making monumental decisions.

*Ruth 1:16*

*But Ruth said, "Do not press me to leave you or to turn*
*back from following you! Where you go, I will go;*
*where you lodge, I will lodge; your people*
*shall be my people, and your God my God."*

You know the symptoms of a divorce diet all too well —your stomach won't willingly accept any food. In fact, you're afraid you might vomit if you try to ingest a complete meal. You are so tense, anxious, nervous, stressed and uptight about your separation or divorce that food is absolutely the last thing on your mind. You may not even care about eating at all!

These feelings are entirely normal, and quite commonplace among women who are separated and divorced. Sometimes a woman will lose so much weight in three or four months that she shrinks from a size 16 dress with an elastic waist to a size 10 with a fitted waistband. She might begin her separation at 160 pounds, only to weigh 130 three months later due to her inability to eat. While such drastic weight loss is not healthy, it frequently accompanies wild emotional swings. You might have even guessed that a friend is having marital difficulty because of a sudden, extreme weight loss.

Occasionally, a woman will diet in the reverse and comfort herself with food as a means to cope with her marriage falling apart. One friend weighed 145 pounds during most of her 15 year marriage, but ballooned up to 182 pounds during her year of separation. Food was her one true comfort. "Ice cream felt good when nothing else did," she said.

Women are emotional creatures by design, and sometimes we will use food—either a lack or an excess —to help us cope with whatever problem life may hurl our way. Pray daily that God will help you to use his strength, instead of food, to cope with your problems.

*Daniel 6:10*

*He continued to go to his house, which had windows in its upper room open toward Jerusalem, and to get down on his knees three times a day to pray to his God and praise him, just as he had done previously.*

It feels great to stretch your muscles after an exercise class, gardening, or a night of hard sleep. Just pulling your arms high up overhead or giving yourself a big hug by wrapping your arms around both shoulders is a wonderful way to get rid of tension. A favorite stretch involves bending your head down to the side, close to your shoulder, and holding for five or ten seconds. You can also get an instant energy charge by clasping your hands behind your back, pulling up slightly, and then holding the stretch for a few seconds before releasing.

Stretching can help you to feel better, have more energy, prevent injury during exercise, and keep your joints more flexible. Stretching doesn't have to take lots of time, and you can even stretch while sitting at your desk. These simple exercises can help you shake off the blues on a cold day if you're cramped in the house during a snow blizzard. You might even be less grouchy with your children on a particularly rough day if you just slow down and stretch a little bit.

Just as you can stretch your physical body and its muscles, you can also stretch your spiritual body. Pray, not asking for six or seven things from God, but talk with him and have a simple conversation. Rest in his presence today as you stretch your prayer life.

Reading the Holy Word also stretches your faith. Study the Bible and apply the lessons learned in your daily Christian walk. If you can't understand the specific translation that you have in your home, go to a Christian bookstore and ask for a recommendation.

Your faith can definitely grow with exercise and stretching.

*Romans 14:1*

*Welcome those who are weak in faith,*
*but not for the purpose of quarreling over opinions.*

The Lord is your shepherd, and he wants a relationship with you.

Shepherds always care for their sheep. A shepherd's main functions are to provide protection for his sheep and to steer the flock toward grass for eating and water for drinking. In fact, sheep are totally dependent on their shepherd for almost everything in life. A sheep certainly can't fight off a hungry lion or wolf, but will rely on its shepherd as a shield from harm. The shepherd will steer the sheep to a hillside in the event of a storm in order to insure their safety, and the trusting sheep will follow wherever their shepherd leads them. A shepherd will always go search for a single lost sheep, hoping to keep his flock intact, because each sheep is special.

Likewise, God always cares for you. Your Father will provide food; he won't let you go hungry. You can probably attest to a couple of times after divorce when you couldn't quite afford to pay your grocery bill, but some financial miracle came your way that enabled you to buy food. That miracle came from God! Your Shepherd also completely protects you. You will probably never know of all the times that God has kept you from physical danger—perhaps in your car during a blinding rainstorm. As your Shepherd, God will search for you in the event you are physically or spiritually lost, because you are very precious to him.

Jesus is constantly protecting and guiding you because he loves you deeply. He will supply your needs, and you don't have to constantly worry about the everyday necessities of life. The Good Shepherd wants you to always follow his divine leading, just like the sheep on a hillside always follow the leading of their shepherd.

*Psalm 23:1*

*The Lord is my shepherd, I shall not want.*

Visualize the very familiar 23rd Psalm, one that you've probably heard and read many times throughout your life.

Lying down in green pastures is such an immensely soothing image. Just thinking about lying down in green grass can lower your blood pressure by a few points. You are able to relax, close your eyes, and think of the sun on your eyelids. You might even be able to take a little nap, enjoying the warmth. It is wonderful to remember that your Shepherd is the One who has led you to these beautiful pastures. This was an intentional trip, and most certainly not an accidental wandering. Notice that the Scriptures tell us that God wants us to lie down and enjoy the calm. He doesn't always want us working or cleaning or cooking or driving car pool. He desires for us to have rest!

Your Shepherd will also guide you toward still waters. These waters are not loud, threatening or dangerous. Instead, they are calm, smooth and still—made for resting and enjoying. Remember, it was the Shepherd who guided you to this place when he knew that you desperately needed refreshing during these turbulent months. You're also assured in this Psalm that God stays right beside you, because he wants you to be constantly reassured that you are safe and protected. The Lord of the vast universe still desires a very personal relationship with you.

Thank God for these lush green pastures and glorious still waters.

*Psalm 23:2*

*He makes me lie down in green pastures;*
*he leads me beside still waters.*

God can restore your soul and make you whole once again. Sounds wonderful, doesn't it? Although you may feel broken and battered, or worn and torn by divorce, you can be a new woman in the Lord.

Healing and restoration are readily available to you on a spiritual level. Your Father may not completely heal you according to your hurried timetable, but he does indeed have a plan for your life. You might not be able to understand each step of the plan, but God has it all mapped out for you. This plan is positive, full, and unbelievably wonderful because God wants only your very best! A friend once reassured me, "God is painting the beautiful canvas of your life and each day is a big new brush stroke."

You can trust that he can heal you from all your emotional wounds of the last few years. Only God can mend your broken heart and sew your spirit back together to enable you to begin life again after divorce. You might seem frazzled and ripped apart, but he can restore you in order to form an entirely new woman. Sometimes it might seem impossible that you can ever be restored, because you feel that no one in the world has suffered the hurt and trauma that you've experienced. But remember that God knows every intimate detail of your marriage and separation, every hurt you've experienced, every tear you've shed, and every sleepless night you've survived while you waited for your husband to return. And your Father has been there all along, lovingly caring for you.

Step into God's presence, and look forward to restoration by the Great Physician.

*Psalm 23:3*

*He restores my soul.*

As your Shepherd, God will lead you down righteous paths—of safety, truth and goodness—that are desirable and lead to happiness. No matter how appealing a self-serving path may appear, your Father simply will not point you in that direction. Of course, you do have free will and can choose that path if you want, but God won't direct you toward anything harmful. God loves you and has a purpose for your life, and he will guide you toward himself.

In fact, God will actually place barriers in your path if you try to take a wrong turn. During the period of her separation, a friend discovered that her cholesterol level was high for the first time. This made her angry, because her physical health had always been excellent. In her forties, she naturally had a few aches and pains, but was generally healthy. Being a bit stubborn, she refused to truly believe that her cholesterol level was elevated. One day she was driving past a fast food restaurant that served her favorite ice cream and she was tempted. "I can work on my cholesterol tomorrow," she thought. After all, her divorce would soon be final. She needed some comfort, and rationalized that she deserved that fatty dessert. So she pulled into that parking lot, and got out of the car to order the ice cream. In fact, she had decided to get the extra large size!

She opened her pocketbook to check the money supply, and discovered that she had only four pennies in her purse. Then she remembered that her daughter had needed extra money that morning for a school event, and had practically emptied her mom's pocketbook of money.

I believe that was God directing her in a right path away from an even higher cholesterol level!

*Psalm 23:3*

*He leads me in right paths for his name's sake.*

Right now you may feel as though you're in a dark valley—that very dark valley known as marital separation or divorce.

You might be fearful of what will come in the months and years ahead. You could be worried, numb with grief, alone, in shock, angry, helpless, hurting or depressed in this valley. Have you become sick during these trials? Are your children incredibly disappointed that their parents have been unable to reconcile? That valley stretching out before you probably looks very deep and wide, bleak and barren. Like many other women in your situation, you wonder how in the world you will ever make it across this vast rugged valley to get to the other side.

The best way to make it through the struggles of separation or divorce is with guidance of God, your Shepherd. You don't have to fear evil because he is protecting you. Your Father will deliver you from tests that come your way during this time—tests of patience, finances and emotional swings. He is faithful, and is with you every hour of every day.

Just as a staff reassures sheep that their shepherd is near, evidence of God's love can give you that same assurance. His name, presence, provision and protection can be of immense comfort to a grieving woman, just as promised in this Psalm. Indeed, your Shepherd is your strength, your courage and your comfort in the valley of marital confusion.

*Psalm 23:4*

*Even though I walk through the darkest valley, I fear no evil; for you are with me; your rod and your staff—they comfort me.*

What are your enemies—fear, a sour attitude, your former husband, blame of God for your divorce, or your children's lack of faith since marital breakup?

God is already at work, handling every single one of these concerns. He knows about your problems even before you confess in prayer, and is working out solutions to these situations as you ask. In fact, God is preparing a table for you in the midst of your enemies.

During a friend's separation from her husband of 12 years, she needed to attend a community event at which her husband and his girlfriend would probably also be present. She dreaded seeing them, and actually tried to avoid going to the banquet altogether. But she eventually decided to fulfill her social obligation, arranged to ride with another friend, and planned to sit with her companion during dinner. This Christian woman prayed diligently that there would be so many people at this public function that she wouldn't be forced to see her husband. Then she prayed that she could calmly smile and walk away if he approached her for any reason. Further, she asked for God's complete protection and guidance during this hideous night that she was dreading.

God answered her prayers. The crowd was huge and she never even had to see her husband and his partner. The people who attended told her that they admired her civil attitude, and she was able to serve as a godly witness with her behaviors.

God had prepared the way for her by preparing a table of grace, in the literal presence of her perceived enemies, and filled her cup to the point of overflowing.

*Psalm 23:5*

*You prepare a table before me in the presence of my enemies; you anoint my head with oil; my cup overflows.*

Trust that God's promises of goodness and mercy will follow you through each day of your life. Claim that bountiful promise each morning as you pray. You simply cannot lose if you have the Almighty's merciful goodness!

You have access to God's blessings due to your faith, and because you are striving to be a woman of obedience during separation and divorce.

God wants your life to be one that is truly good, and he wants you to thrive in your marital separation and divorce. He wants you to be peaceful, joyful, strong and grounded in your faith. God wants your church family to support and love you. He wants you to have strong relationships with your extended family members, who can bolster you during your struggles. Your Father wants your job to be one that you like, one that will help you buy the basics of food, clothing and shelter—and maybe a few extra surprises as well!

Likewise, God wants your children to believe in him and follow his directions for their lives. He wants only the very best for them because he deeply loves them. Your heavenly Father wants your son and daughter to be happy in their home, and with newly adjusted grandparent relationships. He wants them to be happy and successful at school, and with their friends.

God wants you to have many, many days of his goodness and mercy—an open mind, an open heart and an open door into your future.

*Psalm 23:6*

*Surely goodness and mercy shall*
*follow me all the days of my life.*

God promises that you can live in his house forever—his house with all the goodness, strength, peace, joy, hope, abundance, love and completeness that he has to offer. One day, you can certainly be in heaven in direct communion with God.

But wonderfully, this promise can apply to your earthly existence as well as your heavenly one; it isn't necessary to wait until death to be able to dwell with God. What incredible security this can be to a woman who is divorced. Dwelling with God means that you aren't ever alone, and you are always safe in his perfect protection and care. He will shepherd you through this present life and onto heavenly glories thereafter.

What blessed assurance this is to be able to abide with the Lord both now and forever. You have eternal hope through God. Hope in the knowledge that you will indeed survive this marital separation that you never wanted or dreamed about, as you loved your husband unconditionally. Hope that you will be blessed at work and at home. Hope in the certainty of calm as you obey God's Word and follow him every day of your divorce proceedings.

More and more joy will come into your life as you abide in God's house daily, a house that is secure and a refuge from life's storms.

*Psalm 23:6*

*And I shall dwell in the house of the Lord
my whole life long.*

Do you feel like you've been sitting in the back seat for the length of your entire marriage?

A casual acquaintance was separated from her husband of many years when she called one Saturday morning and asked if I'd take her to the grocery store. Assuming that her car was in the shop for repair, I drove over to her house in my old-but-dependable car. She confessed on our trip to the supermarket that she had never gotten a driver's license even though she was in her late forties. Her husband, it seemed, thought that she didn't need a license to drive because he had always taken her anywhere she needed to go.

Now she was realizing that she had been in the back seat through all her years of marriage, and that had been one more way in which her husband was controlling her. She had never held a job outside the home, even when her children started school, because her husband said that he could make enough money for their family. Sadly, this wasn't the case, as they were consumed with financial debt. And, of course, he reasoned that he couldn't take her to work because then he'd be late for his own job.

This sweet woman eventually obtained her driver's license, and got a job that would help her to financially provide for herself after her husband divorced her. She began to attend church regularly, where she gained a great deal of strength and confidence from God as well as fellow believers. She made the decision to serve God alone, and to allow only him to navigate her life.

*Joshua 24:15*

*"Now if you are unwilling to serve the Lord, choose this day whom you will serve, whether the gods your ancestors served in the region beyond the River or the gods of the Amorites in whose land you are living; but as for me and my household, we will serve the Lord."*

Take a few minutes today to examine the well-known scripture verse from the book of Philippians listed below. Look at each work separately.

"I." You can do all things—not your neighbor, parent, friend, or work colleague. You must go through separation and divorce yourself; as no one else can serve as your substitute.

"Can do." These are action words, affirming words, assuring words. You can do it. There is work to be done during divorce, and you will be able to actively work through this process. You can most certainly learn how to manage your home alone, maneuver your way through a separation agreement, and survive a marriage anniversary date alone.

"All things." With heavenly help, you can do all the things required of you right now. All of the necessary housework, financial management, emotional analysis, single parenting and spiritual decisions. You will face unimaginable difficulties, but you can survive each one of them.

"Through him." This is the most important part of this wonderful verse—Christ is present now, and will help you. You are not alone. He is always available! Your Heavenly Father will not desert you as you face the challenges and pressures of life right now.

"Who strengthens me." God strengthens you. The powerful, loving, present God who created the universe cares enough for you to provide strength to face troubles and trials if you ask him to reside in your heart. Don't even try to survive divorce all by yourself; you need God to uphold you and steer you to your final destination.

Memorize this verse, and live by it.

*Philippians 4:13*

*I can do all things through him who strengthens me.*

One divorced woman thought she was doing okay. She had somehow survived the first year, paying most of her bills, working full-time, and continuing to love her children dearly. Also, her faith in the Almighty had deepened and her extended family had become more precious to her than ever before. Therefore, she had the impression that all was generally well.

One gloomy Friday afternoon, a friend who was separated came over to her house for their regular prayer time. These two women connected through a Bible study at their church, became prayer partners, and discovered that they were able to survive by praying about the devastation in their marriages. The two women listed their answered prayers in the journal used for that purpose, and then began to write down any prayer concerns on their hearts. The divorced woman was amazed when her friend listed her former husband as a person who needed prayer and needed the Lord in his life. She had never been able to utter that prayer. Her prayer partner correctly observed, "Well, you still have a few raw nerve endings there, don't you?"

It can take quite a long time to heal from a marriage to a man that you deeply loved, and it is okay to have some raw nerve endings! But her friend's comment showed her that she needed to pray more regularly and pray differently. Instead of refusing to pray for her former husband, she tried to ask God to control his life in order for him to be the best possible father to their children.

God is healing her raw nerve endings. He can do the same for you, if you ask for his help.

*James 5:16*

*Therefore confess your sins to one another, and pray for one another, so that you may be healed. The prayer of the righteous is powerful and effective.*

Some dates are particularly hard for a woman of divorce, and cause acute pain. Missed wedding anniversaries most certainly fall into this category.

A friend at work asked for prayer one morning as she walked in the door to begin her work week. When she walked into the office that day she was not her usual bubbly self, but was sitting alone quietly and looking a bit pale. She shared with her work colleagues that she was expecting a particularly bad day because it would have been her wedding anniversary—her 25th, a big milestone.

Everyone at work knew what this woman had endured. Her husband had left their family after she had worked to help put him through medical school and his residency. Immediately upon leaving, he moved in with one of his classmates from medical school and avoided his family commitments of helping his wife raise their three toddlers.

She later shared that she had known that her husband was unhappy for a good while; he had his first marital affair as a second year medical student. She had hoped that somehow her marriage could begin to heal after that assault, but it just began to further unravel. While she was sad to be missing a 25th wedding anniversary, she wasn't sad that her husband's behavior was out of her life. She had finally concluded that God didn't intend for her to live in an adulterous marriage.

Acknowledge big events, such as an un-anniversary. Grieve, and tell God of your heart.

*Isaiah 43:2*

*When you pass through the waters, I will be with you;*
*and through the rivers, they shall not overwhelm you;*
*when you walk through fire you shall not be burned,*
*and the flame shall not consume you.*

Give thanks to God on this Thanksgiving Day as you reflect upon all your blessings for which to be grateful. Make a mental list of reasons to be thankful, and then begin to write that long list down in your journal.

You can include God's great love for you, your marriage, wonderful children, dependable work, your home, your old car that continues to run and the incredible support of your parents during the period of separation. Do you have a family member who is also divorced, who has been especially helpful? Make sure to include your siblings, as many brothers and sisters are a tremendous assistance during separation and after divorce.

How about friends at church? Others on your list might be your pastor, neighbors who help with yard work, or teachers at school who have been especially attentive to your daughter as she struggles through your divorce.

You could also be thankful for almost enough money to pay your bills each month, a concert that you attended last week with your son, a song on the radio that has lifted your spirits, going to dinner with your girlfriends, attending exercise class, repair of your faulty kitchen stove and your newly-discovered smile.

Be thankful for the joy that you have in the Lord. Thank God for Christ Jesus—his birth, death, burial and resurrection. Are you thankful for hope, peace and calmness that are found only through the Lord?

Your list will probably be long, and you can continue to add to it each day. God is good.

*1 Thessalonians 5:18*

*Give thanks in all circumstances; for this is
the will of God in Christ Jesus for you.*

Christ will be your faithful companion during marital separation and divorce. He is always with you, and will not leave. You can walk with him, talk with him, abide in him and rest in his constant presence.

He will walk you through hard times and lift you up on those days when your spirits sag. You can talk with him and tell him all of the terrible things that have happened, even though he is already fully aware. Pour out your heart and tell him what is weighing you down, that very thing that is pulling you to the very bottom of that pit called despair. Cry to the Lord on the day that your son screams at you for being divorced from his father and then cry again whenever your former husband fails to show up at your daughter's violin recital.

The Lord will also rejoice with you on the happy days when your heart sings. Share those wonderful times with God, just as you've shared the ugly moments. Shout with joy when your daughter hugs you and says that she loves you more than ever. Shout again when your son is accepted into the college of his choice. Give God the praise if you're able to refinance your house due to lower interest rates.

Christ's continued presence can be wonderfully reassuring every day of your life, and most especially during your marriage difficulties. Pray to your Father and thank him for his companionship.

*Romans 8:31*

*What then are we to say about these things?*
*If God is for us, who is against us?*

Practice the art of compassion—every day.

It might be easy to retaliate if your husband is late with a child support payment one month. You could very easily get angry, let that anger fester until you're miserable, and then say something very hurtful to your husband—an ugly comment that you daughter might overhear. However, try extending some mercy instead. You should certainly insist that he meet his financial obligations, but if he has a very good reason to be a few days late with money owed, try to graciously forgive while informing him that you need the next payment promptly.

Exhibit some sympathy for your hurting son as he copes with divorce, a development that he never anticipated. Even if you had a horrible day at work and are sick of having to cook supper when you're dead on your feet, listen to him as he tells you what's on his heart about separation from his father. He needs your tenderness, especially at this critical moment.

Take pity on the woman in your church who has separated from her husband and is dating another man the following week. She needs your support—not judgment. Show some compassion and love her as a child of God.

Look for opportunities to display compassion, just as Jesus did when feeding his hungry followers.

*Matthew 15:32*

*Then Jesus called his disciples to him and said, "I have compassion for the crowd, because they have been with me now for three days and have nothing to eat; and I do not want to send them away hungry, for they might faint on the way."*

Sitting in church without your spouse can be especially painful and emotionally precarious, for a woman who is separated or divorced.

When separated for only a few short days, one woman had to decide whether to attend church without her husband. She dreaded this day in the worst possible way, because her family had attended that particular church together for 12 years. This woman was not eagerly looking forward to the questions that would inevitably come her way, but she pulled herself out of bed, and told her children that they were still going to church. That was certainly a tear-filled church worship service, as well as an incredibly difficult one for her children.

A friend who had been divorced for two years went to church one Sunday morning, only to be assaulted by "former family feelings." She simply saw a husband and wife holding hands sitting in the pew beside her, and she became completely unglued. Tears flowed during the hymns and she began to wonder if she would have to leave the service because she was so emotionally distraught. This woman said that she was shocked by the intensity of her feelings of loss, as her former husband had already married someone else by that point in time. But the hurt was still there, in some hidden form or fashion.

If you're in church and begin to feel that you are spinning out of emotional control, take a very slow deep breath. Get a tissue out of your pocketbook, blow your nose, and force yourself to smile at your children. Then pray, asking God to bring you comfort during the next hour.

*Luke 4:16*

*When he came to Nazareth, where he had been brought up, he went to the synagogue on the sabbath day, as was his custom.*

Participating in a work meeting a couple of weeks after separating from her husband, a woman began to cry. She couldn't seem to help the tears as they rolled silently down her cheeks, while thinking of lost dreams instead of a work assignment.

A colleague slipped her a mint under the table and whispered, "You can't cry when you're sucking on a mint." She unwrapped that piece of peppermint candy, quickly put it in her mouth, sucked furiously, and found that this advice worked. It is indeed impossible to cry while sucking a mint.

Pick the flavor that you like best—peppermint, cinnamon, licorice, butterscotch, lemon or spearmint. Go out and buy a large bag of mints if you need an effective, although temporary, stop for your public torrent of tears.

Mint therapy can work in many emergency situations such as attending an infant baptism, driving a child to summer camp, participating in a friend's wedding, sitting in a daughter's high school graduation and taking a son to his first day of kindergarten. Keep an abundant supply in your purse, because you never know when a mint could come in handy. As women, it seems that we have an incredibly endless supply of tears.

God cares about all your problems, large or small, and solutions are available to you. All you have to do is ask your Father in heaven.

*Genesis 50:1*

*Then Joseph threw himself on his father's face and wept over him and kissed him.*

The season surrounding the birth of Jesus Christ is filled with many wonderful events—church services, family gatherings, holiday shopping expeditions, a special coconut cake, Christmas cookies and a gingerbread house. Others include eating turkey, putting up a Christmas tree in its designated spot in the family room, reading favorite Bible passages again, attending candlelight Christmas Eve worship and sponsoring a needy family at church or work.

Also present in this frenzied month are Christmas carols on the radio, those traditional holiday movies repeated on television, musical concerts, hanging of stockings, the wreath on the front door and putting lights on an outdoor tree. Even more—ribbons on light fixtures, smiles of surprise, snow, a new Christmas dress for your daughter to wear to church, wrapping paper, an Advent wreath, fatigue and memories.

It's very natural for you to have many emotional and tear-filled moments during this month, so be prepared. You might even be remembering years of Christmas past, perhaps one year when your husband gave you a special piece of jewelry as a gift. Slow down and take time to allow yourself these times of reflection, as they can lead toward emotional healing. You are continuing to walk through the fire of grief.

During this year of marital separation or divorce, make every effort to let Christ's birth be the center of your many holiday celebrations. Don't place marital turmoil or secular celebrations in the center of your heart. Consciously put Christ first in word and action and affirm this decision on the first day of December. After all, Jesus is most certainly the true reason for the season of Advent. Honoring him can bring untold comfort. His birth is that of our Savior, God's son, Redeemer, Prince of Peace, and Everlasting.

*Matthew 1:23*

*"Look, the virgin shall conceive and bear a son, and they shall name him Emmanuel," which means, "God is with us."*

One woman, who had married her high school sweetheart, dreaded her first Christmas season as a divorced woman. Their marriage had lasted for 19 years before her husband left their home. She was absolutely overwhelmed and was flooded with countless memories during this particular holiday.

She and her children retrieved the Christmas tree ornament boxes from their attic, in an effort to brighten up their home. Everyone was in a dejected and rather sad mood, but this woman was determined to continue with their established holiday tradition of decorating a fir tree and placing it in their living room in front of the large bay window. But as she opened one particular box, she started to cry. On the bottom, underneath the ornaments that her children had made over the years, lay two decorations that she had hand-painted for her husband very early in their marriage. Seeing these visual reminders of a marriage for which she had grieved for months was just too much for her to bear at that precise moment.

Her children saw her tears and stood by helplessly. She drew them to her, wrapped them in her arms, cried some more, and assured them of her unending love for them. Then she decided to let them place those ornaments on the tree, even though one angry part of her wanted to smash them into pieces and hurl them in the general vicinity of the trash can.

Ask God to guide you in a general sense, and then in specific situations that you will most assuredly encounter this Christmas.

*Matthew 6:10*

*"Your kingdom come, Your will be done,
on earth as it is in heaven."*

Do you wonder if there will eventually be an end to this thing called separation? Will it somehow get better? Right now your heart feels like you've lost everything you ever desired.

Yes, there is some sort of end to separation. Your separation could end when you and your husband are able to reconcile through hard work and counseling. Or it will end in divorce if it is not possible to repair your marriage, or if one of you isn't willing to attempt marital reconciliation. It is a blessing that separation doesn't last forever, because it can be a no-man's land without a sense of direction.

On the other hand, divorce lasts a long, long time. In fact, you may be divorced for the remainder of your life. The effects of divorce may always be with you and your children, but you don't have to let your divorced status dictate your entire life. Instead, rejoice in the Lord!

Things will indeed get better for you. No matter what month of the year, keep your eyes on God and trust in him. He is fully in charge of your life, and has wonderful provisions that you cannot even comprehend. Pray regularly, and passionately. Tell God what is on your mind and in your heart, and wait for him to answer.

Read the book of Job if you ever feel as though you've lost everything. Your material possessions may be fewer than when married, and you might be unable to figure out how to pay your bills. But keep the faith! At the end of separation and divorce, you may find that you have more than you had at the beginning of your marital troubles—more faith, joy, dependence on God, strength, peace and hope—more of the good and lasting qualities of a Christian woman.

*Job 42:12*

*The Lord blessed the latter days of Job more than his beginning; and he had fourteen thousand sheep, six thousand camels, a thousand yoke of oxen, and a thousand donkeys.*

Have you ever wondered if God has heard your prayer and earnest pleading to put your marriage back together? It's normal for you to sometimes wonder if God answers prayers. Your broken heart may be preventing you from praying to God as you want, or your mind might be so clouded that you don't even know if you could recognize an answer if it came your way.

God is not always obvious with answers to prayer, but he does indeed answer. The answer may be an emphatic "yes," as in the case of one divorced woman who was praying about the possibility of changing churches. Her former husband was still attending her church, and she had left the marriage due to his violent behaviors which had shown no improvement over many years and had gotten much worse just prior to separation. God pointed her toward a different church to attend, one where no one knew her family history and where she could be free to worship without feeling as though she were the object of gossip.

A pastor once said that other possible answers from God were "No," "Wait," "The request was a human impossibility" or "The request could be possible only with my help." The latter was most definitely the case when one woman began to pray every day to be healed from years of verbal abuse that had completely destroyed her self-esteem during marriage. This healing was possible only with divine intervention.

Our Father does not grant every wish of our hearts, and prayer is not a laundry list to be presented before God for our immediate gratification. Rather, the privilege to pray is a communication with your Creator. Talk with God, be still, and listen for certain answers.

*Psalm 4:1*

*Answer me when I call, O God of my right! You gave me
room when I was in distress. Be gracious
to me, and hear my prayer.*

Perhaps your Christmas season this year is just a heavy burden for you to bear and you feel weighed down. You simply have too much on your plate to juggle at one time—too much shopping, not enough money, lack of time, an abundance of family gatherings, lots of cooking, memories, and excessive church activities.

You may feel tense and uptight, and unable to enjoy the holidays. Your children may even sense your anxiety, and it might be affecting them at home and at school.

Relax. You don't have to do it all, and you don't have to do it alone.

Closely examine your past traditions, and decide if you want to do every single thing that your family has done for the past ten or twelve years. You may want to leave some out or add some different twists to your celebrations. As a single mother, it might not be possible to attend a holiday activity five nights a week and still maintain your sanity. You just might have to decline a party invitation from your neighbors down the street, if you feel that you need to be at home to bake those chocolate cupcakes for your son's kindergarten class Christmas party the next day. Or you could choose to stay home onc Saturday night to play a board game with your children and get to bed before midnight, instead of attending a concert. Your house doesn't have to be perfectly clean. That dust will still be there the first week in January!

The status of being separated or divorced often seems magnified during the month of December. Therefore, remember that you are never alone. God is with you—providing for you, holding your hand, caring for you, enabling you, guiding you, helping you and always loving you.

*Exodus 18:18*

*"You will surely wear yourself out, both you and these
people with you. For the task is too heavy
for you; you cannot do it alone."*

You may feel like one of the Israelites, wandering around in the wilderness of divorce without direction. That particular wilderness can get terribly thick, dark, out of control and full of thorns. Divorce is frequently accompanied by verbal ugliness, emotional wounds and physical illnesses of various sorts due to stress. A woman who is separated from a man that she still deeply loves or loved at one time may keep stumbling and repeating the same mistakes over and over while hoping for a different end result.

One good friend kept opening her heart and her arms to her husband, despite his continuing affairs with other women. She kept hoping that he would change and love her as a Christian man should. Unfortunately, the repetitious cycles of infidelity got much worse until he ultimately left their home to live with a woman thirty years younger who was married to another man. When someone finally told this woman to make a decision whether to stay or leave, she divorced her husband and managed to regain her self-respect, sanity and spiritual direction.

It is almost impossible to make progress toward emotional and spiritual healing if you are still grumbling, complaining and blaming for marital woes. A poor attitude can keep you in the wilderness for many years. However, a Spirit-filled attitude will lead you directly through separation and divorce into God's land of promises—promises of peace, calm, comfort, trust, obedience, truth and light.

*Deuteronomy 1:6–7*

*The Lord our God spoke to us at Horeb, saying, "You have stayed long enough at this mountain. Resume your journey."*

Ask God to help you to quit being so focused on yourself and your own pain, in order that you might see the needs of others. Separation and divorce can be a terrible time of tears, aches and self-centeredness because your marriage has exploded into a thousand little pieces. And the tunnel vision associated with marital disintegration is normal for a while.

But stop and look around.

Your son may desperately want his father to throw the baseball with him, but you're the parent who is present. Or your daughter might be crying while practicing her cello recital piece because her father is out of town and won't be attending her performance. How about your neighbor who had surgery and needs a hot meal? Is your church in need of youth leaders? Your mother and father are probably very worried about your emotional state. Your parents are also concerned about how their grandchildren will fare during a divorce and its aftermath. You have a friend who is also separated from her husband and crying herself to sleep every night. There may be a Sunday School classmate who has just lost his job.

There are many spiritual, emotional, social, financial and physical needs all around you. You can't solve them all, but you can be sensitive and pray for others even if you are still grieving for the loss of your own marriage. In fact, you will discover that your own pain and grief finds healing in the process.

*2 Chronicles 30:27*

*Then the priests and the Levites stood up and blessed the people, and their voice was heard; their prayer came to his holy dwelling in heaven.*

Stop for just a minute during this busy day and think. In a parable, Jesus likened our response to the Word to seed falling on a variety of soil. What kind of soil are you?

Have you grown so hardened and bitter because of your divorce that you are not ready to hear God's Word and let it take root? Bitterness is very common after periods of neglect or abuse from a mate—someone you trusted and had planned to be with your entire life. Maybe your soil is hard, too rocky, and you don't feel ready to even listen to God right now.

Your soil might be too shallow, having nothing available to allow a seed to actually grow past an initial burst of germination. Unless you are spiritually fed and nourished through the Word, you will drift away from your Father due to lack of soil depth.

Or you may represent the soil that is crowded with thorns and cares of the world. You might be too distracted as you hear the Word. Perhaps you reason that you just can't deal with God and a divorce at the same time. You're far too busy and your soil yields no spiritual growth at all.

We want to be good fertile soil—receptive to God's Word, seeking to understand and apply it to our lives. My family had a vegetable garden when I was small, where beans and corn certainly grew best in dark rich soil that had been cultivated and fertilized. We regularly watered and pulled weeds to help the garden be productive. These same principles apply to Christian women in separation or divorce. We can prepare our hearts, remain open to God's Word, continually feed our faith and remove unwanted growth. These actions can yield a tremendous harvest in our lives.

*Matthew 13:23*

*"But as for what was sown on good soil, this is the one who heard the word and understands it, who indeed bears fruit and yields, in one case a hundredfold, in another sixty, and in another thirty."*

About a year after her divorce was final, a friend decided that she might like to go on a date—one distant day, with an unknown man. She had no specific plans, but just a possibility of some future encounter with that special man that God was already choosing.

While reading the newspaper one morning, she noticed that one of the larger department stores at the local mall was offering a free makeover at their cosmetic counter. So she called and scheduled an appointment for a professional re-do. She left work a couple of hours early one Friday afternoon in order to see what miracle was coming her way and was quite excited!

She sat on a tall stool and proceeded to have her face cleaned, toned, moisturized, firmed, concealed and otherwise prepared for makeup. This was a wonderful treat. As her pampering continued, the makeup artist reshaped her eyebrows and then used a large brush to apply foundation. First, the artist chose a great color of blush for her fair skin, and then beautiful eye shadows. Next, she used an eye liner and coated her eyelashes with purple tinted mascara. For a finishing touch, the artist applied a purple-pink color of lipstick. Finally, she put a high gloss on this woman's lips. For the first time in many months, she looked and felt beautiful!

Treat yourself to something to boost your self-esteem, such as a free makeover. You deserve something special, to be refreshed. This can help you feel more feminine, and you just might learn a few tricks of the trade that you can use in front of your own mirror at home.

Likewise, you can be made over as you accept Christ into your heart. Your old self will be gone, and the new will be present—a spiritual makeover.

*Acts 3:20*

*"So that times of refreshing may come from the presence of the Lord, and that he may send the Messiah appointed for you, that is, Jesus."*

Research has shown that the verse below from the book of Psalms is the exact center of the Bible. What is the center of your life?

At the heart of God's Word, you are encouraged to put your trust in the Lord, and not in man. Spouses may disappoint, children might stray, parents will die, neighbors can let you down, friends could change, and work colleagues will one day retire. But God is always the same, faithful and everlasting. Don't place your ultimate confidence in your work, a computer, a Christmas gift, your marriage, an education, a new car or other possessions such as a home. It's foolish to trust anyone or anything on earth more than you trust your father in heaven.

It might be easy for you to remove some things at the center of your life that are hindering your relationship with God, like one woman's habit of watching three hours of daily soap operas on television. On the other hand, you might have to make an extra effort to block some distractions, such as a strong addiction to work that interferes with church and family life.

You might not be able to see God's plan, and you might not understand it. But God does not forget those who are faithful to him, even though his timetable may not be what you expect.

Put your trust in God that he will guide, love, protect and provide. In this Christmas season, and always, choose to make God the center of your life.

*Psalm 118:8*

*It is better to take refuge in the Lord than to put confidence in mortals.*

What do you believe about Jesus, the Christ?

Slow down, stop and think about that question for a minute. It is important to examine your own spiritual beliefs, and not merely those of other people. Even though there may be some merit to what others say about God, but you must decide for yourself precisely what you believe. What do you believe about Jesus Christ—down deep in your soul?

When asked this question during a sermon by my pastor, I determined that I believe the following:

Christ is God's only Son.

Jesus is the way to salvation.

God's Son is my Savior.

He is Lord and Master of my life.

Christ is Power.

Jesus is part of the Trinity.

He died, was buried and rose again.

Christ is of God and from God.

Christ is in God's image.

Jesus is my Teacher.

He is my hope.

Pray, asking God to reveal the things of Christ that will allow him to master your life. Each person's list may be different, but we are all God's children.

*Mark 8:29*

*He asked them, "But who do you say that I am?"*
*Peter answered him, "You are the Messiah."*

God has promised to deliver you from the hurt, pain, misery, abuse, neglect and darkness in your life right now. Your heavenly Father will care for you and bring light into the dim corners. He will bring you out of the uncertainty of separation or divorce into the certainty of everlasting love. God will shield you, provide for you and protect you from harm.

Claim these glorious promises, along with others sprinkled throughout the Bible, as you trudge through an absolutely terrible day—or week.

It might seem humanly impossible that you will ever smile again, that your children will recover from their parents' divorce, or that you will get a job that can help you pay your bills. You might see yourself as always struggling in every way and doubting. But look to what you have been promised.

Of course God won't make you deliriously happy without another problem in your future, but he can bring you inner joy and peace. He won't zap your children with a feel-better pill, but can minister to them through their pain and hurt, and bring them to a better place in life. And most certainly, God won't make you an instant millionaire, but he can help you gain a sense of financial equilibrium if you follow some basic economic principles. There are numerous resources available to the Christian woman for financial guidance if needed.

Believe, endure, pray, trust and obey.

By following these ideals, you will receive God's promises and they will be far more than you ever thought possible. Read about Abraham, draw on your faith, and believe God's promises.

*Romans 4:18, 21*

*Hoping against hope, he believed . . . being fully convinced that God was able to do what he had promised.*

I had a young friend whose marriage dissolved, even before she was able to wed.

This young woman graduated from college, began a ministerial position in a church and then received a marriage proposal from a wonderful Christian man. Life was truly looking grand and the future seemed bright with hope. After one year of satisfying church work, she felt a strong call to serve as a foreign missionary in Asia. But her groom-to-be was hesitant as he tried to talk his future wife out of mission work, pleading and bargaining with her. However, she could not be shaken in her belief that God was calling her to missions.

Her fiancé then flatly refused to even consider accompanying her on a foreign mission trip at any point in his life and suddenly broke their engagement. Four months before the wedding date, her groom abruptly moved back home to his parents and told her never to attempt contact again.

Her romantic dreams were shattered into many pieces, and she began to grieve for a marriage that apparently would never be. This friend wrote a letter to me a few weeks after their breakup, emphasizing that she was keeping the faith, and stated that God was "refining" her.

A refiner heats metal compounds to very hot temperatures, where impurities will rise to the surface to be skimmed off, resulting in pure metal. As the metal becomes more and more pure, the refiner can eventually even see his own reflection in its surface. God wants the same for us—pure lives in order that he may be reflected in us.

*Malachi 3:3*

*He will sit as a refiner and purifier of silver, and he will purify the descendants of Levi and refine them like gold and silver, until they present offerings to the Lord in righteousness.*

Do you ever wonder what God wants of you? Just exactly what must you do for him, as he has done so very much for you?

We certainly know that God does not need animal sacrifices, as Christ was the ultimate sacrifice and we no longer need the symbolic ritual of burning animals to please him. Our religious traditions such as church attendance aren't enough, either. Neither are our monetary sacrifices, nor our gifts of time and service.

What God wants and desires from his children, instead, is a life pleasing to him—a life of honesty, goodness and mercy. A life of humility spent walking with him—a life characterized by peacefulness and simply doing the right thing.

If you're a mother, you probably have fond memories of your toddlers wanting to spend time with you. Remember when they begged to have books read just before going to sleep at night? How about the times that you played with them in the yard instead of cleaning the house? They probably felt like they were the center of the universe because, after all, Mom had paid special attention to them.

If you don't have children, reflect back on a special childhood memory with your own mother. Can you recall a special shopping trip to buy a dress for the Christmas season? You just adored that time with your own mother that no one else could claim—time that she gave to you alone because of her intense love for you.

Likewise, God deeply loves you and wants you to spend time with him, and do what is good, right, and true.

*Micah 6:8*

*He has told you, O mortal, what is good; and what does
the Lord require of you but to do justice, and to love
kindness, and to walk humbly with your God?*

It is critically important to finish what you have started. Don't quit!

Do not let the past overcome you, but determine to go forward from today. Acknowledge the past, deal with it, and leave it there—in the past. Don't get stuck in past marital issues to such a degree that you can't live in the present.

You began your marital separation as a Christian woman grounded in the Word, and you need to complete this period in the same way. God has a purpose for your life, and you will discover what it might be. Don't feel defeated, because God is watching out for you and intervening on your behalf. Your period of separation and divorce can be one that is worthy, noble and honorable if you are firm in your commitment to Christ. Don't get sidetracked by earthly temptations, and veer off the path chosen for you.

Encouragement to stick with your Christian ideals can come from friends, family, reading, prayer and just plain old everyday persistence. Continue to fight, no matter what circumstances come your way. Your reward will be incredible richness in God.

God's strength will carry you from day to day; you don't have to do it alone. Help is available, and he has a wider vision than what you might possess today. Tap into that spring that never runs dry—your living hope—and finish what you have begun. Keep the faith and don't abandon God, because he hasn't abandoned you.

*2 Timothy 4:7*

*I have fought the good fight, I have finished
the race, I have kept the faith.*

God wants you to have an abundant life, one that is joyful and full of love.

One woman was trying to keep the family home after divorce, even though home repairs were becoming quite costly for her. She had a leaking skylight in a bathroom and called a roofing company to come and give her a cost estimate. As the repairman was investigating the skylight, he noticed that her gutters were pulling away from the house because of some rotting timbers. Furthermore, the man decided that the entire roof really needed to be replaced. Her house was only 14 years old with its original roof, and he had found several areas of rotten, splitting shingles while he was up there examining the skylight damage. She was shocked to learn of all this damage! And then she panicked as she sat at her kitchen table to discuss finances with the roofer. She managed to thank him for coming, told him that she'd have to think about the money involved, and began to cry out of sheer frustration. Then she called her earthly father, who gave her some advice along with the name of a less costly repairman to consider. And she called on her Heavenly Father in prayer, asking him to protect and guide her.

God wants you to rejoice in your ability to call on him in both good and bad situations of life. The good can be even better as you celebrate with your loving Father, and the bad will certainly be more bearable because he is faithful enough to bring you through it. Your joy does not have to be dependent on outward circumstances.

Celebrate a life in Christ—one of abundance, fullness, guidance and love.

*John 10:10*

*The thief comes only to steal and kill and destroy.*
*I came that they may have life, and have it abundantly.*

Some women in separation or divorce think more highly of themselves than they should.

They have a tendency to consider their own behaviors above reproach, while at the same time openly condemning their former husband's actions. Perhaps your husband was an alcoholic, committed adultery, allowed street drugs to ruin his life, or abandoned his family. Maybe you were even guilty of these actions as well, but understand that those actions are totally in the past and behind you. It is important to remember that God loves everybody, and is available to all—every single person.

Someone at church once taught a lesson on the Lord's Prayer and emphasized the word "our" in the phrase "Our Father." This little three-letter word reveals that God can be God of each person. He is not just a Father to people who attend church or those women whose lives are in disarray because of unwanted divorce. Instead, God wants to be a Father to everyone, because God will forgive anyone who asks. And that includes your former husband who may have been abusive, but now has repented of his behaviors while exhibiting true change. We have all missed the mark of perfection, and God earnestly desires our repentance and changing of behaviors.

Another friend phrased it differently when she said, "If someone is headed in the wrong direction, God does allow a U-turn!"

*Matthew 6:9*

*"Pray then in this way: Our Father in heaven,*
*hallowed be your name."*

Everyday life is filled with simple annoyances, mundane chores and tasks to be completed.

Dirty baby diapers, runny noses of toddlers, a burned casserole dish, weeds, getting up very early to take the bus to work, a colleague at work who gossips incessantly about co-workers, a dead car battery, cleaning the toilet bowl, cooking supper, talking with a telemarketer and car pooling. How about mopping the water out of your basement after the rain storm, buying new tires for your car, taking the car in for an oil change, helping with homework or going back to the grocery store for the second time in the same day because you forgot to buy the milk?

This is the stuff of everyday life, and it will pass quickly enough. So relax, have some fun and celebrate life.

God has given you work to do. Offer everything you do to the Lord, even raking leaves or picking up toys, and it can become much less of a chore. Some of the drudgery might even be relieved as you tell God what's on your heart. It's possible to learn about discipline while sweeping the kitchen floor for the third time in one day. Along the way, you just might find some purpose and joy in these everyday, common things of life.

*Colossians 3:23*

*Whatever your task, put yourselves into it,*
*as done for the Lord and not for your masters.*

We are only human, and sometimes in a weak moment we might wonder if God actually hears our prayers. Wonderfully, we can be emphatically assured that he does.

One woman, prior to the Internet shopping era, was desperate to complete her Christmas shopping by the beginning of November because her second baby was due to be born around December 1st. She had made lists for all her family members, and was crossing off those names at lightning speed. However, she was having one huge problem. Her son wanted a pair of cowboy chaps for his Christmas gift, and that was all he wanted. In fact, he had told everyone that he was getting chaps for his gift. He informed his grandmother, preschool teacher, neighbors, and anyone else who would listen that he couldn't wait to dress up like a real cowboy.

Unfortunately, his mother couldn't locate any chaps. She had visited every costume store in their small town, called nearby stores, and scoured catalogs without any success. As a last resort, she decided to pray about her son's Christmas gift. Around Thanksgiving, after many frustrating and fruitless shopping trips, she recalls praying aloud, "Dear God, I know you're busy and I know this is small in the grand scheme of things. But do you have any chaps?"

The very next day, she received a catalog in the mail from a western wear company. She had not requested that specific catalog. In fact, she didn't know that the company even existed. Opening the catalog through tears of joy, she saw a children's ad that featured brown suede cowboy chaps. Needless to say, she was on the phone to place a rush order immediately.

Yes, God hears prayers. And yes, he cares about everything in our lives—including cowboy chaps.

*1 John 5:14*

*And this is the boldness we have in him, that if we ask anything according to his will, he hears us.*

The verse below is one of the most calming in the entire Bible.

It brings to mind an image of God truly holding you—and all of your conflicts, desires, hopes, dreams, heartbreaks, Christmas shopping lists, court dates and uncertainties—in his big hands. God's hands are very wide, large enough to hold us all. And what could be more restful than being held by the Creator of the universe?

God is in the lead, and is the Teacher. He is showing you his ways of trust and faith, even as you stumble along the rocky path of marital separation or divorce.

All of the circumstances in your jumbled life are under God's ultimate control, and he is helping you to lean on him instead of yourself. You may not understand God's perfect timing or his plan for your life and those of your children, but trust is important. He will deliver you into a land of plenty when the hour is right, in his time. And right now in the interim, during this time of waiting, you have a great opportunity for growth and maturity.

Retire to God's waiting area, remain calm, and rest as you are assured that you're in his steady and capable hands.

*Psalm 31:15*

*My times are in your hand; deliver me from the hand of my enemies and persecutors.*

There is good news for you, even as you suffer today.

Of course, you have been hurt in your marriage and its breakup. The agony that you have endured has, at times, been hideous and you may feel utterly destroyed. Do you feel worthless due to abuse, or like a failure because your marriage didn't survive?

Your children have also been hurt by their parents' broken marriage, and they may be displaying various types of pain in their mourning. Are they sullen and silent children who are bottling up all of their anger inside, ready to explode at any moment? Or are they openly resentful in both words and action?

God wants to give you beauty for all of these ashes of separation and divorce. He wants only good for you and your children. Your Father in heaven loves you and your children. He wants you to accept yourself just as you are and wants you to be able to love others. If you are grounded in God's ultimate love, the resulting fruit in your life will be his glorious peace and joy.

You are a special and valuable woman, created by God.

God can give you a garland for these ashes. He wants to remove the refuse from your life if you will ask him.

*Isaiah 61:3*

*To provide for those who mourn in Zion—to give them a garland instead of ashes, the oil of gladness instead of mourning, the mantle of praise instead of a faint spirit. They will be called oaks of righteousness, the planting of the Lord, to display his glory.*

A friend had been divorced for well over a year, not dating anyone regularly, when she began to have wonderful dreams about a man to whom she was attracted. He had not even asked her out, but she was dreaming about him two or three nights a week. His hugs and kisses played prominently in these dreams, along with trips they would someday be taking together. One night, she even dreamed about the Christmas present he was going to give her!

Was she going crazy? She e-mailed a Christian girlfriend, one of her many "counselors," and asked her opinion. Her friend gave her some sound and comforting advice, which she took to heart. Her suggestions were excellent and they might apply to you right now:

Allow yourself to dream again.

Dreams can be a sign of emotional progress.

Celebrate your dreams and don't feel guilty for having them.

You have a right to live again. External forces may have occurred which ended your marriage, but internal forces of God's Holy Spirit are bringing healing to you.

These dreams mean you're moving along in the right direction, instead of continuing to cry yourself to sleep or focusing on revenge against your former husband.

Dreams can be a healthy outlet for your emotions. Her girlfriend didn't diagnose her as crazy, but instead reassured her that she was totally normal to have such dreams. Prepare your heart to receive God's guidance about your dreams, your hopes and your life.

*Matthew 2:13*

*Now after they had left, an angel of the Lord
appeared to Joseph in a dream.*

Is there a special woman who is helping you through this period of marital difficulty that you are currently experiencing? A godly woman who is praying for you, praying with you, and assisting you to navigate the fog of divorce?

An older lady in my church, who was leading a women's Bible study group, served as a mentor for three participants in the group during periods of marital stress. This dear woman listened to us, counseled, ate lunch with us, helped us to be reasonable, and allowed us to intrude into her home when we needed comfort. She instructed us in God's wisdom and prayed that our marriages could be reconciled if at all possible. Very gently, she also helped us see that the behaviors within our marriages could potentially endanger our spiritual and emotional health.

She was a true mentor, a woman willing to engage in a lifelong relationship with us in order to help us reach our God-given potential. This woman never had children herself, and we honestly considered her to be another mother. Wonderfully, her mentoring and caring actions didn't stop at the moment of separation, and she continued to guide us during divorce and for years afterward. She wanted us to become more Christ-like, even though we were experiencing one of the biggest hurdles of our entire lives.

Christ, God's only Son, is our ultimate mentor. He will never disappoint us. He shares, he guides, he cares, he loves and he builds.

*James 1:22*

*But be doers of the word, and not merely hearers who deceive themselves.*

Is your heart prepared for tomorrow, the birthday celebration of Christ the Lord? Pray that the Messiah will be the focus of your day, instead of tears and sorrow over your marriage. Be ready for an emotional avalanche, as you attempt to make the best of a sad situation.

If you are attempting to reconcile with your husband, you might consider spending the holiday itself as a family unit. Be careful not to give your children false hope as you undertake your annual pilgrimage to their grandmother's house. They are quite naturally hoping for a reunited family, and may see a temporary reunion as a more permanent one. Therefore, you need to exercise caution as you explain to them the particular circumstances of your home life.

On the other hand, if your court date for divorce is scheduled for the first week of January, you probably don't want to spend Christmas day with your husband. Ask God to grant you the mercy to allow your children to spend time with their father, and insist that the children's time be equally divided between their two parents. Be gentle with your children, especially if it is the first Christmas holiday associated with divorce. It will be unbelievably difficult, but you can do this. Brace yourself.

Make plans for the hours that you will spend alone on Christmas day. Have a quiet time with God, attend a church service, serve a meal at a homeless shelter, visit your aunt, call a friend who is also separated, cook for your parents or take a nap. Just make sure to have some strategy mapped out, so that you are able to find some joy in this wonderful Christian holiday.

Pray for strength and peace, and focus on Jesus. Celebrate Christ's birth!

*Isaiah 40:5*

*"Then the glory of the Lord shall be revealed, and all
people shall see it together, for the mouth
of the Lord has spoken."*

Thank God and give him praise as you celebrate the birth of the Christ child today. Our Savior, God's only Son, has been born. Jesus Christ has been called Wonderful, Prince of Peace, the One, Messiah, Lord, Good News, Master and Deliverer. And he is all those things—plus more!

Jesus is truly the best Christmas gift possible. God is now fully human and fully divine, and his Son is the atonement for all our sins.

As you wake up on this Christmas morning, smile and rejoice in Christ's birth. Share your joy and this good news with your children, as you hug them and wish them a very Merry Christmas. Whether you're alone or with other family members on this holiday, read a scriptural account of Jesus' birth and offer prayers of gratitude to God. Focus on the Lord and what he can bring to your life and the lives of your children—hope, strength, comfort, healing and peace.

If your ability to rejoice is dimmed because of recent marital breakup, remember that Christmas Day is but a single day and life will continue on tomorrow. You can survive memories, tears, and an empty house with God's help and the comfort that the Holy Spirit brings. Jesus can be the balm for your wounds, and he can provide immense consolation as you are continuing to grieve for the loss of your marriage.

Jesus Christ, our Lord and Savior, is born. Glory to God! Hallelujah!

*Luke 2:11*

*"To you is born this day in the city of David a Savior, who is the Messiah, the Lord."*

A friend called one day, saying that she was a victim of parental guilt—consuming, terrible, overwhelming guilt because of the absence of her child's father in their home and everyday lives. She and her husband were divorced because of his continued domestic violence. He had been physically abusive for years, and these behaviors had come to a full climax one day when he pulled a gun and threatened her.

She had attempted to compensate for his absence in her daughter's life by buying her some quite expensive gifts, but this strategy hadn't worked out too well. Because her teenage daughter's birthday was close to Christmas, she had splurged early and leased a new car for her around the first of December. Sadly, her daughter had wrecked the car only two weeks later, and mom received the astronomical repair bill in the mail the day after Christmas. As she reflected on the reasons for the car purchase, this woman readily acknowledged that she was trying to make up for the fact that her daughter had no father at home.

Try to remember that you are just one parent. Extravagant gifts and purchases don't make you a better parent—only a poorer one. Presents most certainly do not make a divorce any more palatable for your children. In reality, they are only a temporary diversion from the real pain and problems facing them.

Guilt can lead to weariness of your soul, and can weigh you down. Ask God to help reduce your burden of guilt as you maneuver your way through this maze called single motherhood.

*Matthew 11:30*

*"For my yoke is easy, and my burden is light."*

"How deep can you go and come back up?"

A friend asked that question soon after she separated from her husband. She was devastated, sickened, furious and shocked that her dreams had dissolved. Depression was insidiously creeping into her emotional being. Her husband arrogantly continued to tell her that he had just changed, and she simply wasn't making him happy any longer. He didn't want to grow old with her. He insisted that he needed someone different, younger and exciting.

Every woman who has been through separation and divorce knows just how deep it is possible to sink in the emotional abyss of marital woe. You might begin to doubt yourself, and everything you've believed in for years. Do you find yourself crying every single day? Are you so angry that you can almost feel your blood pressure rising? There may be days that you even question your sanity, as you struggle to stay afloat.

Recognize that you have a problem, and ask for help. Call your pastor, talk with a friend, arrange for an appointment with a counselor and allow yourself to cry. Continue to hug your children, read your Bible, talk with God while praying daily and take medication if your doctor prescribes it for you in order to prevent an unending downward spiral.

You can live a better life! There is hope through Christ, strength through God, joy in the Lord despite external circumstances and a supreme peace available to you. God loves you greatly, and has sent his Holy Spirit to minister to you and pull you out of the deep.

*John 5:6*

*When Jesus saw him lying there and knew that he had been there a long time, he said to him, "Do you want to be made well?"*

Life can become more difficult when faced with an empty nest, after being a mother to active children in your home every day for many years. Indeed, your divorce may seem more final and quite pronounced at this time, because your house is suddenly neat and quiet since your children have left home for work or college opportunities. You might be alone for the first time in years, or for the very first time in your entire life, and a bit sad over this development.

For years you helped with your children's homework, drove your son to a piano lesson, took your daughter to the soccer field for a Saturday morning game and car pooled for your church youth group. You attended football games at the local high school to watch your daughter as a cheerleader, went shopping with your children for new school clothes and chaperoned a church youth camping trip. You cooked for your husband, washed his laundry and cleaned the house during your entire married life. Remember the time that your daughter prepared her version of a gourmet dinner, a handmade child's card, the day your daughter got her ears pierced, being pregnant with your firstborn or sewing a dress for a special dance recital?

You can reflect positively on these growing up years, with a sense of satisfaction over a job well done.

Your children now have new developmental tasks before them, and you do as well. Enjoy some silence for a while as you nestle into your favorite chair for a week of reading. If you feel lonely, call a friend. Become active in your church singles group, take a course at a community college or put yourself into work. You have a new course of life stretching out before you!

Pray, asking God to direct you as you move forward and fill your empty nest with his plans.

*Philemon 1:7*

*I have indeed received much joy
and encouragement from your love.*

About three years after separation from her husband of many years, one woman felt as though she was finally beginning to awaken from sleep—a very long and deep sleep. Looking back, she realized that she had functioned for countless months in an auto-pilot mode with cooking, working, cleaning, paying bills, and caring for children. She was often emotionally numb and just existing day to day, while trying to cope with all of life's changes and staggering developments of separation, child custody agreements, counseling and divorce.

But finally her head was clearing of some of the anger and bitterness of her former husband's actions. She was on a more even emotional plane and found herself smiling.

She didn't know what had changed. She still had lonely times of missing her marital mate, tears would occasionally rise to the surface, and she was continuing to struggle financially. But she was seeing a very bright light at the end of the divorce tunnel and feeling like she was alive once again.

This woman mentioned her feelings to a Christian friend, who proclaimed that God was healing her. She decided that it must be true! Her wounds were forming scabs, she had re-discovered her joy that had been temporarily hidden from view, and her recovery process was in full gear. She was even ready to go out with a guy for dinner and a movie.

God is good, all the time. He heals broken lives, and he will bring you through every challenge of your separation, reconciliation or divorce.

*Matthew 15:30*

*Great crowds came to him, bringing with them the lame, the maimed, the blind, the mute, and many others. They put them at his feet, and he cured them.*

True happiness comes from accepting God's love for you, and loving him in return. You can be a partner with God, and delight in him while you choose good paths for your own life and the lives of your children.

You have the wonderful opportunity of walking with God, leaning on him, getting to know him, praying to him and depending on him. As you yield your marriage to God, you can be fully assured that he knows what is best for you. He will care for you as you trust him with your very life each and every day.

As you reflect over this past year of life, you can probably remember many times when God has provided for you, meeting your needs in unlikely places. You've made much progress in your spiritual journey and have discovered that you have countless reasons to rejoice and be thankful. You have deep and abiding hope for a fulfilling and positive future. You are now firmly convinced that God keeps his promises and that he will provide you with a fresh start in life.

You can find wonderfully great joy in life with God.

*Psalm 1:1–2*

*Happy are those who do not follow the advice of the wicked, or take the path that sinners tread, or sit in the seat of scoffers; but their delight is in the law of the Lord, and on his law they meditate day and night.*

Say a prayer of thanksgiving to God, the Creator and Master of your life. Then smile broadly because you have endured this past year of your life, with its good times and bad!

Good times filled with hugs from children, God's love, friends at church, reconciliation possibilities, supportive work colleagues, parents who believe in you, and a pastor who continues to give you godly counsel. Good times including wonderful dinners with your single girlfriends, dreams of a better future, hard work, Bible study that has deepened your belief in Christ and peace.

Bad times when you were crying at night and unable to sleep, seeing your husband with another woman, witnessing your children's anger at separation, going to the courthouse for a divorce proceeding, and meeting with your attorney to hammer out legal details. Bad times when you were struggling financially, repairing a broken stove, seeing your husband continue in his cycle of abuse and violence, arguing with your husband about child care and paying legal bills.

God has been with you every step of the way, lovingly guiding you and providing protection from harm. His perfect plan for your life is slowly being revealed to you in his time.

You have kept the faith, been tenacious, stood firm and not wavered in your belief that Christ's example for life is the best. You have stayed the course, feared God, respected yourself, loved your children and persevered in the face of unbelievable difficulties. Your focus has been on your Father in heaven, Jesus as Lord, and the Comfort of the Spirit instead of worldly pursuits of temporary pleasures.

You have done well, and your faith can be a standard of excellence to others. Keep your eyes on God and then you can look forward to another glorious year.

*Proverbs 31:29*

*"Many women have done excellently,*
*but you surpass them all."*

## About the Author

Mona Brown Ketner is the mother of two grown children, Adam and Amanda. She is a member of New Philadelphia Moravian Church in Winston-Salem, North Carolina, where she enjoys mission work and playing the flute. Mona is a nurse. She received a Bachelor of Science in Nursing from the University of North Carolina-Chapel Hill and a Master of Science in Nursing from the University of North Carolina-Greensboro. She holds the position of Perinatal Outreach Coordinator at Wake Forest University School of Medicine in Winston-Salem.

ISBN: 978-1-935130-10-9

51699

9 781935 130109

U.S. $16.99